Martial Arts Business 101

Hooya - Living the Dream

By Allie Alberigo
6th Degree Black Belt

This publication is designed to provide the reader with competent matter and reliable information in regards to the information covered. It is expressly sold with the understanding the authors and publishers are not engaged in rendering legal, financial, or other professional advice or services. Laws and practices often vary from state to state and if legal or other expert assistance is required with a service professional in that specific area it is your obligation to find qualified professionals. The authors and publisher specifically disclaim any liability that is incurred from the use or application of the contents of this book.

Copyright Allie Alberigo, 2008 All rights reserved.

Contact information

Allie Alberigo
Taking it to the Next Level
Takingittothenextlevel.com
235 Union Blvd.
West Islip, N.Y. 11795
631 – 321-5432
renshilininja@aol.com

First Edition July 2008
Cover Art by Chuck Wilson
www.AtouchofZen.com
chuck.wilson@atouchofzen.com

I went to your site and - WOW. I just changed my answering machine message with the one you recommended. I'm at the end of my rope and you have inspired me. I NEED THIS! Thanks for coming through. Just wanted to let you know that the improvements we made by implementing the first months of your program have been crucial for Royal Court Academy. The instructors, students and parents feel the new professionalism that has taken hold of our school and what a positive impact it has made. For the first time the majority of our comments are more positive then negative. I couldn't be happier.

Having a full time job at Harley Davidson makes the changes slower then I would like. I have access up to month five on your site but I'm just working on month two. It's a slow process and I make sure I'm consistent with doing a little bit every day. **The point is your system works.** *It's because you supply the information with implementation in an easy to follow file system. Thanks for making it so easy, effective and affordable. Taking it to the next level is the best consulting tool I have found. I Wanted to let you know that, Thanks again.* **Jeff C. Growel**

My wife talked to you yesterday and joined your online training program at Takingittothenextlevel.com. I just wanted to say **THANKS** *for all the great information! This is, in my estimation, one of the smartest moves we have ever made. I honestly think after 9 years of blood, sweat and tears, (literally), in this business, we'll finally be able to hit the "big time" in income and success at our school. We look forward to working with you for many years to come!* **Steve Gupton, from NC, a MSI client.**

As far as your company goes, I had a chance to view the DVD you sent. There are many others that have more to offer or so they think. Just because they charge more does not make them better, but none takes the care at beginning level and beyond as yours does. Your DVD has really filled in the gaps that were holding me back and maybe causing me to lose even MORE money. Thank You

The Next Level program was a life-saver. Allie helped me take the school from 5 students to nearly 100 students in 10 months. His system is simply the best. He is also one of the more caring individuals that you will meet in the martial arts community.
James Liu - OC Jiu Jitsu and MMA

Allie's Next Level consulting service provides a systematic approach to martial business success. Each month affords copious material to invent, restructure, or re-align business systems, marketing strategies, communication efforts, and/or instruction methods. When fully applied, "Taking it to the Next Level," opens the space for extraordinary results. Furthermore, Allie is always adding something, so be cognizant of each month at all times. Basically, if you want to be brilliant in martial arts business, then welcome aboard! **David Kaye, Sensei - Chief Instructor**

I just wanted to say hi and let you know how things are going up here. I know you're probably really busy this time of year like us. Speaking of being busy we have had 27 new enrollments in the past 7 business days, that's signed up and paid! All with no advertising other than the yellow pages and our website I hope we can have you up again soon. We are approaching 600 paying students on our roster and only after 3 years and lot a work and a lot of help from you. We've just been doing what you say and it works, but like you say the trick is to actually do it! Thanks again. **Chris Gifford - Ottawa Academy of Martial Arts - 613.728.0880**

We all know the saying "when the student is ready the teacher appears" however let us flip this around to "when the teacher is ready the students appear". This is more like it in our industry. There are some schools that are stuck in a rut and will continue to be that way till they make a decision to move and grow their business. Some instructors are quite happy (meanwhile they will whine about it) with where they currently are. We are where we are today because of the choices that WE have made – not the choices that anyone else has made. So unfortunately no matter what you do or anyone else does for some school owners until THEY are ready to choose to move forward they never will.

We are eager to move forward and are currently re-introducing our 2-4-6 week call procedure. We have had this information for soooooo long and yet have never done anything about it. So it is back to square one and I have told the staff to get ready for some changes as we all need to pull up our socks and service our students.

Thank you for all your support and we look forward to a prosperous future.

Helen Yuen - YUENS FAMILY MARTIAL ARTS CENTRE Coquitlam, BC

I received your email right when I was thinking about a student that quit because he didn't pass the test. I just wanted to let you know I appreciate you showing us you're going through similar problem as we do... on a different level but regardless similar. You gave me strength and reassurance that I'm doing the right thing by not passing who do not deserve to. Anyways still to this day I read and save all your emails and even show it to my staff for encouragement... **James from Victorville TKD.**

Foreword

It is amazing to hear business success stories. Over the decades that I have been a success and business strategist, I have had the opportunity to work with businesses ranging from sole proprietors to large behemoths of corporations. They all have one thing in common – strategies ranging from marketing, sales, accounting, tax, management and personnel strategies and the list could go on and on. The reality is that we have strategies for everything we do in our businesses and in life for that matter. A strategy is simply the syntax in which we do what we do. Unfortunately, many entrepreneurs and businesses also have something else in common – many of their strategies are unconscious. No, I didn't say the entrepreneur was unconscious…although some I have seen may have been better off if they were unconscious when they made their decisions. What I really mean is that many times in business we make specific choices consciously. In other words we have specifically thought about it, considered the options and alternatives and made an informed decision. Yet, we all often make choices in business that we are not conscious of. Many times these choices are in areas that we are unfamiliar with or feel less qualified to do and we tend to avoid these areas. What we fail to see is that not making specific choices and decisions is a choice and a decision in and of itself.

Those that have heard me speak or worked with me personally have heard me say, "Change is inevitable – But Progress is Intentional." The businesses and entrepreneurs that I have had the opportunity to work with that have achieved the greatest and most consistent success are those that intentionally make decisions and choices within their businesses. They operate from a conscious level until the processes and systems become who they are and then they operate from a place of "unconscious competence". In order to achieve your greatest success you must make intentional decisions and choices. In order to do that, you then must have an understanding of the various areas that impact your business. Don't misinterpret what I'm saying. You do not need to be an expert in everything you do. I do believe, and experience proves, that you have to be well informed and understand all areas of your business.

Other traits I found to be consistent with what I have called the "Synergistically Successful Entrepreneur" is that they are in control of their future in their minds through the appropriate setting of goals. Not a to do list but real, solid goals set in a SMART® format – meaning that they are Specific, Measurable, Actionable, Realistic and Time-Driven. The last two items are they have a life of balance and they are focused on a purpose beyond themselves.

In this book Allie Alberigo gives you the information you need to succeed. He deals with many of these issues and does so from a practical and real-world experience. Allie gives you a perspective on everything about a business ranging from marketing, sales, employees, systems to customer service, goal setting and the psychology of success. The tools and skills you will learn from this book will give you a great foundation and launching point for the business of your dreams. Allie has had many decades as a successful entrepreneur, consultant, coach and teacher and encapsulates these decades of "hard-knocks" and lessons in the pages. This manuscript will allow you to learn from his "skinned knees and bloody noses" without having to go through the same pains that Allie did.

If you were to hire a coach – would you want the one that has had no experience, very little experience or a boatload of experience? I always tell my clients that I want a person that has proven they can do it not once, but many times – someone that has had consistent results in many types of environments. That is what you get in this book. He has effectively distilled it down to the prime elements of success that are needed to make the dream a reality. This book is the first step to your new vision for you and your business. You will come out of this realizing how much you thought you knew but had no clue and with the pathway to understanding it now.

Lastly, if you want to learn the key strategies to build, grow and flourish, take this information, integrate into your business as well as your life as T. Harv Ecker says, "how you do one thing is how you do everything". By taking these principles, many of which are cross-contextual, you will see greater purpose, greater passion, greater success and greater fulfillment. So take the journey, and remember that any journey worth taking is worth enjoying so enjoy your journey with this guidebook and begin to make progress through intentional decisions because remember "Change is Inevitable – Yet Progress is Intentional."

Mel H Abraham, CPA, CVA, ABV, ASA, CSP
Master Success Strategist • Coach • Consultant • Speaker
mel@melabraham.com

Chapter 1
Customer Service – The key to a thriving business
14

Chapter 2 –
The key to success – Goal setting and time management
34

Chapter 3 –
Common Mistakes of an Entrepreneur
43

Chapter 4 –
Ninja marketing tactics – Build your marketing arsenal
60

Chapter 5 –
Systemization of your Business
90

Chapter 6 –
Student Retention – The Goose that laid the golden student
111

Chapter 7 –
Employee Management –Heartache to riches
119

Chapter 8 –
In The Trenches – Stories from the staff
133

Chapter 9 –
Always be a student of higher education
146

Chapter 10 –
Life Lessons from someone who cares
152

Chapter 11 –
Sales 101
158

Chapter 12 –
Developing Rules for your business
181

Chapter 13 –
Ending on a good note - What happens when you are done?
185

Chapter 14 –
Income Generators - To tip the scales in your favor
189

Chapter 15 –
Building your empire –
Become a Real Estate Entrepreneur
194

Chapter 16 –
Developing a Winning Curriculum
198

Chapter 17 –
Developing a Retail Wonderland
202

Chapter 18 –
Commonly Asked Questions of the Business Owner
207

Chapter 19 –
The Psychology of Entrepreneur
211

Chapter 20 –
The Art of Organization
220

Chapter 21 –
Finding a Business Mentor
224

Chapter 22 –
Branding
226

Dedication

I must say I would have never thought I would be here writing this book. I was not the best student in school...heck, I have to be honest - I was terrible. If someone were to ask my teachers what they thought would become of me, I am sure they would have said something like I am not sure but maybe a job in a local slaughter house or some sort of menial labor.

It's not because I wasn't smart, I was very witty, mostly with comebacks or being a wise guy during class, but all in all they could see I had quick wit and was a trouble-maker at the same time. At some point I guess the word got around and I was labeled as a trouble-maker. I used to get in fights at school mostly due to my mom. One time when I was about 5 or 6 years old another boy in my neighborhood and I got into a fight. He ended up losing control and biting me on the cheek. I ran home crying. My mother immediately marched me down to the house of the other boy and talked to the parents. She didn't get a very favorable response to say the least. We exited quickly with her grabbing me by the hand and dragging me home. She then told me if I ever came home crying again, she would make it even worse by teaching me a lesson at home. I never truly knew what she meant by that but it had its impact on me.

I don't want to paint a picture of my mom being abusive because it was absolutely not the case, she was a stern European woman born in war-torn Malta, during World War II. She came to the U.S. at around the age of 9 and basically fended for herself. To say the least she was one tough cookie. Anyway, I never wanted to let that happen again, and I put my martial arts skills to work. There were no more times with me coming home crying. I think my mom may have regretted the monster she built. I had over 50+ street fights before I got out of high school.

This book would not be possible without all of my students, family and friends who are the catalyst that made me what I am today. This is my third book, the first being "The Beginner's Guide to Ninpo" the second "21st Century Ninjutsu – A Warrior's Mindset" and now this. I am highly honored that I am now being heard by many people and I guess for a child who was brought up in West Islip on Long Island there can be no better success story. During my childhood I was brought up listening to Elvis Presley and then rock and roll greats such as The Beatles, Kiss, Van Halen and all the other metal giants. I started in music at the age of 10 years old performing in movie theaters and then small nightclubs at a very young age. I always wanted to be famous.

As I look back on my career, I may not have become a rock star or a movie star yet, but I am certainly honored that individuals such as you are reading this book right now and hearing what I have to say. Thank you.

I dedicate the motivation to write this book to my daughter Kiara. Kiara, you are the most amazing child I have seen and I have seen many. Maybe I am biased because you are my daughter but no matter, you are the sun in the sky to me. You are my entire being. I love you with all of my heart.

To my Mom and Dad, thanks for being you and for giving me everything that you did. I know how hard it is to be a dad and supply your child with what they need on a daily basis. For all other parents out there, we all know what a hard job it is. I love you both tremendously. I also want to thank Judy, my step mom. She and my dad have been together for many years. I am so happy my dad found someone who is there for him. Thanks.

Thanks to all my friends in the martial arts. I want to say, if for some reason you are not on this list, it is not because you are not in this category. The real reason is I have so many great friends I can't remember them all. I am a really lucky guy. Thanks again to Soke Olshlager, Randy Weekley, Andy Stigliano, John Busto, Frank Olmeda, Robert Sugar Crosson, Cung Le, Mark Sperranza, Joe Puleio, Cliff Wolfe and everyone else I know.

I also want to thank all the people in the martial arts industry who have motivated me to become better at what I do and to continue consulting. First and foremost, Jeff Cohen from Member Solutions (formerly of A.P.S.). Jeff is the one who asked me to become a consultant, hosted me as a Keynote speaker at many of his events and got me started. I would also like to thank Dina Engel, who is an amazing person at Member Solutions and a good friend. I would not be doing thank you's any justice if I didn't mention Joe Galea, who has become a very good friend over the years and was an inspiration to me long before I ever met him, due to the articles he wrote for different consulting companies. Joe and I are both Maltese and he is a good guy and we share a kinship.

I must thank my friend Pat Maritato – you are not really a friend but more like my brother from another mother. You are an amazing dad and a great businessman. Without you, I would not have grown my Landscape Construction Company to what it was, enabling me to sell it and really concentrate on martial arts. Dude, you are awesome.

Chapter 1
Customer Service
The key to a thriving business

It's sort of ironic when you think about it. The problem for business in the 21st century isn't a lack of information – it's too much information. As quoted in one of the super hero movies "with knowledge comes great responsibility." Access to virtually any information is as easy as a touch of a keyboard now. What many people don't realize, however, is that just having the knowledge sometimes creates more problems then not having the knowledge at all.

An analogy could be that of the fisherman who was searching for food for his family. He went to the ocean and sat on the shore looking for fish. Once he found some he slowly waded into the water and began grabbing at them, but they proved to be too elusive. He was a man of tenacity and determination and knew he had to continue or his family might go unfed.

He tried all day and then night fell upon him. He had to decide whether to return to his hut without any food or stay longer, when all of a sudden it began to rain. He sought protection from the weather and found a cave. Deciding this would be a good place to stay for the night, he made a campfire. Once the cave was lit from the flames he noticed cave drawings. On them were pictorial descriptions of a man hunting fish. He had a spear with prongs on it and was spearing them. The man immediately knew what to do.

The next morning the man was out at the break of dawn building a spear and soon he was spearing fish. He had the best yield of fish ever, proving the age old saying "you can catch a man a fish and feed him for the day or teach him how to fish and feed him for a lifetime." The one thing this story depicts is how the proper instruction at the correct time can make all the difference. There would have been an entirely different issue if the cave were filled with 20 different ways and theory, like much of the information you get out of books or programs. What the man needed was clear, concise, proven no nonsense instructions and this is what he received. Sometimes in business too much information is simply too much.

We've all heard the saying "Practice makes perfect." Well, this statement couldn't be any further from the truth. Only perfect practice makes perfect. Allow me to clarify – if you are practicing something incorrectly, no matter how much you practice it will not make you better at the activity. Sometimes bad habits are developed and they take more time to erase than slowly practicing perfectly. A perfect example of this rings true with golf. Most players are better off getting lessons before they start the game. I personally know this first hand. My first time I hit the gold ball was at a range. I didn't know how to hold the club or how to stand. I had a fun day, but in those few hours didn't really learn a thing. About a year later I was invited to play golf on a team at a golf outing. My partner was semi professional and was assigned my coach. The day proved to be a great deal of fun and now I really love the sport of golf. It is amazing how a little hand-grip or the right stance can make a difference. Knowledge is everything and in business could mean the difference between being profitable or bankrupt.

Listen Up Everyone!

Ah . . . the art of listening. It's indispensable for good customer service. But it's not as easy as it may seem. Even though you claim to be listening, and respond at the right moment with the typical ahs, uhuhs, and yups, you may still find yourself not really listening. This can be true even though the auditory process is working and the sound is going to the ears and the ear-drum is vibrating in order for your brain to process the sound into clear understandable communication.

During my one-on-one consulting calls with clients, I spend 20 minutes covering topics that are important to the client. We speak on a wide array of topics, but there are times that I want to stop the conversation and say – "Hello. Is anybody out there?" I think that even though the client made the effort to set up the call and took the time to be there on the phone; still the client is not 100% attentive. Or due to the client's expectations or desire to get an answer to a specific question, my answers may fall on deaf ears. People need to realize that they are not always going to get the answer they are expecting. For example, someone may ask me how do I get more clients/students through the doors of my school or business. Their thoughts may be on marketing or advertising. My reply may not pertain to marketing in the traditional sense but could deal with referral programs or retention tools. The end result is the same, more clients, but the approach may be different.

I have some rules for listening and they can apply to you and your business. The very lessons that I am speaking of can help you with your clients as well. If you don't listen, don't expect that they will. If you become a better communicator then you will be able to reach them and get them focused on communicating with you. You can even utilize this with your students as a way to teach them to listen better.

Four Tips for Better Listening!

1. Make sure you are not distracted. Eliminate any outside factors that may take away your concentration.

2. When you listen, *really* listen. Do not let anything interfere, such as background noise, music, etc. Stay focused on the topic at hand.

3. Look at the person directly; do not shuffle through papers and do not engage in any other activity. Remember, eye contact or at least face contact is important.

4. Provide feedback on what you have heard. "So this is what I understand that you're saying. Is this correct?" Make sure you are on the same page.

Becoming an effective listener takes practice. I notice while teaching my classes at my school or my Team Leadership Character Development program that only a portion of what goes into a person's head is retained. This is especially true when teaching children. Even parents of our students don't give you their undivided attention when you are talking to them. Nonetheless, the best place to start is with you. Follow rules one through four and you will be well on your way to becoming a better listener. I assure you that this is something that will improve your communications with clients, and will also benefit many other areas of your life. You will become a better salesperson, a better friend, and also a better spouse. Just listen!

At the end of this book we have set aside some pages for notes called the Epiphany page. Every time you find something you are reading to be of interest take the time to go to the end of the book and write down the page number and a reminder on what you found and how you want to institute it.

Greet Your Students As If They Were the President

In any business the most truthful statement of all is: The Customer Is Always Right. Without customers you are out of business.

Every successful owner knows that in order to have a thriving business your staff needs to understand that each current and potential client needs to feel comfortable in your school. As a business owner I always focus on diligently training my staff, team leaders and instructors in the proper way to greet new members, existing members and their families.

Sometimes we take for granted the power of creating an environment that encourages everyone to feel like they are part of an extended family. It is very easy to forget why it is so important to greet each student every day and make them feel special; regardless of how long they have been training in your studio or have been a client. Every client wants to feel connected, and wants to believe they are all a vital part of your school. In simpler terms: they want to feel special!

When I speak to business and school owners a very common question is how do I retain or sign up more clients. Normally they are looking for what they believe to be marketing knowledge. I normally will ask how they meet or greet potential and existing clients. Most business owners don't realize how important the meet and greet process is. Remember, there is only one time to make a first impression. Uniquely you would think business owners know this but in reality only some of the businesses I come in contact with actually make this part of their daily repertoire. This is the basics in customer service but could also be the advanced level as well. Much like the martial arts the basics become the mastery level.

Here are 6 simple rules to accomplish this on a daily basis:

1) Take the time each and every day to speak to your clients and their guests when you see them, understanding that the clients are not the only important people, but the people with them as well, for example, siblings and friends. Your audience is anyone standing in front of you – they are all potential clients.

2) A quick hello goes a long way in making them feel personally connected to you.

3) Greet each person who walks through your door with a smile. Sometimes a simple smile is all you need to make your clients and their families feel welcome, and at home. If you are engaged in conversation with another client or on the telephone a quick hand gesture or polite "I'll be right with you," will suffice.

4) Inquire about their health and progress and ask them how they are doing in their personal lives. For example: "how is your training going or how are the wife and kids? What was your day like? Are we meeting your expectations for training or business? I am sure that you can come up with a few on your own. A simple inquiry allows the client to see you take an interest in their health and their success.

5) Ask if they are in need of any assistance, or have any questions. This is a great way, again, to show you care for their well-being- but it's also a great way to uncover any future or current objections which may take them off of the current client list. Any occasion when you take the time to speak to the client opens up opportunities for sales, upgrades and additional product packages.

6) Single out a few people each day and pay special attention to their achievements. In a martial arts school bring the class' attention to how well they have performed a movement or a drill. Compliment their attitude, or just simply recognize them for what they are doing. For any business you can also send notes home to individual clients/students with compliments. Highlighting their achievements or as little as a simple thank you will go a long way to encourage them to continue on and stay a part of your client base. In our schools we do at minimum 15 motivational postcards per week. This is as easy as saying "Dear John – on Tuesday you really impressed me – keep up the great work – Signed Kyoshi."

These tips may appear to be so simple that you may feel them unimportant. However, take a good look around your school/business. Where are you located when your clients/students and their parents arrive? Are you accessible? Do you have a staff member at the entrance greeting your members by their names if you are unable to do so? Wal-Mart made this a huge part of their customer service program and it really boosted business. Are all of your staff members upbeat and friendly in front of your customers? Take these tips and this opportunity to analyze how you are greeting your clients. You will be surprised at what you find. These simple six ways to greet your clients will make a tremendous difference. Take the time today to remind your staff exactly how they should be greeting your clients, and explain why it is so important. Make this a part of your daily routine, and watch the energy in your business soar to new heights!

Communication - Opening up a can of worms

When things are good, they are good; when things are bad... well, hopefully we won't have to go there. That's when the hand goes up and people say: "talk to the hand." This is an adage spoken over and over again. In general people tend to want to hear the good news first, and deal with the bad news as it comes up. Or even play what I call the Ostrich game of life by putting their head in the sand until all goes away.

People assume the good news will overshadow the bad, but sometimes avoiding the inevitable will only result in problems you can't overcome or deal with properly. Quickly nipping it in the bud is probably the best approach for any situation but the optimum goal is stop it before it happens.

Here is an example:
Mrs. Smith comes in to sign up her child Johnny. After going through an exciting intro class, he loves it and wants to join. Seeing Johnny's enthusiasm, Mr. Karate instructor goes over all the programs with Mrs. Smith and she agrees to sign Johnny up for the yearly program. Mr. Karate Instructor is very happy, signs all necessary paperwork and gives Johnny his uniform and schedule and of course for **"Taking it to the Next Level"** clients they would then explain and give the client their "welcome to the family" packet after he welcomes them to the family. He sends Mrs. Smith and his new student Johnny on their way.

A few weeks go by and Mrs. Smith isn't bringing Johnny to class anymore. As the diligent Karate teacher, Mr. Instructor calls a few times doing what we call "we miss you calls" and gets no response. After repeated attempts he finally reaches Mrs. Smith because she has forgotten to look at her caller I.D before picking up the phone. She tells Mr. Karate Instructor that Johnny has lost interest and they are discontinuing the program. At that point he tries to re-motivate her to bring him, but she declines. He goes through a laundry list of items that can help her, but nothing he says at this point could bring her back.

As martial artists we usually think on the defensive in regard to particular reactions to a movement. For instance, someone throws a punch at your face: You don't block with your chin, you bob and weave or slip and slide to avoid the punch. You never stand by and get punched in the face! Sometimes to overcome your opponent you even fake a move to draw an opening. This process is "opening a can of worms."

We as martial artists look for the warning signs and prepare for the worst. As teachers, martial artists and business owners it is our job to take the guesswork out of our relationships with clients. As they say, the truth will set you free. So, after the initial sign up or first business purchase I encourage you to take the time to speak to

Mrs. Smith and explain to her the honest truth about her child's training and the benefits of doing business with your company. This may be done on the telephone or in person in what we call our 2 week orientation. Discuss some challenges that she may or may not experience. This doesn't have to be accomplished on the same day, it can be done a day or so afterwards or as you implement another very important system practiced by Next Level clients: the 2, 4, 6, 8, 10 week call system. It can be done in person or on the telephone. Here is an example of the conversation:

"Mrs. Smith, we have found there are some things you may come up against while training in our school. The reason I am bringing this up is not to stress the negative, but to enhance the positive benefits of training at our school, and truly show what a learning experience this will be for the both of us. I just want to make sure we are both on the same page and you are fully prepared for any situation. We believe in order for you to defend yourself in a street fight or to help your child learn and grow as an individual the better prepared you are ahead of time the greater the likelihood of your child succeeding becomes.

"Letting Johnny acquire the skills to achieve his black belt and be the best that he can be in every area of his life is not going to be an easy task. After all, nothing that is worth anything is achieved easily. At our school we consider every obstacle a small speed bump; to us speed bumps are made to slow us down and give us the opportunity to take notice of all that is going on around us. Achieving yours and Johnny's goals is worth the hard work."

That being said, if we don't address these pitfalls now, they will be overwhelming and you may not know how to deal with them when they arise. A pre-emptive mentality is what we need when we run our businesses. It is imperative to make sure you are thinking way ahead of time. A great example is global warming. Not trying to get political here but in reality if we think with the future in mind and not only about profits, we will not have to go back and make corrections. Many business owners prefer to learn through trial and error. I personally do not like to waste time and money if I do not have to.

Education is the key to success – not only educating yourself but also your client, builds great customer retention. Some of these answers are geared toward a martial arts business but clearly you can see the application in any business - Consider the following:

1) You or your child will want to stop at some point in their training; in fact they may want to stop many times during their training. If this occurs, what will you do about it?

2) All students experience some form of burnout or de-motivation. This is commonly misperceived as boredom, when in fact it is not. If this occurs, what will you do about it?

3) All students at some point feel frustrated. There are hundreds of reasons why this may happen, but we have been through them all and know exactly how to help you deal with them. If this occurs, what will you do about it?

Will you allow us to help you through these situations?

This communication only lists a few of the most common examples of what may occur throughout any client's lifespan. I am sure that if you and your staff were to brainstorm you could come up with a ton more on your own.

Questions like these may seem as though you are inviting trouble, but in fact you are putting a fail-safe system into place. These types of questions will not only open the eyes of the clients but they will also help them to expect, understand and overcome any issues that may come up. You are taking down perceived barriers and creating a relationship that encourages open communication. Lack of communication is one of the leading common causes of failed relationships.

Many parents or students do not even know what to expect and are continually searching for signs that will prove to them that they made the correct decision. Sharing with them the challenges that will occur and some suggested solutions gives them time to prepare themselves with answers should any issues arise. If you empower your customers with other alternatives then they will react in a manner that will be more beneficial to both you and them.

Isn't it every school's goal to prepare students to defend themselves? If so, where is the focus on setting them up for success at any cost? The only enemy that will lead them to quit is ignorance. If we prepare them with an arsenal of defenses for those moments when they feel like they want to quit they will be able to overcome and succeed. So next time you sign a student up or get a new client, take the time to open up a can of worms.

Satisfied or Motivated

I often eat at a local diner on Long Island, Bayshore, New York called "The Peter Pan Diner". The restaurant has good food and fast service. The staff knows me and I feel like it is a comfortable place to take people I know. I usually do most of my networking over lunch or breakfast, and have brought many of my out of state guests there. It remains a good place to spend my time talking about the Martial Arts and business and meeting with friends. It is a safe bet and I know that very rarely will I be disappointed. Plus the owners are great supporters of all I do in regards to sponsorship, cross marketing and just overall great people.

There is a very exclusive Italian restaurant right around the corner from my martial arts school which I used to eat at every Friday night. At one point I would bring my staff out to dinner at least two times per month spending hundreds even thousands of dollars. Sometimes I would walk in and feel like the president of the United States while other times I was lost in the crowd and left feeling unsatisfied. A missed drink, a missed appetizer and at some point waiting for hours to be served without even an apology. As long I was with people I liked and we were enjoying ourselves it really didn't matter how much time we spent waiting. Yet, even though the food and the service was good, the staff treated me well and I was satisfied, many times I wasn't treated as well as I should have been. I don't find myself raving all that often about the place and going there anymore. Why?

Well, there is a big difference between satisfied and motivated. Let me explain. There is another restaurant that I frequent that I often speak about with high regards. It is an Indian Fusion restaurant and I love it. The food is outstanding and the service is equally good. Every meal I have ever had at this restaurant has not only met but far exceeded my expectations in every possible way. Plus the service is just as outstanding as the other place I frequent. I continually tell friends about this restaurant and recommend it regularly. What makes me motivated to tell people about this place and not the other? *It is the difference between satisfied and motivated.* If you draw a line on a piece of paper and on the far left write "Dissatisfied," in the center write "Satisfied," and on the far right, write "Motivated," you'll have a "visual" of the range of feelings clients may have about a business.

The far left is the zone of indifference. Customers who are at this end have the impression that they have been slighted, treated poorly or feel that they haven't received the service they expected, and these customers will be unsatisfied. If you respond to these people with remedies in a timely fashion there is some chance for recovery; if not these customers will remember all the little things and look at everything you do under a microscope; if things are not corrected they are lost forever.

Clients who come into your establishment regularly and don't have any complaints may be considered satisfied customers; they may come back regularly and continue buying from you but they may never refer a new client or talk about you to others in a positive way. They would be in the center column of your piece of paper: "satisfied."

Now listen carefully here, because this is critical to your success: when you have clients who are *totally* satisfied, who really feel that they are getting even more than their money's worth and who appreciate the nuances of all you do, then they will be highly motivated. And when that happens that will tell everyone about you and your business.

Are your clients motivated or are they simply satisfied? Think about this example with relationships. If your spouse, friends, or acquaintances feel you always give them as much time, effort or love as you are able to give them, they usually will feel excited and motivated. If they feel you are doing at least the minimum of what needs to get done, they will feel satisfied. This satisfied feeling usually ends badly; we have been programmed to expect to be "wowed" by everything we encounter. Maybe it is Hollywood's fault but we all look for the fairy tale experience. Most people realize that life is very different from a fairy tale, yet they still find themselves wanting the best experience ever.

What is it you need to do to take your customers from satisfied to motivated?

Five Suggestions

1. Keep your word and never fall short - I know someone who would always talk the talk but not walk the walk. In fact at one point I had to sever my relationship with this person because of it. He actually had a movie night in his school where he forgot to bring the movie. No joke! The staff basically sat there and told the movie as a story to try to make up for his mishap. Everyone occasionally makes mistakes but this person did it far too often. Always keep your word.

2. Always give more than you promise - Over-provide and undersell. Make it a positive experience. Talk to the client to hear about what they think. Recently I was eating at a restaurant with a friend. I spoke highly of the restaurant and built it up on the entire ride there. When we arrived the ambiance of the place proved to paint the picture of what I had spoken about. Well, when we sat down for service the waitress came over and was pleasant. I was off to a great start. Soon after we realized she forgot our drink order, then apologized when she remembered – I shrugged and my friend and I kept talking. We finally (and I say that with an eye roll) got to order and continued talking. The food finally arrived but was incorrectly made. Did I mention I am a vegetarian? They brought me a chicken dish. How way off, so I had to send it back. The person I was with had to wait, while they re-did my meal. The waitress didn't offer to keep her food warm.

A little time had gone by and the food finally arrived. Still the drink order was not correct. Well we ate, had great conversation and continued to enjoy our evening, but the service created much conversation. The person I was with was a waitress at a high-end restaurant. She was used to making some mistakes, but she knew how to deal with them and keep the customer happy. All in all, the service proved to be poor, the food was equally as poor and it really ruined my idea of the restaurant. When I asked if the owner was in, the waitress told me she had the night off. I know her and she takes pride in her restaurant. The writing was on the wall at that point. All in all, the waitress didn't bother to make amends by giving us dessert or a drink for free. She just said her good byes and left the bill. I haven't been back since.

3. Educate clients - as to why you are the best, how what you provide is the best, and how people using your business are fortunate to be customers. Now don't brag, but teach. Sometimes people, especially in the Martial Arts, don't know the difference between what we do and what others do. Many clients are not taught the difference. Sometimes they need something to be proud of and to verify they made the correct choice. Make sure you help them do that.

4. Don't come across as a salesperson - I once had a parent tell me that I was the best salesman ever. It was frustrating talking to this person. He saw everything I said as a pitch. I talked to him about ideas on how to help his child and he stood there and smirked at me as if he was waiting for the punch line. I stopped recommending things to him. He eventually got the point, but lost out on many benefits. Be careful of how you approach the education process.

5. Last but not least, show people you care - Make sure they know they are the most important people in the world to you. And yes, you *can* have 40 or 4,000 people who are the most important people in the world to you, which is why customer service is a very important part of growing your business.

Remember, it is much easier to keep an existing client than it is to get a new one. So put a good portion of your effort into keeping your current clients happy. Every little thing you do matters to them. Sometimes it is the little things that count the most. Keep your clients happy and you will see your business grow exponentially.

10 Tips for Building Customer Loyalty

Getting customers is great. Keeping customers is a blessing. So don't let your customers leave after only one sale. Keep them coming back for more.

Follow-up is extremely important when building any business, but it is one of the most neglected activities in martial arts schools as well as retail businesses. Like any crucial business activity, it is worth putting time and effort into doing it right. Sometimes following up is difficult and takes a large amount of work, but in the long run it will pay off for you 100 times over. Don't let your customers slip away. A happy customer is someone who will continue to study at your school and who will bring other customers into your business as well, and keeping an existing customer costs far less than getting a new one.

I have many "Elite Consulting Clients – E.C.C" in which I do a 40 minute phone call with each and every week. These clients have at a minimum doubled their businesses and sometimes as much as quadrupled their companies in less then two years. This is amazing growth by any standard. Just recently while speaking to one of my clients I asked them to develop what I call a student grid. This could be a client grid if you are not in the martial arts business. We categorized the clients in many different areas. First their name, address and phone number. Second, the program they are currently enrolled in, thirdly, their purchasing algorithm.

My goal was to see what the client was like in all categories, what their spending habits were, what they did extra-curricular in our business, etc. When the client finally did this, which took some time, we discovered a few untapped marketplaces. For example, this particular school has a good following of 3-4 year olds. The problem being they do not have any systems in place to service them other than their normal classes. They didn't do special seminars, or have special retail for this client age range. So upon careful investigation we instituted an entirely different set of items for retail and special events netting the business a larger gross and net profit per year. This was all done with investigation of the client and their purchasing algorithm.

Here are 10 tips to keep your customers coming back for more.

1. Send thank-you notes: This seems to be a no-brainer, but you'd be surprised at how many school owners and entrepreneurs neglect to write thank-you notes - especially when things get really busy. Take the time to tell your customers you genuinely appreciate their business. The thought will remain with them for a long time. A small gesture like this will stand out in their minds because most of your competition won't send thank-you notes. I once had a store manager of a large food chain called "Stop and Shop" send me a thank you card. This one gesture certainly made me purchase more often from them, you see even years later I am talking about it.

2. Mail postcards: If you want customers to look forward to receiving your postcards, make the message meaningful. Customers should want to keep the postcards handy, or even send them to friends. Some ideas are "Quote of the month," "Health tip of the month," and "Healthy eating." You can include tips on topics such as time-management, meditation, stretching, bully-proofing your child, stranger danger, conflict resolution, or other areas that interest your customers. Avoid being promotional; just provide the kind of information that customers will appreciate. The added benefit to you is when guests visit your customers' home, they may see your name, potentially leading to conversations about your business.

3. Send e-mail updates: Think of your e-mail updates as your personal press releases and trickle marketing. Provide customers with information on product sales, special events, customer service updates, etc. You should send e-mails to your customers at least once per month to build momentum. This activity keeps students and their parents informed. Over time, it gets them excited to be involved with your school and motivates them to give you referrals. Be careful not to train them not to listen. (we will talk about this later)

4. Get together over coffee or lunch: Spend face time with your customers in a non-sales environment. Ask about their families, hobbies, personal goals and so forth. When you show customers you really care about them on a personal level, they're yours for life.

5. Celebrate birthdays, anniversaries and other special occasions: These occasions are of the utmost importance to your customers and their families. So let them know that you care. I regularly send birthday cards, but I also recommend recognizing anniversaries and other occasions that you know of. Remember their special dates and they will never forget you!

6. Follow up on health issues: If you find out a customer or a family member has been sick, call periodically just to offer support. Send flowers or a card if the situation warrants it. You can also do the same if someone has a baby.

7. Offer referrals: Keep records of which of your customers are self-employed. A great way to encourage loyalty is to refer people to your students' businesses. Scroll through your customer database and make phone calls to find out whether your clients or their parents have their own businesses. If they do, record that information. This will enable you to help them through referrals, and chances are that they will return the favor. You may also include this list in your "Welcome to the Family packet."

8. Entertain: Throw a party for your best customers or top students. You'll be amazed at how much rapport and good will you can build with your students when they feel appreciated. Make them feel like the upper level. You can do this is such a way that you will turn a select few into the many. The word will get around and people will look forward to qualifying to be invited the next time. The top students will help you to build the family environment you are looking for.

9. Ask for post-sale feedback: Demonstrate you care about the quality of your service. Call customers and ask them questions such as: Are you pleased with the service you received? What did you like most about working with us? What would you like to see improved? What product or program would you like to see more of? If you could change anything what would it be?

10. Send out 20 "Great Job!" cards per week: This is something fun and is an exciting task. It helps to boost morale and keeps everyone excited. A simple card that tells a student you think he or she is doing great really goes a long way. Imagine the thrill of receiving a card that says "Great sidekick Tuesday. One day you will be an awesome black belt!" or "Thanks for coming in and talking to me today. I appreciate the opportunity and if I can ever be of service to you, please just call."

These tips will help you take your company to an entirely new level. Following up on all aspects of your customer interactions shows your customers that you are actively involved in keeping them thrilled with the service you provide. And when you ask customers for feedback and implement their suggestions, they feel a sense of ownership in what you're doing and become even more loyal to your school. This is a great way to build your empire.

Providing the Ultimate in "Customer Service"

I purchased a Ford Explorer. Before I bought it I shopped around, as do many customers interested in purchasing a car. First I went to the local Cadillac dealer, where I already have a Cadillac on lease. I was ignored and made to feel like I couldn't afford a Cadillac. This was amazing because I already owned one, but still they managed to make me feel terrible. Then I went to four other dealerships and met with similar responses. When I stopped at the Ford dealership I was met by a salesperson with a huge smile across his face. I could see he was motivated to sell me a vehicle at any cost, and that immediately made me want to deal with him.

Having bought many cars as well as having a few on lease right now for employees and family, I thought I knew what I was in for. I had my guard up, but this person recognized what I was expecting and went to work with my best interest in mind. He knew I was a qualified buyer and he wanted to sell me a vehicle. No exaggeration; I was ready to buy the car, had all the papers filled out and walked out the door within one hour. I was scheduled to pick up the car the next day at 10:30 a.m. I was charged and excited. I was also blown away with the salesman's proficiency and also the dealership's expertise at making it such a painless process.

Early the next morning the salesman himself called and said there had been some delays. I explained I was on a rather tight schedule so he said, "You are such a great customer that I will deliver the vehicle to you personally." I was amazed when at one that afternoon he was there with the truck, showed me how it worked, and personally put the license plate on the truck for me in the parking lot of my own business.

I had just experienced the ultimate in customer service. Three weeks had gone by and I had received a letter each week; one thanking me for the purchase, the next letting me know where to call if I had any questions, and the last letting me know that a customer service questionnaire was in the mail.

Now I could go on and on about how the Martial Arts industry often doesn't provide the greatest customer service, and how that compares to my car-buying experience, but let's start by asking ourselves some questions. Are we providing a level of service to our customers that makes them feel the way I felt buying my car? Are we providing the ultimate in customer service? If not, why not? Well, now is the time to change that and to give our customers the ultimate in customer service.

Ideas to Improve Customer Service to Your Clients

1. Break your students up into three customer service groups. Make one group all new students 0 -6 months; the second, students who've just received a promotion or the 7-12 month; and the third all other students, 12–24 months. You can take this further if you want.

2. Design a customer service package specifically for each group, including a letter letting the clients know how you feel about them and what they mean to you as your students. Include some basic policies and information on what is going on at your studio. Mention other concepts and theories that you teach. Do not be afraid to include information or discounts on other programs and upgrades.

3. While organizing your packets for the three categories of students, decide on how "deep" you want to go. For instance I've received three letters so far and a promise of a questionnaire from the car dealer. Decide on what you want to say to each group and how often you want to communicate with them, so that you may clear up questions and prepare them for the long, fun filled journey ahead.

4. Decide on the message you want to convey to each group and repeat it often.
Now that may sound strong, but ask yourself, "Are the big boys, such as car dealers, skimping on their contacts with their customers?" No, they're not! Well, what makes small business owners think that we become pests when we keep getting our message out there? The reality is, if you do it right you will not be considered a pest but an asset.

5. Once you have set up your systems be disciplined and diligent about using them.
Make it part of your business to get the letters out on time. Set up your time frame: for instance the first letter goes out two days after a student signs up; letter two goes out three weeks later; and the third letter goes out after five weeks. This is something that will help build student loyalty and retention, and will instill the idea that you are a professional organization.

It would be difficult to overstate how important it is to develop business systems. You have heard this before, but here is another slant or reason for it. If you are less professional but have a personal touch, that may be fine, but what it *does* tell people is that you are small time. Even "Mom and Pop" stores are businesses. We need to let our clients know this is our business and we conduct ourselves in a businesslike manner. We are a professional organization. Our professionalism will impact how people purchase from us as well as how they deal with our organizations. We need to be consummate professionals and to provide the ultimate in customer service. We need to keep up with the big boys. Now it is up to you to put the systems into effect. If you do it correctly the client will replace the word business with family and service and not look at it as negative but a huge positive.

Being on the Edge of Excellence

What defines excellence? What is it that takes a client from thinking your service is adequate to feeling that what you provide is excellent? What is it that makes a person disappointed and unhappy? And what moves a person from simply being happy and satisfied to believing that he is a part of excellence? The answers to these questions are vital to business owners.

There are many factors that tip the scale to make a client a raving fan. It is our ultimate goal to have clients who are so overwhelmingly pleased that any chance they get they talk about our schools. Think about this: What products do you use that please you so much that you tell everyone you can about them? What makes those products different from others? What products are you satisfied enough with that you continue to use them regularly but still don't talk about them? Why is it that even though you are satisfied you are not motivated to share your feelings?

The goal of these questions is to have you shift your perspective and to think as a customer. I am sure you have your favorite restaurants and shops toward which you tend to gravitate. Is the gravity pulling you there because going there is a habit, the service is good, and you're "satisfied?" Or do you rave about those establishments and look forward to going to them when the time comes?

I believe that excellence in customer service provides the answer. This has many levels to it. Part of excellence is in the product, part is in the service, and a good amount of your perception of excellence has to do with ambiance. The product doesn't necessarily need to be the best, but it should appear to be the best. It is all in presentation. Of course my core belief keeps me striving for excellence in all I do. I want my product to be the best, as I know you do also. I want to continually improve and do more for my clients. I want them to be raving fans.

What can you do to tip the scales in your favor? Here are a few steps that may take you over the edge.

1. Organize specialty days - For example: Mother's Day and Father's Day car wash. Each parent who comes in for training with his child receives a free car wash. You can do this many ways, such as buying passes at a local car wash. The money invested is well worth it. Or you can hire a team or a group of volunteer students to wash the cars. This can be done on any occasion.

2. Provide advanced training for free - special seminars and events above and beyond what students usually get. Be clear when you explain what it is that students are getting. If you aren't clear and specific, students tend to think it is an ordinary part of the training rather than an "extra" they're getting for free.

3. Keep in touch regularly and ask how your students are doing. Get to know them personally. Besides the obvious benefit of knowing your students and having them know you, personal connections are a great retention tool. If there are connections then clients are less inclined to leave.

4. Take care of "issues" in a timely fashion - Make sure complaints or problems are handled immediately. Most of the time the client is satisfied just being heard. Sometimes the specific resolution means less to the student than your concern for his or her well being. Most doctors involved in malpractice suits have been told that they would not have been sued if they had been better at following up on the illness or issue.

5. Educate your clients - Education is the key to success. Just because they are shopping with us, doesn't mean they know we are the best. Toot your own horn. Let people know what separates you from your competition. Remember that competition is not just other Martial Arts schools; it is any and all activities that can potentially take students away from you program.

6. Continually give - Find ways to be generous and show your appreciation.

7. Give people awards and accolades - Present perfect attendance awards. Perfect attendance awards are a great way to show you appreciate your students' motivation to come to class. If you want more information on this check out months 3 and 4 on our premium site, www.TakingItToTheNextLevel.com.

8. Host open houses - Develop a system to show parents what you do, and to highlight the students. This is also a great way to gain new students.

9. Offer private lessons - Private lessons offer a great opportunity for us to have that one-on-one, personal contact with our clients to help them achieve the results they are looking for. It is of the utmost importance for a client to see progress. A private lesson is the perfect setting for this to happen. Remember, it is not necessary for you to make money on the private lessons. Look at them as a way of saving you money in marketing in the long run. It is much cheaper to keep an existing client than finding a new one.

Developing the Ultimate in School Interaction

Wow, not another Karate school opening up in my area. Okay, let me think here, what can I do to put the bum out of business? How dare he open up in my area, I have been here for 10 years, it is clearly my town. Some nerve!

Then a buzzer goes off and reality sets in. Hello. This is the 21st century, the great American dream is to have the freedom to do what you want, open a business anywhere and take your shot at a piece of the pie.

Who is our competition? The Martial Arts school down the road is *not* who we should worry about; the market in every town usually can be shared by many Martial Arts schools. In fact, in my town I am friendly with almost every Martial Arts instructor and we continuously share ideas and concepts. After all, if an instructor has a student with a friend who is not willing to travel, that instructor may refer the friend to me. If the instructor doesn't, then we all lose. Sharing is the most basic concept of abundant wealth. Don't be stingy!

If the Karate guy down the road is not your competitor, who is? Maybe gymnastics, baseball, soccer or any other activity that takes students away from the Martial Arts. How about this: if we could get Oprah to endorse the Martial Arts, we would have huge lines at our doors.

So why not do the next best thing? We need to educate the public school systems to recognize that what we do is the one tool that they are missing in order to develop the best students.

Here are a few things that we do to connect with teachers and school systems:

1. At the beginning of the school year, we interview every student, asking what he or she has learned from our program and how it has helped the student in life, specifically about how it helped in relation to becoming a better student. Then use the answers to compose a letter of reference from our school to the student's teacher.

For example:

Dear Mrs. Smith:

We have found Robert to be a highly motivated child and we see that he enjoys being in the spotlight. We have determined while working with Robert that he loves quiet praise rather than public praise. His love of dinosaurs really helps us to explain things to him by developing parallels. We think he will be a great student. If you can use our help in any way, please do not hesitate to call us for special visits, cultural days or anything that deals with Martial Arts, self-motivation or focus. We have extensive experience dealing with children and would love to be on your team. This can be done with a little help from the child's parent. If you ask the parent if they will help you they will see this as just another added benefit you offer.

At every promotion we have our students fill out letters of intent (also available on TakingittotheNextLevel.com). In these letters of intent we ask for the approval of the students' teachers, asking them if the children fit the criteria of our school: are they respectful; do they work hard; do they hand in their work and homework on time; are they doing their best exhibiting their "Black Belt attitude?" We ask the parents the same questions relating to the students' home lives, as well as their desire to be respectful to their siblings, their families, and all other people they come in contact with. Then we ask the teachers to sign off, and let them know that we are available for special school visits, cultural days, gym classes or coaching sessions for the teachers. After all, we are master motivators.

2. We encourage all-around healthy lifestyles, so we ask our students to be educated in proper nutrition and diet. Just bringing up this topic is a good way to lead into meaningful discussions in gym classes or health-related classes.

3. We invite school teachers to the tests in which their students are involved. We believe school activities and Martial Arts activities are all interrelated. Both schoolwork and Martial Arts are about the continual pursuit of perfection.

I believe an important piece of the "puzzle" of how to maximize our effectiveness is to work regularly with the school systems. Our paramount goal is to do whatever is best for our students. So if we can work hand-in-hand with parents and school teachers we will share the training responsibility and share in the credit for our students' successes.

Saving the Bad Apples! or Turning "Bad Apples" Into "Good Apples"

Have you ever had a client that has pushed all the right buttons? One who has done everything in his or her power to get you to explode and say, "You, get out of here - or I'll @#$%^&&&*!!!"

Don't hide how you feel; learn how to turn the feelings into a productive situation and turn your and their frowns upside down.

Too many times when we are faced with clients that are either angry or dissatisfied with our services or performance we either run from the situations or sweep them under the carpet, hoping that they will never surface again. In both cases, this is not the correct response. At times you may say to yourself that it is okay to get rid of a troublesome client. I do subscribe to the philosophy that you need to get rid of the bad apples, but sometimes we can help change those bad apples and save them. You see, when clients have good experiences with a company, they tend to tell three other people about them. Positive word-of-mouth is great for business. However, clients (or ex-clients) who are displeased with a situation tell, on average, 11 people about it. So you can see that it's often of benefit to turn a displeased client into a pleased one.

Naturally, no one wants to walk into a bad situation, but I have found over the years when I have dealt with clients that it is easier to attack a difficult situation immediately than to let it fester and become bigger than it originally was. Always consider the value of your client, your reputation, and your company. I would say it is worth your while to face that angry customer and get the situation resolved as quickly as possible.

Here are nine steps to help you turn that frown upside down.

1. Take care of the situation immediately - Nothing is worse than letting a person's displeasure fester and allowing him or her to get even angrier. A quick phone call just to say you know about the situation and you intend to handle it may be enough to cool the flames. Then set an appointment to talk in person. I have realized after years of taking both approaches, immediately addressing problems and working with the students' or clients' best interest in mind always ends up as a win-win situation.

2. Be sure to show your concern and be genuine - Pretending to be concerned is a very easy way to make your clients angrier. You must take the time to walk the path of empathy and deal with the situation from your clients' point of view. At that point, make yourself perfectly clear on how you feel or how you would like to handle the situation. Now, don't get me wrong, you can't always bow down to a client, but letting the client know that you are on the same team usually helps you to work things out more smoothly.

3. Don't rush your clients - Be patient and let them vent. Sometimes it just requires listening. It is not all about you and getting the solutions. Sometimes a client just needs to be heard. Never interrupt or shut them down. In many cases, it is best to just listen. If clients are angry they will eventually wind down. In some cases, they'll realize that they blew the situation out of proportion and they'll feel foolish. Then they're likely to accept nearly any solution you offer.

4. Keep calm - Often, in times of anger, people say and do things they don't mean to say or do. Learn to let those things go. Once, while training with Shihan Steven Seagal, he told me you must take things into your mind, but not into your heart. Don't let people rent space in your heart. Another great quote is, "While you are holding a grudge, the person you are holding a grudge on is out dancing."

5. Ask the correct questions - Your goal in a situation like this should be to get to the bottom of the situation. I learned a long time ago, there is a bit of truth in every story. So even though you may not agree, you should ask yourself, "What can I learn from the client?" Your aim must be to discover the specific things that you can do to correct the problem. Try to get precise information about the difficulties the problem caused, rather than a general venting of grievances.

6. Get clients to give you ideas on solutions - Once you have everything out in the open, then you can work together on solutions to get rid of the problem. Hopefully, at this point the clients are willing to work with you. If not, then you should schedule another appointment for a time when they are calmer and ready to cooperate to make the situation better.

7. Agree together on a solution - Once you have identified the challenge and you have talked about solutions, you are now ready to set some in stone. Agree on a course of action that both of you can live with, and then stick to it.

8. Set up a time frame - Once you've agreed on a solution, set a schedule and a realistic time frame that you both can happily work within. This will give you both time to work at the situation and fix it. The biggest mistake you can make is to agree to something that can't be accomplished, just to smooth things over. Honesty is the best policy. Sometimes, even if you can't work out a solution, clients will be happy because you have been totally honest with them.

9. Live up to your promises - Make sure that your commitments have top priority to you and that they don't get forgotten. The troublesome situation may not have been that big of a deal to you, but if it upset a client that much it meant a lot to them. Validate the client's feelings by being totally professional. Often, this will create a level of customer loyalty that you could never have imagined.

Turning "bad apples" into "good apples" can be done if you address and solve your clients' problems in a professional manner. It will help you in the future because clients will recognize that you are approachable and that if anything ever happens again, rather than getting angry they can come right to you and talk to you. Once you've fixed clients' problems, you'll have earned other opportunities to serve their needs in the future...and the needs of those who'll be told about how well you handled them. And when you've successfully satisfied a difficult client, that can often be the perfect time to promote alternate programs and to upsell. I like to look at every situation as a way to grow, both financially and spiritually. Learn from your problem situations and you will grow and prosper.

Chapter 2
The key to success – Goal setting and time management

Recently, I have noticed a major change in my area in the way schools are being run. The more that consulting companies such as MATA, MAIA, NAPMA or Taking It to the Next Level help make the Martial Arts business more professional, the more schools start popping up. The more Black Belts see the successes of their teachers and the financial benefit, the more people believe that they are capable of the same things. In my area alone over the last 15 years, at least 100 schools have opened with more then half of them already closed. The scary statistic is that many of them are still open. I remain one of the largest schools in New York, but I'm beginning to see the competition is cutting into my profits. As I mentioned earlier, other activities such as Soccer, T-Ball, Baseball, Video Games etc. When there is a small group of people to recruit from, then the competition starts getting fierce.

In the past two years, a typical ad run in a paper has yielded a great deal fewer responses then it had before then. I have found ads that once brought in 20 to 30 calls are now bringing in one or two. I have found that a door hanger campaign with 2,500 flyers that once brought in 25 to 50 calls now brings in two or three. So the scary part is the old stuff is not working any more. I have spoken about this many times in regards to catching the clients' ears and eyes simultaneously. We need to make an impact on the clients. Remember, there is only one opportunity to make a good first impression.

There are two types of businesses: inside-out and outside-in. I believe that most of the time each business has a bit of both, but you can't have multiple approaches simultaneously. You are basically either one or the other. Let me explain a bit more about the differences. An inside-out company concentrates on its clients first. Everything such a company does involves servicing its clients. My perspective on this has drastically changed. I used to have the attitude of take it or leave it. Now don't get me wrong, I was never a tyrant or self-centered; I always did what I did because I believed in the Martial Arts and its ability to change peoples' lives. I just believed that what I said was law and I believed that what I already had was the best there could be. Now things have changed. But before I explain my new mentality let me define an outside-in company. I believe that most Martial Arts schools play a game of revolving doors. As new students come in, others go out. Outside-in companies are continually looking for the newest, greatest advertising campaign, are always looking for ways to get new students and continually grow. This is the outside-in mentality. Advertise and sell.

Let me tell you a story that I heard from one of the marketing and business geniuses of our time - Jay Abraham. He spoke of a building he had purchased that at one time housed a company that manufactured liniment for aching muscles and arthritis. The company had gone out of business due to lack of sales. He started renovation of the building, and while the construction was going on he received thousands of requests from people for the product and a replacement product. He asked the previous owners to sell him the trademarks, mailing lists and product. After the sale was agreed to and done, he approached catalog companies and put a zero dollar advertising campaign together. He told the cataloguers that if they sold the product, he would allow them to retain all the profits, as long as they gave him the mailing list of the buyers. In fact, he even offered to ship to the product for them. He realized that the big business was not in selling the product initially for a profit: it was all about repeat business. There were people who had been using this product for years. Abraham ended up taking in hundreds of millions of dollars on this deal. He realized that the company was thinking outside-in, not inside-out. The money was there to be made by servicing existing clients rather than always and only looking for new ones.

Here are a few questions to ask yourselves. Please write them down and then when you get a free minute, actually fill in the blanks. Doing this is very important.

1. What is it that you are sitting on that may potentially yield a greater profit over this coming year? What can you do to recognize where you are sitting on a pile of gold? What is it that you are not seeing? What is the potential?

2. What can you do to restructure? There are many school owners I speak to who are charging far less than the industry standard. If you don't know the standard, it is around $120-$140 per month for a basic three day per week program. I have determined this based on the many conversations I have had with thousands of clients. Can you charge more? Many times when I consult, my advice is to ask people to raise their prices. Most of the time I hear excuses: this is not New York; this is a low-income area, etc. While some of these reasons are legitimate, most of them are not really relevant. I have often helped schools in low-income areas increase their bottom lines by making one simple decision. All they need to do is do it.

3. Are you trying to excel in too many areas? What is it that makes you who you are? Why do people come to you? Once a consultant asked my staff and I the same question - What makes you special and what makes your school special? You know what we all said? We help change peoples' lives. He pressed for more information. The staff responded with things like increased self-esteem, self-defense and all the things that are written in every Martial Arts ad that is run today. You know what: I didn't think we were that special after all. In fact, I had a hard time believing it. Until I discovered our U.S.P – unique selling proposition - this took some time and deep thought. What is your U.S.P.

4. What can you do to increase the quality of service to your clients? What is it that you can do to make yourself better? What is it that you will do to go above and beyond?

5. Why will people continue to come to your school if all you do is the same stuff over and over? People go to pre-school, then elementary school, then junior high or middle school, high school and then many levels of college. Once they graduate they have other plans for after the schooling is done. What is it that makes your students stick around? You must have tiers or levels to make them want to stick around. If we continue to repackage the same old stuff - selling it as a new move or advanced process - then we are gong to lose people. We need to keep progressing and moving our students and ourselves forward. If we are stagnant then it is our own fault for becoming extinct.

Before you can start to move toward where you want to be personally and professionally, you need to know where you are. Spend some time answering the five questions above. I am often guilty of reading, listening and watching and saying to myself I will get to it, then not doing it. I believe it is imperative to take the time now to do this drill.

Goals We Set Are Goals We Get

The key to success is goal setting. In a study performed by a college professor some twenty years ago, he interviewed nearly 100 people. In his study he asked how many people actively set goals. Out of 100 included in the survey only 2% actually set goals and stuck to them. Some twenty years later he interviewed the entire group again and found that the 2% of the people that set goals had accomplished much more, and had a net worth that was ten times higher than the entire rest of the group. That's quite a powerful testimonial for goal setting!

There are some basic principles a person needs in order to realize the benefits of goal setting and its ultimate affect on their success.

M.A.P.- The Massive Action Plan:

This is a plan that will take you from start to finish. A person who falls short of accomplishing goals may not have a clear plan of how they are going to get to the end result of the plan. Something I have adopted and developed as a student creed at Long Island Ninjutsu Centers I learned from one of the greatest motivational gurus, Tony Robbins. While setting goals you need to set a goal, have a plan, take consistent action, have a success coach, review progress and renew goals accordingly. I teach my students goal setting is imperative to success in all that they do. Whether it be achieving their black belt, or having the best marriage possible.

Consider this: you know what you want; for instance, you want to lose weight. This is an admirable goal. But how do you go about achieving this? You must have a plan - this plan is to set out a daily routine of what you are willing to do to get to that goal. Going to aerobics classes, martial arts or even walking in the neighborhood. A success coach (and this is very important) is absolutely necessary. This should be someone that can keep you on track. Someone who when you want to fall off of the wagon will push you to continue.

Take Consistent Action

Go out every day and work toward your goal. These ideals do not apply to personal goals alone. Many small businesses fail because they do not have set goals, do not have an action plan or don't follow through to the end. If your plan is to double your student enrollment or to increase your bottom line through inside sales, then you need to document this goal and the steps that you plan to take to achieve it.

Update your goal sheet every day or week. Studies show that it takes 21 days to develop a good habit, so be consistent! Review your progress and take the time to see the steps that you are taking and recognize them. See the strides and the accomplishments. If you have not achieved your goal then you will need to re-assess your plan.

Renew Your Goals Regularly

This step is important because it helps you to achieve your goal by realistically prioritizing and re-evaluating each goal independently. You may come home from a seminar or workshop with 100 new ideas. It's important that you prioritize each of them and add them logistically into your action plan.

Having and setting goals is a learned and practiced science. It takes dedication and consistency, but once you have developed the habit of documenting and tracking your progress goal setting is easier than 1,2,3!

Be Prepared

Tony Robbins is one of my role models. I have read his books, listened to all of his audiotapes and been to many of his seminars. In fact, I receive his monthly newsletter. Just recently I listened to an audiotape in which he spoke of how he adhered to the philosophy of preparation. This is so true when it comes to the Martial Arts.

I have done many conference calls on time management and goal setting. The skill needed to efficiently accomplish both of these tasks is preparation. It is better to use two hours preparing for the future than to use two hours each time to organize yourself to get something done. Here are three tips that will help you prepare to achieve your goals.

1) Work on your goals and objectives – If you take a few hours each month and write a set of goals and objectives you want to put into action the next month, you will be a step ahead of the game. You can then methodically take those goals and objectives and break them into steps to systematically achieve each one of them. I believe a person should have one overriding goal, and that is to achieve as many goals as possible. This is my own personal quote. Once you have developed the objectives, then you are on your way to achieving.

2) Take the time ahead of time to set your goals – I have found this to be one of the most important and imperative steps in getting organized. This is the reason I get so many things accomplished. Writing down and prioritizing what you want to accomplish is going to make your days more productive. The fact that you don't waste time getting started is going to get you ahead of the game right from the start. One preparation strategy that I use is to assign specific days to do specific tasks. It helps eliminate guessing and floundering around to accomplish the tasks at hand. For instance, you could assign every day from 9-10 am to marketing: Monday you could focus on referrals; Tuesday you could do door hangers, etc. From 11-12 you might schedule another task such as making networking calls. Make the goal or objective you are trying to achieve a priority, and accomplishing that goal will take your school to the next level.

3) Keep yourself motivated – Find the things that motivate you. Take a weekend and just sit in a hotel or take a quick trip somewhere up in the mountains and bring a pad and paper. Don't relax only; use this time to recharge. Find a group of peers or a person to mentor you. Get a series of audiotapes; join a club for public speakers. Go to seminars with people who will help you achieve success in areas that pertain to your goals in business, finance, investing, etc. These are the activities that we usually put off on a regular basis. Do not put them off. Do not settle.

The definition of insanity is doing the same thing time after time, but expecting different results. When you spend time on preparation, you will do things differently. You will be more effective and productive, and the results will show!

Making Time For The Tasks That Never Get Completed

As the owner of multiple locations I personally understand the meaning of "short on time"! However, I further understand that it is my responsibility to put an effort into not only ensuring that my classes and curriculum are the best that they can be, but also that my location is experiencing growth. The way I am able to achieve this is most certainly by becoming a master at time management and goal setting. I covered what it takes to create an M.A.P – the massive action plan - then I spoke briefly about the steps it takes and the follow up you need. Here are some simple goal setting systems. I must mention that I have attended many seminars with the Franklyn Covey Company and I highly recommend attending some of their events. In fact to this day I still live my life through the Franklyn Covey system and Planner.

Goal setting is a matter of three things: prioritizing, focus and follow up. For example, once you have set your goals, you need to determine what priority status each goal is. The question you need to ask yourself is what goal or task will help you get closer to your final goal. For more clarification, if you want to make more money this year, what is it you need to do to achieve that? It may be one goal or a bunch of mini goals that lead you to your final destination. Once you have determined your goal you need to set in motion your plan of action like we spoke about before. Then you need to prioritize what goals are going to help you get there and place an order of importance on those goals. For example, using the letters A, B and C will help you. A - being the top priority and C being the least. There may be a number of top priorities so you can assign them all the letter A.

At that point you may want to assign numbers to go along with the A's. Not all A's may be of the same importance but still may be more important than they B's and C's, for example A-1, A-2 etc. Then you can do the same down the line with the B's and C's. Once you have established your order it is imperative to follow the discipline of the order so you can achieve your tasks. If you do this diligently you will find you are moving forward quite quickly and seeing your achievements regularly. Little things get in the way. Sometimes they may need immediate attention but they shouldn't slow you down entirely. For example, a phone call from a disgruntled client. You need to pay immediate attention to it. The minute it is done you are back onto your list. This is why I stress doing the list the night before with a clear head and focus on the direction you want to go. If you don't do this you will find that you will get swept up in the day to day madness and find the entire day has gone by and you didn't work on your priority goals and tasks.

Managing the 'Little Things'

When I started my school I had no idea it would develop into the "monster" that it is. I didn't realize that I would need to pay payroll taxes for upwards of 18 people. I didn't realize that I would be buying company cars, doing a simple IRA, dealing with headaches from employees not doing their jobs, doing their jobs and wanting more money, not meeting quotas on financial obligations, etc. I had no idea. Low and behold I am here and it is a fun ride. Rather than focus on the negative stuff, I always try (and I repeat, *try*) to focus on the positive. It is not always easy, but it is better to focus on the positive.

Being a Martial Arts business owner is a blessing. I am able to watch each and every day as someone new walks through my doors and tries the Martial Arts. For those who stay even briefly, it is a life changing experience. It is something that we all as school owners are blessed with. So the good thing is that we are doing what we love. For those of you who aren't able to teach full time and need to work second jobs, I commend you even more. I remember what it was like to work 60 hours per week and then teach another 30. It is beyond tough, so my hat's off to you.

What are the little things that mean a great deal? Well, as I said before, I never realized that I would build this machine that required so much detail and maintenance. The little things are all the things that make a huge difference to your bottom line.

What is a Career Martial Artist?
Someone who sets time aside to see their future!

I look at a career Martial Artist as a Martial Arts business owner, a person who each day is securing his or her future. Career Martial Artists are people who are taking the time to plan, putting money away for retirement, investing in anything from the stock market to real estate, and putting together estates. This way, all their hard work is not wasted if the day comes when something happens and they are no longer there to experience all that they have done.

Why do we usually think so linearly? Well, simply, it is because we are so busy, so overwhelmed with the day-to-day, that there is no time to actually do more.

I know what busy is. In fact, I want to tell you what I did one day recently, from the minute I woke up till I lay down to watch television. For some this may seem like a cakewalk, for others it may seem like a large amount of stuff. I have shared this with some of my clients on a Tele-seminar and they really seemed to like it. Some emailed me later to tell me it was something they were amazed at, while others found it inspirational that so much can be accomplished in one day. I got the idea from Donald Trump in one of his books. I was amazed at how little I did compared to him but that is why he makes the big bucks.

Here goes:

Daily Journal from February 6, 2007

7:00 am: Awakened by cell phone. Tenants. The heat is not working. Ignored call. They called again. I woke up after I realized how cold it was. Called the oil company and set an appointment to repair the problem; coordinated with tenant.

7:05 am: Went back to bed, couldn't sleep. Then read for one hour, got out of bed took shower, got ready.

8:30 am: Got my bagel and breakfast; made it to the office by 8:45.

8:45 am: Put away the corporate kits delivered by my attorney unannounced, found lying on my desk. Ate my breakfast while organizing.

8:50 am: Started typing this journal and eating my breakfast and preparing for the day, while reading some reports dropped off by my team I called in my prescription, finished breakfast.

8:55 am: Checked all e-mails, answered some consulting e-mails and cleaned up junk e-mail.

9:10 am: Checked and balanced nine corporate checking accounts. A mom called from the dojo who is a parent of one of my students about her disappointment in the change of venue of our upcoming Black Belt test. We spoke and she seemed to be fine. I think it is just as upsetting to her, if not more so, than to her son. I started questioning her motives but reminded myself it really didn't make all that much difference, it was handled and I let it go.

9:47 am: Signed certificates for the East Islip School, my second largest location, that had been brought in for me. Talked to Chuck, one of our staff, about "Taking It to the Next Level."

10:00 am: Took a call from my ex-wife about our daughter, and we went over our daughter's schedule for the next five days. It is good to be friends with her; we get along really well.

10:10 am: Recorded audio generators for next level, recorded month nine greeting, "The theory of satisfied to motivated, the theory of the speed bump." (Seven messages in total)

11:45 am: Wrote e-mails and confirmations on dates and consulting. Ordered lunch.

12:15 pm: Ate lunch brought to me by staff member.

12:45 pm: Worked on computer doing flyer for school.

1:30 pm: Stopped working, traveled to my house only 5 minutes from my office to read and relax

3:00 pm: Came back to the school to teach, got dressed and went over classes with staff.

4:00 pm: Taught; then came home.

8:00 pm: Finished teaching, got dressed in my regular clothes and went home by 8:15 to eat dinner and watch television.

Okay, now that you've seen one of my typical days, I want you to write down exactly what one or two of your typical days looks like. Include everything. Don't leave out anything, regardless of how minor it seems. Before you can take care of the "little things" you need to know what you are currently spending your time doing, and then what you should be spending your time doing.

Once you've tracked a day or two, you will clearly see that each of our lives is consumed by "little things." As far as our businesses are concerned, when we open our doors there are so many activities that need to be done. The first is preparation for the day. The problem is, once we enter our schools many little things come up to disturb our process of preparation.

Journaling the Key to your Success

Now that you have gone through the process of writing down a day or two of all your daily activities and started goal setting I have a home work assignment for you. You can continue to read on but you must start the process right away. First I want you to take the time each and every day for two weeks as you did in the previous assignment writing down all your task from the moment you open your eyes till the minute you go to bed and close them drifting off in to dreamland.

The goal is to do this for two solid weeks. If you have staff members you may ask for them to join in the task as well. After the two weeks go by you can review them together or merge them for the following assignment. Once you have completed your two week journaling quest I ask that you categorize your activities in three categories. 1) New Student Generation – this will only pertain to the tasks you have performed that are relevant to generating or securing new students. 2) Existing Student maintenance – this task will involve anything you did over the past two weeks that will help you to retain, motivate or fix any issues involving new students, 3) Administration and finance – these tasks involve all your student inventory, auditing, contract entering, paperwork including anything you need to do to keep proper records of your student body and finances.

Once you have achieved this journey of journaling for two weeks I recommend highly you take three different color highlighters and categorize all of the three groups by color. This task will act as a three fold activity in goal setting. The first being seeing where you time is being spent, or how it is being spent. The second is to find out if you are actually performing the tasks needed to run your school efficiently, for example during that two weeks how much time did you put into the growth of your school securing new members or marketing. Third – see what you can delegate to free up your time. Quite often all good goal setters are excellent at delegating. I sometimes personally feel lazy because I am trying to delegate as much as possible. Well, maybe I am lazy, but then I again, I work on my business not in it as much as possible.

Once you complete the three highlighted categories of your journal you will have a clearer picture on where your school is headed. This section on goal setting will absolutely change your life and your business future. It is imperative that you take action immediately and become a master, just like you did in your martial art life.

Chapter 3
Common Mistakes of an Entrepreneur

Martial Arts Quicksand!

Here is a story for you. Recently I had a conversation with one of my staff members. He is one of my former school managers who failed to make his school successful. I feel responsible for a portion of what happened, but the tools were there and the systems were sound and workable. One of my Elite clients once asked, "Why is it that some people are able to make it work while others can't?"

It is a fact that some are just not right for the job. They may not be capable or intelligent enough or possess the necessary character traits that the position requires. We need to admit that some people don't have the personality and abilities to be self employed while others do better in positions such as an instructor, assistant instructor, program manager or even a salesman. The reality is a majority of the people can't make it work. Who are the people who really have an undying thirst and desire to make it work? The real question is, is it you?

Information overload to some translates to a wealth of information for me. What I believe to be easy may seem like a nightmare for others. My six-year-old daughter spelled it out for me one day. I made her favorite dinner, Pastina in veggie broth - we are both vegetarians. I tasted the food and it was cool enough for me to eat. So I said, "It's fine."

She looked at me and said, "It may be fine for your mouth but maybe not for my little mouth." What a lesson! What I think is easy may seem that way because I have built "bigger muscles" than others have in business.

The question is, are you willing to stop making excuses and get down to being all you can be? Are you ready to become an army of one and build your empire?

Now getting back to the conversation I had with my student and former school manager. Basically he told me that he felt like he was underperforming for many reasons and felt like he was in quicksand. A very small amount of the reasons had to do with laziness while the majority had to do with not following the systems. Some things we have under our control, others we don't. I could go on and on stating that if an employee would simply just follow what they are told to do, they would succeed. But I have learned over the years you just can't make a horse fly, no matter how much you want them to. Again, some people are just not made for the job. Granted, others are capable of being trained and with the proper guidance they can become outstanding.

Lessons are sometimes learned the hard way. I want you to learn from my mistakes. Make sure you pick the correct employee for the job. Take the time to interview enough candidates as well as finding a professional recruiting process. Just recently we invested thousands of dollars developing a screening process with the correct questions so we can find the top employees in the categories needed within our schools. I don't want to beat a dead horse but these systems are also available on the premium section of Takingittothenextlevel.com.

You may still find this strange, but I want to help. I want to make your life easier. I have to admit, my goal is a bit selfish. Whether you teach Ninjutsu, Ju Jutsu or another form, I want to help the world by helping you teach the Martial Arts while realizing a better life for yourself by running a more successful, professional school. Just because you are the owner doesn't mean you are the best at everything. Martial arts may be your skill, but you may be terrible at sales, so go out and hire someone who is better than you. After all, our goal should be to make our students better then us. If that is the case then not why hire people who are better than you are at the things you don't like or prefer to do or are terrible at?

Thoughts of a Small Business Entrepreneur!

My morning began in the typical way. I woke up early and started to get my daughter ready for school. I made her breakfast, prepared her lunch and took out her clothes. I drove her to school as I do every day. Throughout all of this my body was sore from being on my feet the day before at a fair that our school performs at every year, and from the training for my 5th dan test the night before that. I did more grumping and groaning than usual, but as I did so, I also remembered that I am blessed, and no matter how I felt or how I saw things at that particular moment, every day above ground is a beautiful day.

You may ask, "What the heck is this guy talking about?" Well, I know that many of you live similar lives, have similar thoughts and often feel stressed and grumpy like me. This is human nature and we can't do anything about it. The thing that I would like to talk about is that no matter how we feel we cannot let these emotions affect our professional careers, our businesses or our relationships.

I continually ask myself questions that directly relate to how I live my life and run my business. I hope that some of these questions can help you.

1. What am I going to do today to make a difference? The long-term answer to this question will define the legacy that I leave behind me when I'm gone, but in the short term it relates to the daily tasks I need to accomplish. As we spoke about in the chapter on goal setting business owners set goals, sometimes even delegate (which they should do more often) but don't seem to monitor on a regular basis. The follow up and follow through are the most important things you can do as business owners. If you have goals and do not finish them they are nothing but a huge waste of your time. The sad reality is that often people start things but never finish them. In theory the ideas are all practical but ideas in your heads and not in actions are nothing but thoughts.

2. What am I doing to achieve my goals? There are many timeframes for goals – weekly, monthly, quarterly and yearly. I usually set my goals for the year, and then I wrap those big goals around all that I do weekly to accomplish the objectives that are tied into the major plan. I often share my lofty goals with my staff, and they seem to be on the same page (I said seem) and have the same desires. (This relates to my "shade of blue" theory that I will explain at the end.) When all is said and done we leave the meeting and start our days. I am often disappointed when I follow up and follow through, realizing that they either didn't understand or didn't share in my enthusiasm. They didn't see the vision clearly.

Very often we meet or speak with someone and express our own tastes, desires and expectations. The person we are talking to also states preferences, and we believe that we are in agreement. For instance, I meet a colleague, she and I talk, and we both say we love the color blue. Immediately we have a connection. Now "the color blue" is a metaphor for anything that we have in common. My inner dialogue says, "Wow, this person loves the same color as I do or the same food I do. We have something in common to build upon." In fact, when you look at "the color blue" on a chart, there are 50 different shades, and the color I like could be far different then the one my colleague likes. Number one on the chart may be sky blue; number 50 could be dark blue. The thing that is amazing is it is still blue, but in reality her color could be so close to black and mine so close to white that it is not at all similar except for the name. If we realize this can happen, we can move closer to really expressing our vision. My vision is not necessarily my staff's vision, even though we all initially think it is. If you want more info on this read the book ***Blink by author Malcom Gladwell***.

3. What did I accomplish out of the things that I set out to do? This is probably one of the most important questions all successful business people ask themselves. There are those people who are idea based, who are often owners; then there are those who are task masters, who get important things done. Without the idea people, nothing ever happens, but the most important people are the task masters. Those are the people who need to make sure the ideas become reality. If we, as owners, continually monitor our tasks and make sure they are done to the level of proficiency, then we will be ready to move to bigger and better things. Each day will be a stepping-stone to greatness. I believe that we need to consistently monitor our accomplishments in order to achieve successes.

4. Am I really as productive as I can be? This question can be depressing for the person who really wants success. The question is really how much do you want it?

Many times I talk about having balance, not working too hard or too many hours, but then I also talk about working a ton of hours in order to gain the success you want. Balance is a hard thing to achieve. How can you have balance and have success? This is where there is a trade off. The thought that you need to work all the time is painful, but a bitter reality. You must work hard in the beginning, and work long hours, but if you work smart and set up the correct systems and the correct business plan, then after you build the business you can monitor the company as a business owner, not as an employee. The imagery of floating in a pool in the tropics while monitoring your company almost seems unrealistic, but I do it continually (not so much the pool part, but definitely monitoring from afar). I think the most important thing is making sure you are living up to your own expectations. Excuses - the reasons you can't do things - are the major cause of failure. The way I see it is that if you want something bad enough you can have it. The questions you ask yourself in the morning and the evening and the answers to those questions are going to determine the level of success you experience.

In closing, I want to tell you not to be too hard on yourself, but rather to think of each day as a bank of time. We are gifted with 168 hours in a week. What we make of our time is what will determine how successful we are. There are people who experience the most horrific tragedies in their lives, and turn those tragedies into success stories. What can you do to make your life a success story? What price are you willing to pay, what sacrifices will you endure to make that happen?

Common Small Business Pitfalls

In every small business there are common mistakes that can hold us back from the success that we imagine for ourselves. Often times these are a direct effect of a lack of foresight or experience, or perhaps a by-product of moving too quickly into decisions. Regardless of the reason- these are common pitfalls that most Martial Art School owners have experienced and gained wisdom from.

Underestimating cash flow needs:
Lack of operating capitol is the biggest mistake small business owners make, and certainly the biggest downfall for most martial art school owners. The thing to keep in mind is that as your school grows so does your need for increased cash flow. As you grow so do salaries, taxes, supplies, advertising budgets, inventory, insurance, cleaning and higher rent, make a financial plan and use a financial planner to help you project cash flow, establish a working relationship with a bank, and keep a savings. Planning correctly can mean the difference between the life and death of your school.

Failure to broaden teaching skills and curriculum:
Johnny, Karate School owner begins to teach a kid's class and an adult class, then he offers an advanced class 2 times a week as the school grows. He hits the mark of about

50 or so students and then stays there year after year. If Johnny School Owner expands his curriculum to include a tiny tiger class of 3 to 5 - year olds and offers a basic adult fitness kickboxing class, then he can easily add additional 30-40 students and almost double his base. A school owner must remember to expand classes and curriculum along the way to experience success. Broaden your vision and perspective! Your curriculum can include teen classes, day-time classes, stress relief yoga, tai chi or even an after school karate program. The most important thing is expanding the curriculum to fit your vision of success!

Hiring unnecessary employees:
Is the new person that you hired assisting you with your school's vision, growth, and increasing revenue through their activity? Are they allowing you to focus on more revenue increasing activities? This is the key to deciding whether or not an employee is necessary. If you have answered no to a majority of these questions, then you have an unnecessary employee! An unnecessary employee is an additional cost, not a benefit to your plan for success. Determine to add employees only as needed and only at the proper stage of growth. Remember that a school has different needs as it grows. Only hire staff members who are an absolute necessity for a new or additional location or an expanded curriculum

Opening multiple locations too quickly:
The most successful multi-location operations are those with enough staff and revenue to support the new or existing location. It is justified to open an additional location only when you have employed a qualified staff member and you will be providing them with a career opportunity; or, if you have reached a successful peak or saturation point within your current location and have the additional income and staff to support another location entirely on your own. Too many owners let ego drive their ambition and over-step their boundaries with an additional location before they are ready to challenge the operating needs required. Do not make this mistake. Analyze whether you are busting at the seams at your current location before you open another. Quite often the second location will drain the first location and focus will be taken away from the main location, causing it to decline in income and quality. Be very careful. I know, I have lived this and still do on a daily basis.

Failure to share your business/school vision with your staff:
Every business needs to have either weekly or bi-weekly staff meetings. This is absolutely necessary to share your vision with the members of your staff so that there can be a common goal for the entire group. Consistent meetings will ensure that you are all aware of the challenges, goals and expectations and are working towards the same goals. These meetings also are a great method to track progress, reward successes and correct failures. It will also bring to light those employees with good ideas and motivation.

Failure to stay objective on business decisions:

Even though you are the boss and may be the "Master" of the school- bear in mind that you do not know everything involved in operating successfully. Network with other owners, peers, business associates, friends, and relatives. Get their opinions and their advice. If you notice, the film industry runs test screenings and premiers to test a film in its market before fully releasing the mass marketing. They use this to gauge how the film will be received and get the market's opinion to know if changes or revisions are needed. You need to run your ideas past those who have been down the same path and had successes and failures. Be open minded and seek advice. It's important to remember that it is okay to not to know everything!

Do you ever ask yourself, "Where am I missing the boat?" We all know that there is always room for growth and improvement. We often create a glass ceiling for ourselves by not considering important areas of our businesses. Here are some areas of staff management and marketing that are commonly overlooked:

Keep Your Staff Managed and Informed:

As a small business owner with limited time and resources one of your most important support systems is definitely the staff that you employ. A well informed and managed staff can make all the difference in the world - and can be a major contributor to your success and quality of life! But without properly outlining expectations, commending success and creating a good management plan your staff could turn into a very detrimental entity in your school.

You should be using the following systems for management:

Employee Handbook- Every business needs an employee handbook. The handbook should clearly and concisely cover all policies, procedures and expectations. Handbooks keep your staff informed, and are a great reference point should any questions or challenges arise.

Employee Contracts- Protecting your investment is of the utmost importance. Your staff is a reflection of your school, and directly impacts your livelihood. Contracts should create a promise that each member acknowledges the employee/employer relationship, staff/student relationships, and also the non-compete issues. This should be a part of your employee handbook and signed by every employee. It simply eliminates the scenarios when people claim "you never told me that."

Have a Backup Staff- What if your main instructor is out sick? Or worse, quits or is unable to continue in their teaching capacity? This has happened to me more than once. The sad reality is sometimes you don't see it coming. One of my good friends who runs a very successful martial arts organization on Long Island once told me "your best student or employee can leave you tomorrow." This is one of the most profound statements I have heard in my life. I have had people who left work on Friday stating they loved their job, only to come in on Monday and quit. I often ask myself how did I not see it coming, but the reality is sometimes people will deceive you. Schools need a back up staff available to pick up the slack for occasions that impact your current staff. Create a back up staff from current employees. You can easily build staff training and responsibilities into the curriculum for your Leadership, Black Belt or Masters Teams so if a situation arises a well trained staff member is waiting in the wings to get in the game! It may surprise you how many people are interested in helping you and become a part of something great.

Are you putting yourself out of business a little at a time?

Being a Ninja I pride myself in my stealth abilities and my expertise in collecting" Intel." Sometimes, during my consulting one on one calls, or when I have free time (which is very rare), I pick peoples' brains. I believe the key to being a good consultant is to have an open mind, to learn from my mistakes and to network actively with knowledgeable people. There are no criteria that would eliminate any businessperson from my list of people I can learn from. Simply put, I learn from everyone. So I want to thank all of you for helping me spread my wings.

In my travels around the country and through my dealings with schools, I have found a few practices that are incredibly dangerous and detrimental to the health of any business. Here's an everyday example of poor business practice, and one of great business practice: you may find them immediately relevant to a martial arts school.

Some time ago I went to a new restaurant with my family. I made a reservation over the telephone for 6:30. When I arrived at 6:15, no one came to greet me or tell me where to sit. I went to the counter myself and introduced myself and explained how happy I was to see their new business in my town. The response was worse than not friendly, it was uncaring. I thought, this may be due to the rush of business. I asked where the restroom was. As I walked through the restaurant I saw many empty tables. I wondered, *why am I waiting when the restaurant could seat me?* I came out of the restroom and spoke to the person in charge. She told me the empty tables were reserved. I explained that I had a reservation. She checked and then told me they were reserved for other people. Anyway, I waited until 7 before I started getting upset. They finally told me that they were going to give me someone else's reservations. I let them know how displeased I was with their service. I told my family that I expected this restaurant to be gone in six months if they didn't change their ways. Well, I was wrong: it only took four months before they were out of business!

Just recently I ordered a vegetarian breakfast burrito in an I-Hop while visiting a friend in Colorado. The cook made it wrong twice. The manager came over to me, kneeled on one knee and said, "Please accept my apology, I am going into the kitchen to cook that burrito myself." I was shocked and overjoyed that he really did make it himself. Now that is customer service. The employee failed, but the manager made it all right.

I highly recommend the book *The E-Myth*, by Michael Gerber. This is a great book on putting together a turnkey systemized business that can help you run your business in such a way that you stay in business for a long, long time.

Here are some tips on keeping yourself in business and growing.

1. Don't forget to look at the long term of your business. Most of the time businesses don't look any further then the next week or the next pay period. Why is that? Generally it's a lack of time and foresight. Business owners get caught up in what I call "life, the hustle and bustle of every day activities." Owners forget that it is not just day-to-day stuff that gets you to grow; it is taking care of the days so the weeks and years take care of themselves. You need to put together systems that work and will continue to work forever. That's not to say that you may not upgrade or change them, but if left alone they will do the job. I travel a great deal, so that's the time that I take to recharge and come up with ideas. If you don't travel that much, I recommend taking some time and going to a hotel to just think and write down your new ideas for long-term business health.

2. Pay attention to good manners. Have you ever walked into store and seen a group of employees engaged in personal chit chat as you waited for service. Under your breath you've probably said, "Hello, doesn't anyone see me?"

Well, this happens all the time. The staff wasn't trained to understand that the customer is most important, not what they did yesterday or what happened in their lives. When you're working, whether as an owner or an employee, life is not about you, it is about the business. Properly train your staff to have good manners and to take care of the clients as though they were as important to them personally as they are to the business. Treat them as though they were the President of the United States. Sometimes it is even worth paying a receptionist simply to greet people as they walk into your establishment.

3. Keep your school spotlessly clean and neat. The days of the dungeon dojos and gyms are all gone. Even the so-called tough guys like to have things cleaned professionally. Having a desk that is cluttered, a bathroom that is not clean and a lobby that is in disarray is bad for your business. Most people will develop an immediate perception of your business, believing if that is the way your business looks, then that is the way you run your business. Remember, you only have one opportunity to make a great first impression.

4. Put serious thought into your advertising. A well thought out ad is imperative if you want to insure success from your advertising. There are no valid excuses any more for amateurish ads, with all the consulting companies ready to give you camera-ready artwork and ad copy. Make sure you are building an appealing visual for your clients to see.

5. Train your employees well. There's a huge gap between big businesses and small businesses when it comes to training. Most big businesses have standard operating procedures and training manuals. It is not all that common to see a training manual in small businesses, let alone martial arts schools, I've yet to see a training manual—even though I'm sure they're out there-for an independently owned martial arts small business. But most schools sure could use one! We have spent thousands of dollars on developing our training manual. By the way did I mention – it's on Takingitothenextlevel.com. Sorry, I had to mention it.

6. Network with businesses in your area. All small businesses can benefit from helping each other out. In the interest of networking, in our "Welcome to the Family" packets we include a booklet with all the businesses in town that advertise our business in their establishments, along with any special coupons or advertisements that they want us to give to all of our new students.

The packets are given out to all new students on the first day that they join. In each packet is a host of different items: a postcard for our website, five free gift passes for new members, a flyer for our birthday parties, our "Welcome to the Family" newsletter and pictorial, and the journal from our latest black belt test (a powerful motivator). In the interest of networking, we also include a booklet with all the businesses in town that advertise our business in their establishments, along with any special coupons or advertisements that they want us to give to all of our new students. It is a win/win for everyone.

7. Separate yourself from the crowd. Find out what your "unique selling proposition" is. I've found that only about one small business in 100 can tell me in 50 words or less why I or any other consumer should deal with them as opposed to their competition. A great way to identify your unique advantage is to play the benefit game with your staff, and with your students as well. To play, assign someone the task of writing all the benefits of your school, and then pick one topic. Everyone then says something relevant to the school about that topic. Then you move on to any other benefit you've identified as associated with your school. Have staff or students fill in what the school does to help them achieve that benefit.

8. Treat people how you would like to be treated. As I have gotten older, things have changed for me in my life. I work long and hard, and really all I want out of life is to be treated fairly, at minimum. But to make me feel good, treat me as though I'm special. You will have my loyalty for eternity. In fact, if I like you and feel as though you have treated me specially, then I will not even care if you charge me more or are not the quickest with providing a product. I just feel good about being treated as though I am special. If I spend my money in your business, and you show me that you genuinely appreciate me, then you will never lose me as your client. There are simple things you can do to let your customers know they're important to you. One way is by simply staying in touch with them. I don't know of any business that can't increase sales by using a quarterly newsletter mailed to their customers —none!

In addition to this I used to deal with a graphic artist, he still to this date is one of the most talented I have ever dealt with. On a regular basis I would spend between 20-30 thousand dollars per year printing marketing material, coming up with new ads, and developing new products. I got so used to him and liked his work so much I would call up and say just design this thing for me and bill me later, never asking price or pressuring him. The only problem was his service. He continually made me what I wanted, but when I asked him about projects he spoke to me rudely and treated my staff the same way. He also did this with other friends and business associates. I spoke to him and he really made no effort to correct his behavior. I no longer work with him due to his methods and attitude. At first he didn't seem to care, but now I can see he is suffering due to the loss of my $30 thousand dollar account.

9. Treat your employees like family. Some companies consider their employees as tools in a tool shed. They think that employees are only there to make the company money. I have seen this more and more with the big conglomerate companies these days. Although the truth is an employee should be making you money or else they are not doing their job, you must remember to build a positive environment in your company. They think that the bottom line is really all that matters. In my company I believe that synergy is the most important thing that you can develop. You need to put together a family bond that is unbreakable. Take care of your business family and watch out for their well-being. This will create employee loyalty, as you never imagined possible. Finding and keeping good people has never been harder, and it's only going to get worse. And the cost of training a new employee can be astronomical, not only in terms of the time and money it takes, but also because you may lose customers in the process. As consumers, we value consistency over everything else, so when you change employees, you risk losing your consistency, especially if you don't have a formal training program in place. And if your business isn't consistent in how it serves its customers then those customers will leave you at the first opportunity-guaranteed. One recommendation I do have is cycle your staff, so no one person becomes to comfortable. Complacency breeds contempt. This goes for your clients as well. Make every effort to get your staff and clients used to change, so they won't be affected if one of your key players decides to quit or open their own location.

Follow these tips and you'll take important steps to make sure that you stay in business and flourish. Sometimes just paying attention to some basic good practices that others overlook can make all the difference.

Get Rid of the Molehill

You have probably heard the saying, "You're making a mountain out of a molehill." I know I was brought up on sayings such as this. To some people problems always seem bigger than they truly are. The most important thing to remember is that perception is reality. What that means is that what people *perceive* is truly their reality. A situation that may upset one person may elate another or vice versa. The fact to remember is that people's perceptions are their realities. For example, a rollercoaster may be extremely thrilling for one person and sickening for another. What is really the difference? The answer is perception. One person may be deathly afraid of spiders while another may want to have tarantulas as pets.

Really it is all about a person's make-up, the mental DNA. Many times people think in a particular way due to their upbringing or their experiences. For example, people who have never been to a foreign-speaking country may feel fear and discomfort with foreigners. If those people were taught that foreigners may be terrorists, then their feelings could very well be colored by statements which are not at all real. Our perception forges our beliefs and compels us to feel and act in a specific way.

Why use the molehill as an example? Many people make situations bigger than they really are. Not to say the situation is not big to them, but in reality it may not objectively be big at all. No matter what an outsider may feel, to the person experiencing the emotion nothing could be more real. There is a concept that stems from Buddhism and that is the training of the mind. In fact, it is a Martial Arts principal, but all in all it is really about perception and how you train yourself to see things. A person with enough training may not eliminate fear entirely but will certainly learn how to harness or limit that fear.

If we tend to see problems as bigger then they actually are, we need to think about the reality and remind ourselves that we can get through this and force ourselves to see things from another's point of view, or in reality, with our new perception or perspective.

What can you do to change your perception? What can you do to see things through the eyes of a warrior? What can you do to create a new reality for you? What was once scary can now be elating; what once filled you with fear can now become fun. It is all up to you and how you perceive the world around you. It is up to you to make some choices and get rid of the molehill.

Not another "Ground Hog Day"

Remember the movie with Bill Murray – *Ground Hog Day*? You heard me mention the saying, "The definition of insanity is doing the same thing over and over and expecting different results?" Well, the script for Bill's movie was basically written on that concept, and unfortunately, some of us run our businesses in an "insane" way.

Ask yourself why we set goals in the first month of the New Year. I would venture to say that such goal setting is to make up for all the screw-ups of the previous year. Experts will tell you that goal setting should be done all the time. It should be an ongoing process and part of your daily life. In the chapter on goal setting we spoke about time management and many other tactics you can use to become efficient. The Bill Murray movie, or at least the message it is trying to give us is quite clear: stop doing the same thing over and over again.

First off, if you know me personally, heard any of my conference calls or read any of my weekly emails, you know that I love movies. Many of my ideas are ripped from their plotlines. I don't actually steal them, they just stimulate the thought process and help me to create new and exciting ideas, concepts and plans that I can utilize in my school or business. Understand that a good movie has to be made from a good script and a great movie from a great script. It doesn't matter who stars in it, or who the other key players are in the film, if the script is bad, then the movie is bad. The analogy is perfect for your business.

I want to share with you some of my mistakes I had to work on correcting. I am not sure how good this is for my consulting career, but I am going to take a shot and be honest. I will let the ego go, and just be open with you. When I started I expanded tremendously, opening three schools within a 14-month period. My ego was flying, my spirit was high and I was at one of the peaks in my career. I had built my small school into an empire, one that most people would not be able to imagine. I had between 1,000 and 1,200 students at any given time and they were all doing the Martial Arts that I loved so much. I was proud, but to be honest, I was scared that it couldn't last forever; that things were too good to be true. I entered 2005 with a crazy travel schedule and within the year, I traveled once to Florida, England, Canada, Thailand, Costa Rica, and Las Vegas, and twice to Los Angeles, Japan, Colorado and Bermuda. My business ran smoothly while I was gone, profits were still good, but there were a few things that I was neglecting.

I started to realize that I had a problem with my employees. While I would estimate that at least 90% of them were fully dedicated, I also saw that 60% of them were not fully qualified. This one problem had the potential to manifest itself into a major crisis, eventually affecting my life, my attitude and the overall growth and future of my business. Not only would it make me work harder, it could easily end up costing me profits and possibly causing the closing of my schools, or at minimum a few of them.

I pay my people very well, so well that I have had offers from other school owners to close their locations and come and work for me. I even had a guy tell me he would give me his school and work for me, if I guaranteed him this kind of paycheck. I was honored but shocked at the same time.

A major flaw that I didn't see in myself was one that an employee said was the very reason why he stayed working for me. *It was that I was so understanding, compassionate and lenient.* Well, why wouldn't anyone stay working for someone like that? The job was the lazy man's vacation, one where employees do what they want, make mistakes and don't have a worry, because they know it will all be forgiven.

Most recently I took a personality profile by a consulting company and one of my biggest flaws was that I was too quick to hire and too slow to fire. I couldn't argue that for a second. The profile pegged me 100%.

I began looking closely at all I was doing. I enforced many of the processes and procedures that I had told my staff to follow and I started holding myself to a higher standard as well. I was inspecting what I expected. Once I started doing that, the lack of quality started to rear its ugly head. For example, the very person who had told me that I was a great guy now thought I wasn't that great anymore and that he really needed to go to someone else for work, as he considered me a tyrant. The only difference was that I was following up to make sure that his job was done properly, and was not giving him the leniency to do an inadequate job. I was now demanding that things be done right. The time had come that he needed to move on.

I realized that for years things had been done incorrectly but I had let it slide. In reality, that employee wasn't responsible, I was. I blamed him, but in essence it was my fault. I was the one letting it happen.

Another person I had working for me was a dedicated student who just couldn't say no to any of my requests. I realized that the desire to please me far out weighed her ability to do her job. So even though she was saying yes to requests, I was constantly frustrated because the results never came close to what I had asked for. I realized tons of money and time had been wasted. That person remains a student of mine and loyal, just not in my employment. We both agreed that it was the best choice for us.

Here are important questions I asked myself - you may want to do the same.

1. Have I taken a long hard look at my school/ business?

2. Am I working smart?

3. What is it that I want for and from my business?

4. What is it that I desire in life?

5. What is my exit strategy, what will I do when I retire or do I want to retire?

Take some time this week to think about these questions and your answers. Be honest with yourself. Remember, there are *no* wrong answers. The way you answer the questions will give you some insight into how to proceed.

Now let me take some time to briefly describe what I mean and why the questions are so important.

1. Have I taken a long hard look at my School/ Business? I looked for areas of waste and loss of profit. Now this could be in any area. Am I paying too much for my phone bill, is the interest rate too high on my credit card, are my gear prices too high, etc. Are my employees working to maximum efficiency? Are they doing the job that I asked them to do? Are they earning money for me? Are they a thorn in my side? Are their positions a profit center for my school? These are all questions to ask yourself.

2. Am I working smart? This means can I be delegating more, can I be more efficient. Can I improve in any area of my business? If so why am I not doing it?

3. What is it that I want for my business? Have I set out a long-term guide or goal-setting sheet as to where I want to be and how I want to get there? Do I goal set, have I made this a part of my routine? If not again, why not?

4. What is it that I desire in life? In a perfect world if I could go ahead in time 20 years, were would I like to be, what would I be doing, what would my life be like? This is part of a level three process we work on, on our premium section of Takingittothenextlevel called the Maboroshi – vision quest.

5. What is my exit strategy? What am I going to put in place now, so that when I decide I'm ready, I can exit with grace with my finances in good shape, and just relax and live my life to the fullest?

I am not done! There is so much more, more than I could ever put into one chapter. Ask yourself these questions about what you're currently doing:

1. Am I doing the same things over and over again, expecting different results? Very often when I do consulting calls, people use the excuse, "I don't know what to do." I tell them about this amazing resource of information called the public library. They usually laugh and take it as a joke, but I would estimate that half of them hadn't ever read anything on how to improve their businesses or their lives. Some of them say that they don't like to read. So I recommend getting books on audio tape. We live in an age of information. With the Internet, you literally have all information at your fingertips. Many schools' tuitions are still far below the national average. We spoke about the average previously, which billing companies claim to be around $129 per month. I believe that amount is still far too low. A few of my friends have schools that charge at least $179 per month. I would say the goal is to get somewhere in between. Lo and behold, even though I tell school owners to raise their prices, they have a host of different excuses as to why they can't or won't do it. It's Groundhog Day!

2. Is my school growing? Again, during consulting calls, I ask what people are doing for marketing? A good number of them have no campaign whatsoever. This, to me, is perplexing, especially when you have many top consultants at your beck and call to help you with marketing plans. Secondly, I offer e-mail consulting all the time don't hesitate to email me. There is certainly no shortage of information on audio so don't drive in your car and only listen to music, take the time to listen to something that will benefit you in the future – knowledge - and have every one of those CDs in your car. If you are driving and listening to music, then you are not really taking advantage of your down time.

3. Am I utilizing my consulting library and other resources? This is a sore spot for me. As most of you know I founded Takingittothenextlevel.com. I believe this to be one of the top consulting resources you ever will come across. I have offered free memberships to try it out. Many people have not taken advantage of this offer. This leads me to believe that we are not focused on things that are of utmost importance. Look for my offer at the end of this book if you want to take advantage of this offer or just email me.

The bottom line question is, are you really interested in taking your business to the next level? Do you really have it in you to run a business? If you have the desire, this is a good thing but it is not all that you need. Recently I have started watching "American Idol." It seems that the first few weeks are dedicated to the tryouts that are absolutely hysterical. I am amazed at how many people believe they have talent, when it is clear to see that they are not capable of doing what they think they can.

Fortunately, on "American Idol," their evaluations are only based on a raw talent of singing. Some of them may have career opportunities in other areas of the entertainment business. Remember, find out what you do well and utilize that skill. I guess the simple question is, do you have what it takes to be a business owner? You don't have to have knowledge of everything. Just do what you are good at and hire the people who are good at the other things. Push yourself to be a good business person, educate yourself, and become what you probably want to be, a true professional. If you don't adopt this attitude, then we all need to yell out "Groundhog Day."

Setting goals is easy. Briefly, put a list of objectives on paper and prioritize them in order of importance. Then get them done in that order. As you do this more often, you will become better at doing the tasks and you will be able to accomplish more and more as you improve. The most important thing is to learn what a "K.R.A." is: this is a Key Result Area. Key result areas are your top priority tasks, the activities that are going to make the most difference in your life and your business, to get the most out of your day.

What is the snag? To be honest, it is self-discipline, the very essence of what we teach in our schools. But if you look at society at large, we are not a country of self-discipline. For example, obesity is on the rise, and recent studies have shown that up to 80% of the people in the U.S. are obese. An important contributing cause of this "epidemic" is lack of self-discipline.

We need to train ourselves to be task-orientated, developing self-discipline to get things done.

Here are five tips:

1. Set specific times in the week to do specific tasks. Don't leave the scheduling of these tasks open. For example: Mondays and Thursdays between 10 and 12 I am going to deliver door hangers. I will do at minimum 1,000 per week. No excuses. No whining that it's raining, it's too cold, my foot hurts. If you want to be lazy, then delegate, but make sure the task gets done. Set other times throughout your week to accomplish other activities.

2. Set weekly and monthly goals. For example, review your finances for a minimum of two hours per week. Review interest rates on credit cards once a month, review costs of supplies, etc. Again, this takes discipline.

3. Look at your stats. Determine how many active students you have on a weekly basis. See who is not attending classes, which memberships are ready to expire, which students seem unmotivated, etc. These activities give you information that is essential to improve retention.

4. Once you have all your student information, set time aside to improve the retention in your school. Institute a new system every week; make sure you always do your 2, 4, 6, 8, and 10 week calls and your "We miss you" and attendance calls, and send out motivational postcards or do motivational calls.

5. Set up a system for upgrading students, and establish special programs and clubs within your school.

Even though I have given you five tips, it is really up to you to dig deep. The very essence of this is to get you to realize that if you are going to be a success you are going to have to understand the mentality of the Bill Murray movie, "Groundhog Day." Realize that you have a script in life. The script started being written when you were a little child. From the day you started to walk, you looked for people to start adding to your script. If you fell and were motivated to keep going, it built the desire to try; if you got yelled at or criticized it may have added the feeling of apprehension to your script. Your script determines who you are today, but not necessarily forever. For example, a person who has a few bad breaks in relationships may currently think that all potential partners are bad or will act a specific way. This is part of that person's script. That person may think that the existing script will always determine who he or she is, but with some work and soul searching the script can be rewritten.

You can put a new script together, but it takes some real soul searching and hard work. You need to accept the parts of yourself that cannot be changed, and to determine which, specific areas of your life can or should be changed. Remember, if you chose not to change your script, you may suffer, but if there is something that is not changeable or that you have no desire to change, then you need to find someone who will complement you and provide your business with those characteristics you lack. It is really all a learning experience, and you must have the self-discipline to realize that if change is going to happen, it is totally up to you to make it happen.

I hope that this is helpful to you; I hope that you are able to utilize the information here and take your life and your school to another level.

Remember that success is up to you. If it is going to happen, you need to look deep. The good thing is that we are here to help you.

Chapter 4
Ninja Marketing tactics
Build your Marketing Arsenal

Marketing Through White Noise

I see 10,000 ads per week? Is that possible? When I first heard this statistic, I thought, *No way!* Ten thousand is far more ads than I see in one week, especially since I don't read the paper, watch the news, etc. But then I jumped in my car and drove my daughter to school. It was 8 a.m. and the drive was only about 10 minutes, but before I knew it, I'd probably seen about 200 ads. You may ask, "How did you do *that?*" I didn't even have my radio turned on. The first ads I saw were on a series of cars and trucks, advertising everything from Mary Kay makeup to plumbers, construction companies, and cement services. I soon realized that I was singing a 1-800-Mattres ad, leaving off the last "S" for whatever they said I should. Then I noticed a sale poster in the front window of a golf store getting ready for spring, and boom - it hit me.

I was being bombarded with marketing. So it's no wonder that when we tell our students in the school and their parents that we have a special activity going on, they seem to ignore us. It truly isn't disrespect or negligence on their part, it is life. They are just doing what they do normally and filtering through the mounds of messages that are thrown at them. Sometimes information they really would like to know gets filtered out with the "trash."

So what do we do to get through? What is it that will separate us from the rest? Well, this remains a huge problem with marketing today. I just recently read that marketers intend to get more personal helping people with their purchase decisions. For example, a person will walk into his or her favorite clothes store and a computer will recognize the customer and say, "Hi, Mrs. Smith, welcome back. Do you know there are specials on that blouse you bought last month?" Well, if this is how marketing will be done, where do we stand as Martial Arts schools?

Here is my opinion of our situation. I believe, and I have always believed, that the only way to expand your business is by personal contact. If we were selling products, we could be less personal and still market our wares. We could just do more direct mail to sell more "t-shirts," and although you should be doing direct mail, to have a really strong impact on students, parents and prospects you need to connect with them. You need to ensure that you and your company are the most important thing on their minds when you are talking.

When was the last time that you gave someone a call and asked to have 10 minutes of the person's undivided attention? If the person is busy and can't talk then, ask if you can call back at a better time. Confirm the best time to call so that you can have his or her undivided attention. Another good strategy to get through the clutter is to set up review appointments with clients and with parents to go over their children's progress. What you really want is some quiet time with them away from all the white noise of all the other marketing companies breathing down their necks. A bit of quiet time will enhance your relationship, and will give them a chance to think about what you are saying.

This is a time for you to sell upgrades, deal with student issues, make sure that the parents are on the same page as you are, and talk to them about special events. Sometimes it is not possible to get an appointment personally to sit with the student and the client, but you must make every effort to speak to them personally. In our school we have many systems in place that help us communicate.

Below is a list:

8 Ideas for Personalized "Marketing"

1. Regular e-mail to all clients with an e-mail newsletter and positive stories.

2. Direct mail for all of our specialty programs: Black Belt Club; Team Leadership; Master Elite; special events; etc.

3. Flyers for seminars handed directly to the clients, to enhance word-of-mouth advertising.

4. A free yearly calendar either in paper form or on your website with notations for all of your events, school closings etc.

5. Scheduled telephone calls to students and clients at 2,4,6,8 and 10 week intervals.

6. Missed attendance calls and "we miss you" calls.

7. Sales calls, former student calls, missed trial class calls, etc.

8. Announcements in class.

These are just a few of the ways that we promote our programs and get the word out. Even with all of this information, there are still people who do not know about events that are going on, Holiday school closings, and so on. This is not their fault; our messages may be getting lost amidst the white noise of marketing. The most important tip that I have for you is to be in touch with your clients regularly and to try to get your clients to understand that your messages are much more relevant to them than all the white noise they are ignoring. They should want your communications with them to be picked up on their radar. They must know that you are deserving of their attention, along with their favorite places, things and people.

Marketing Items To Never Forget!

The Martial Arts Industry is a relatively new industry. Not until 10 years ago did many school owners keep records of their statistics or track marketing results. To this day there is not enough market saturation in the industry to bring martial arts to the forefront and get people to realize the endless stream of benefits. We, as individual school owners have to carve out our little piece of the pie in order to succeed. Marketing is a huge component of this success.

The following are marketing ideas that should be incorporated into every campaign that you run from your school. Use these to further analyze your current marketing strategies or take on challenges where improvement is needed:

Important Marketing Ideas - Variety Is The Spice Of Successful Marketing.

It is not only one source of marketing that will make your company grow, but a combination of many different modes that will yield the best results.

Consistency Is Key!

Using consistency in your ads is of the utmost importance. Research has shown that consumers may not react until they have seen any particular ad a minimum of 4-7 times.

When Is Enough- Enough?

Many school owners will ask me questions ranging from when they should stop advertising to when they should change their marketing design or what time to call a particular person. This should directly relate to customer value. When your customer value exceeds your expenses, then you stop advertising to that particular person.

Advertise- Regardless Of Your Budget!

Whether you are planning to market in the form of phone, radio, print Ads or television will depend entirely on your budget. However, even on a shoe-string budget there are many things that you can, and should be doing to advertise inexpensively. If you build your business and you have increased your budget there are certainly more expensive forms of advertising that may benefit you. Regardless of budget you need to constantly be marketing your school.

These ideas will help you to further analyze where you currently stand in regard marketing and then plan a detailed strategy for the future of all of your marketing efforts. Marketing is not something that should be planned a week or a few days before hand. Every business needs to have a schedule planned out that includes all of the details listed above. Not only will this help you to be more effective in your marketing, but will also save you a ton of time and frustration!

Marketing 101- Concepts For The Small Business Owner

When I first started my small business over 20 years ago there wasn't much information around to help me. As I became knowledgeable on where I could locate that information, I realized that it was not so much that the information wasn't available, but that it was just not easily accessible. Fast forward to the 21st Century, with technology such as the Internet readily available and information immediately accessible at the touch of a finger, this information is so abundant we probably could never read through it in our lifetime.

This leads me to share with you my crash course in Marketing. As a small business owner I have found that there are many "get rich" schemes, many "perfect ideas," many systems that are "proven to gain results." The one thing that I have found is time tested and true is that there is nothing more powerful than an education and the value of one's personal experience.

Sifting through the myriad of information on marketing and sales out there can be next to impossible. It's important that we realize the fundamentals of these business cornerstones, and the importance of prioritizing these items according to your current level of business. .

Let's focus on a quick assessment of your current marketing strategies, and how to ascertain your current growth.

How much growth have I had, both in income and number of clients in the past year? In the past 3 years? In the past 5 years? This number should represent the number of new students that you have gained, figured against those who you have lost over the same period of time.

What is the average length of time that I retain a typical client? Retention of members is just as important as sales efforts to gain new ones. Why would you focus all of your efforts on having a steady flow of new members when your back door is open and you are losing just as many?

How have I obtained most of my clients to date? Make a working list of any and all marketing materials, special events, demos, call campaigns or referral efforts you have used since your school opened its doors.

Which marketing strategies have worked well for me so far? Which ones haven't? You should maintain a working and detailed list of all of your marketing efforts, how many students you have gained through each specific marketing effort and the retention details of each. If you are not tracking this information, you should start doing so immediately. This information is crucial to determining whether or not to continue with any one piece of marketing.

What readily identifiable "niche", if any, do my clients fall into? Are most of your student's children, adults or teenagers? Middle class or upper class? Having this information at hand is also a barometer for potential growth. Do you need to increase your membership of adults or teens? Can you maximize on your children's classes by offering more special events like "movie nights?"

What system, if any, do I have to ensure a steady flow of referrals? Are you actively asking for renewals? Are you sending home "buddy passes," or hosting "buddy weeks"? It is imperative to track all of these efforts and the success of each. To be successful, ask yourself the question what changes do I need to make in the way that I do business? Where are the strengths and weaknesses in your business? Once you acknowledge these you can knowledgably formulate a strategy to overcome the challenges that are currently facing you, and optimize on your successes.

A Marketing Idea That Makes Sense

I recently uncovered some interesting statistics relating to my schools that prompted a conversation between myself and my graphic arts and marketing advisor. As I was looking over my stats from 2004 I noted that I had paid about $60,000.00 in advertising this past year. To some school owners that may sound like a lot, but according to marketing experts this is a drop in the bucket for a school/business of my size. A business of my size should budget at least 3 times that amount of money for marketing. I'm sure that this sounds like a great deal of money to most, and it does to me as well!

I further analyzed some of the campaigns that I had been running. I had just completed a rather lengthy radio advertising campaign that cost a large amount for the return on the investment. We ran for nearly 5 months, which was an investment of roughly $21,000.00. We received about 8 inquiries and signed up 3 people. However, radio advertising is an effort that touches many areas of marketing. Research tells me that radio advertising not only effects immediate response ratios, but also contributes to community branding of the Long Island Ninjutsu name.

I then analyzed my print ads. We are currently running ads in the local papers, with cost in the area of $15,000.00 annually. This does not include the amount that we budget towards grass roots marketing: door hangers, flyers, VIP passes and the like. All of these marketing campaigns are instrumental in creating a buzz and bringing new students through the door.

My marketing advisor, asked me to pin-point what my strongest source of new enrollment is currently, and what I realized was that I fell back on the same subject that I have been harping continually. My referral program! Here are some staggering statistics from 2004. All 5 of my schools combined signed up nearly 500 new students in 2004. Out of that 500 - 275 of them were referrals!

This is a statistic that cannot be ignored. We run a very simple referral program at Long Island Ninjutsu. I encourage you to stop whatever you are doing and think about how you are currently running your referral program. Are you asking for referrals? Are you offering referral incentives? Does it appear to be successful? Most successful schools will tell you when asked that their referral program continues to be one of their largest sources of new enrollment. For those of you who are not currently running a referral program, or who are not experiencing an increase in numbers through referrals, I welcome you to visit www.TakingItToTheNextLevel.com or email me to find out more details about Long Island Ninjutsu's referral programs.

Considering this marketing statistic, I was compelled to think that referrals were where I should be investing the majority of my money in order to increase my return on investment. I am currently investing $60,000.00 per year on marketing. What better way to take that amount and turn it easily into hundreds of thousands of dollars? New enrollments through referrals translate to approximately $3000.00 per student, which I already know through analyzing my customer value. If I am netting $3000.00 from each new referral, up to what amount would I want to invest per student through a marketing campaign? Determining the value of a client is nothing more than knowing on average how long a student stays in your school times the amount of your monthly tuition. You can also factor in if they refer you members and the average amount of members who join. This will give you the customer value.

Once that is determined you may look at all of your calls divided by the amount of total advertising dollars you spend. Take the money spent and divide it by the amount of calls to determine how much it costs per phone call. Another interesting statistic to evaluate is analyzing how many inquiry calls you get to convert to trial classes and then trial classes or membership to actual members and this will give you an accurate picture of how much it costs to receive a new client.

In thinking these things out I came up with a comprehensive and simple marketing campaign, and determined how much I wanted to and could afford to spend.

Without knowing where you currently stand, you cannot make an informed choice about the best path to continue on!

Top Ten Marketing Tips For Schools of All Sizes

Marketing your school seems simple enough, right? Send out flyers every so often, run a yellow page ad, perhaps have a few lead boxes out in the community...

The basic fact remains that there are simple marketing ideas for schools of all sizes that many school owners overlook consistently! Putting marketing projects and tasks into your monthly schedule is imperative to the success of your school- regardless of whether you are just starting out; you are a smaller school - or a school with 15 years and 500 students under your belt. Let's look at this analogy. If your marketing was an electric generator it would power your lights and keep your school either cool or hot. If the generator shut off you would be without power and not able to heat or cool your establishment or have light. You would need to keep your generator running continuously during all hours of business operation. Let's say the generator instead of giving you power to heat or cool your school, gave you students. In order to keep the business open and operating you need a continual flow of new people coming through the doors. If the generator turned off, so would your business.

With this analogy you must also ask yourself the question, how many hours does your marketing generator work? Is it on continuously, a few hours per week or hardly at all? What are you doing to power (fill) your school with students? How much time are you actually putting in to fuel the marketing generator?

Let's go over some marketing concepts you should be thinking about and have in action currently, or put into action right away! Start by analyzing these marketing tips - which are you performing on a consistent basis? Adding these marketing tips to your daily/weekly/monthly tasks will give you community exposure, and drive a constant flow of prospective students!

Establish your target market: Many martial arts schools advertise blindly, running ads in print, radio or television without any focus. I have found that if you target your ad you will have more success. The less information you have listed will provide you with more quality responses. Remember - Less is more! The focus of the ad should not be spread too thin, allowing that the consumer is not darting from area to area to figure out what you actually specialize in. For example: if you are actually looking for children, advertise to parents and explain the benefit your program has for children.

Don't put your eggs in one basket: Don't utilize only one source of advertising. There are many sources of marketing at both low and high cost for martial arts schools. Try to put as many in effect as your budget allows.

Make your school a household name within your community: Make sure that when someone thinks of martial arts: they think of your school. This cannot be stressed enough. The goal is to get your name out into the spotlight regularly so that you become the school of choice.

Become the martial arts expert in your area: Becoming the expert is easier than you think. It is all a matter of getting the right press. Write a press release and send it to all the local papers in your area. Write about everything going on in your school that could be considered news worthy. Write a blurb about the last test with 20 little ninjas or your latest black belt test. This is a fantastic way to gain credibility and have the community recognize you as the ultimate martial arts school in your area.

Put one new idea into effect that will bring your school to the next level: You've thought of one in the past, or maybe your notes are full of them- Great ideas that you still have not put into action! Create a Black Belt Club, run a referral contest, or create an innovative income generator.

Get on the phone and call old or inactive members: Pull out your inactive lists and call up some old members. Encourage them through some type of incentive to come back, refer a friend, write a testimonial, or even offer some feedback. This task is a must, and it's a great way to turn some unsatisfied customers around or even have an opportunity to learn more about why people leave your school to begin with.

Get in contact with your local PTA: You know that your program can benefit children in your area, and Parent Teacher Associations or PTA's are a great vehicle to gain access to those children! Contact your local PTA and ask them if you can be an official sponsor. Let them know that you can provide them with demonstrations and passes for all of their functions and that you are so confident that your program will benefit their students that you will donate the first month of tuition directly to the PTA. Arrange to have parents write out the first tuition check directly to the PTA!

Hold a parent seminar: A great way to increase retention in your children's programming is by having your students' parents get more involved. Hold a seminar teaching them how to coach their children in the martial arts! Not only will they see the direct benefits for their child- but they will also be helping to get students to the next level in their training, so that they can help their children - your students.

Officially kick off your referral program: At Long Island Ninjutsu Centers our referral program is one of our biggest resources of new enrollment. Referrals are based on motivation and even compensation. For every student who joins a particular program you should award them a gift of either a "rebate" off of pro-shop purchases, special training classes, or another reward of value. Each member at L.I. Ninjutsu that refers a new member to our core program of a year enrollment or more will have their referral counted toward a free year membership. If any member refers 5 or more new students that sign up for a year membership they will qualify for the free year. This may need to be adjusted to suit your location and curriculum. This program brings hundreds of referrals into L.I. Ninjutsu every year and for every free membership that I give away, I have five more new students signing up. Not a bad return on investment!

These marketing tips may seem to be simple, run of the mill recommendations. However, if you look deeper into your marketing plan- I would venture to guess that most school owners are not using every one of these ideas- or any of them! So decide what your goals are for the next year- then implement these ideas today to start on the path to exceeding every goal that you've set!

Five of the Biggest Marketing Mistakes People Make

1) Stop trying to reinvent the wheel. It is not always necessary to put your own spin on things. Why bother wasting the time. I know it is a matter of pride or a feeling of accomplishment but often it is not necessary and is a pure waste of time.

2) Use systems that are proven. Do not change them. You can tailor them slightly if they are not suitable for your system, but do not change what works. Only enhance it. I find that people do this all the time.

3) Don't be penny wise and dollar foolish. I've given you many no-nonsense, very affordable ideas to market your school. After all, if you are following them you are guaranteed to get new students. The question is will you use them and will you use them right?

4) Don't do things half way the first time. Make sure that you do it right from the start. For example, a poorly executed door hanger or ad will only discourage potential buyers. There is only one time to make a first impression. Spend the money one time on quality hand-outs, ads, welcome books, etc.

5) Make sure you are the consummate professional. If you want, just e-mail me and I will go over with you how to get started, or what I call my flowchart. This is how you can test yourself and see what grade you will achieve on the issues you need to work on and which are most prominent in your school. The easiest way to learn this information is to enlist five moms in your school, pay them a nominal fee such as a $20 Starbucks gift certificate, give them a pad and pen, and have them go through the school noting for you all the things they think should be done better. Tell them to consider everything, from the look, smell, colors, decorations, all the way to the curriculum. Take their comments objectively and never get offended. You need their honest opinions. We call this "**Karate-scaping.**" We are running a school make-over contest with all four of my schools. For a $750 budget we are redecorating, and the school that does the best job will win a night on the town - a play and dinner in Manhattan. It is going to be fun, but it will also act as a way to see what can be done to make an important difference for a small amount of money.

Ten Important Tips to Make Sure You're Doing the Best You Can

1) No one cares about what rank you are or what title you carry. So don't use ranks or titles as marketing tools.

2) Your style is important only to people who already know about it. For me, the art of the Ninja is an allure, but 99% of my students come to me due to my quality of marketing and the benefits, not to become Ninja.

3) Do not think for a minute that people will stay with you if they are unhappy. So don't have the "it's my way or the highway" attitude. Be ready to serve people.

4) Make sure you don't drop the ball and think that people will let it happen. People see everything. If you make promises that you don't keep they will remember. It takes a long time for people to forget your mistakes. So make sure you are consistent. If you don't live with this mentality then you can't be successful in business.

5) The quality of your service is of the utmost importance. If you are not providing "above and beyond" service you are missing the boat.

6) Make use of professionals. Find a good graphic artist to help you design your ads.

7) Use a good web designer, someone that is really an expert. Remember millions of people each day surf the web. If they happen to stumble on your site and it is bad, hard to navigate, and doesn't have relevant information, then your website is a negative.

8) Think about your clients and what they want, not what you want. When marketing, make sure they are your first concern. Benefits are the only reason why people are in your school. I always quote Tony Robbins - he says that people have only one desire and that is to experience pleasure. Even if some people like being hit on the head with a hammer, this is their form of pleasure and they will do it. Sometimes short term pleasures such as addictive habits become long term pains. It is our goal to enhance peoples' lives, so only consider actions that are beneficial to them.

9) Make sure you follow up and are consistent. When marketing or doing any activity in your school, you need to make sure that it is not a half attempt at what you want to do. Do not start things and let them fade away. Be consistent and make sure your clients see you as a rock.

10) Do not rely on tomorrow. There is only one time to do something and that is now. You can't make excuses why you haven't done this or that. It is a common problem in all small businesses. You need to do it now, get on it, do the marketing, and set the systems in place. Remember one day lost, can never be regained.

Spreading The Word-
Asking For And Utilizing Community Involvement

As we all know, the reason that all of us teach the Martial Arts is to share knowledge, strength and all of the many values and benefits that we can provide to our students.

I was recently asked a few questions by a consulting client whose sole focus is giving back to the community year round. As a Non-Profit organization, their ultimate goal is to better the people who participate at their school, in turn giving back to the community around them. These questions pose a very important message to all of us in the Martial Arts community. For those of us who strive to find ways to give back, or for schools who would like to find a way to be successful while still dedicating themselves to the bettering of the community around them, these questions are fundamental in finding the balance between success and giving back to those around you!

Q: "What are the best ways to gain more community involvement?"
A: Community involvement is often a hard-won effort. Ramping up to consistent and abundant community involvement often means a few years of constantly beating the streets.

Here are some tips about getting your message out there clearly:

It is important that you clearly define to your audience why you strive to give back to the community. What are your goals, who do you aim to benefit, and what is the driving force behind your intentions?

Continually, and LOUDLY ask for volunteer involvement.

Explain how volunteer involvement, whether it's financial or otherwise, is going to help you to provide the community with an even greater benefit.

Find a central core of people who are involved in community and charity work that will be dedicated to assisting you in your vision.

Sometimes you will find yourself constantly looking for a group of good people to assist your school; many times you will find that people consider themselves to be too busy, and don't want to be bothered. But don't let this slow you down! Don't give up until you have the team of community individuals that you need!

Q: "Our school works with a specialty group in our area to benefit children every year. What is the best way to go about getting media attention, and then utilizing that media attention for future enrollment?"

A: The best way to get media attention is to beat the streets and contact all of your local news agencies: Papers, T.V. and Radio. Many of these agencies will help you advertise your event for free, as the event you are hosting is an altruistic activity, and a great lead in for a story about community involvement. Once you've gotten these agencies' attention, you need to write up your own press releases to be published after the event has been held. These short blurbs highlight the event, its attendees and its purpose. It's also a good way to highlight your school's name and contact information.

Q: What is the best way to set up a Scholarship Fund so that underprivileged individuals can take advantage of the Martial Arts?
A: Scholarship funds can be tricky for many schools. This is an area where you will want to get your accountant involved, since for schools that are not set up as Non-Profit locations will have to claim these funds as income and then pay taxes on that income. If you are a Non-Profit location, raising money can be done through community events, and again through a lot of leg-work. The key is to ask for contributions through flyers, conversations, advertisements and relationships with local businesses and officials. Once you begin to receive contributions it is crucial that you have a system in place to accurately track all funds given, and by whom.

Sometimes people consider these funds, given for charity to be more effort than it is worth. However, done correctly, scholarship funds are immensely rewarding. Just knowing you have changed lives and helped people in need is fulfilling in itself, when looking at the many benefits you may receive besides being altruistic, such as the lasting good will and name in the community. It is nothing more than a win/win.

That being said, finding the right candidate to receive these funds requires you to be discerning and very straightforward in clearly defining the recipient's responsibilities to your school. It can be very disheartening to elect a candidate and then have them not commit to consistent training and school involvement. Look for potential scholarship students who need the Martial Arts in their lives, will be enriched significantly through training, but who truly cannot afford tuition.

Q: How can a school use, but not "prostitute" these activities in order to increase overall enrollment?"
A: It is a common misconception that to give back to the community is to take on a life of poverty, or a life of smaller means. When you boil it down, a Martial Arts School at its very core is benefiting those students who are training there and helping the community on a daily basis. The more people you teach how to live a more productive life the better off the community will be. The owner of any school is running a business, and deserves to be successful in doing so! As should a school that is a non-profit and has the clear intention of helping the community, it's important to remember that the larger your school gets- the more you will be able to give back.

Focus on selling memberships to those that can afford the Martial Arts and then enlist them to help you spread the word throughout your community. These students will all know someone who needs your help, or an organization that can provide you with the help that you need! Your students are your most powerful promotion tool! The more students you have - the larger number of bodies to tell the world what a powerful tool your school has been in bettering their lives!

Remember: The Martial Arts is a gift to be given. We have all been blessed with the opportunity to be teachers, and to instill the values of the Martial Arts into our students. This is a time to reflect on how important it is to share the wealth, which the Martial Arts have provided us!

So you've decided to begin further motivating your students and parents to become an unstoppable sales force? But how can you help them to achieve that goal?

There is both leg-work that needs to be accomplished at the school, as well as tools that need to be passed along to your students in order to give them the necessary resources.

By involving your parents and students in your most common forms of grass-roots marketing you are allowing them to contribute to their own success, as well as the success of the school.

I am not asking that you give away the farm. But schools are always looking for new and innovative ways to get new students through the door. If our goals are to sign up more students so that we can experience more success - then why not keep that success in the family! What would be the harm in monetarily motivating those students that have been so loyal to your school for so many years? What better way to have everyone feel as though they have a vested interest in the school's growth!

Utilizing "Business Appreciation" As a Source of Referrals

When thinking of referrals we enlist many different areas of the community as sources for referrals. Although our students and their families and friends are the largest contributors to our success with referrals, there are numerous other sources of referral revenue that can easily be tapped into. When looking for other sources, I encourage you to reach out to your community for additional support for your business.

One way to build community support is by developing connections to businesses local to your school. The goal is to establish reciprocal relationships where you contribute to one another's success by buying products and by fostering relationships with each other's customers.

Supporting Local Businesses

Patronize Local Businesses to Outfit Your School - The first step in building relationships that are conducive to increasing referrals is by using local businesses' services for the needs of your school. For example, use local pizza parlors to supply the pizzas for each of your birthday parties, and local party supply stores for your birthday party supplies. Become familiar with the employees in all of the establishments that you patronize, introduce yourself to the managers, and let them know that you intend to patronize their businesses continuously.

Building relationships this way will allow you further access to the customers of each business. Having a professional relationship with the owners and managers will make them more likely to get creative when it comes to using their consumer base as a source of referrals.

Provide Local Businesses with Gift Certificates Discounting Your Services - Approach businesses within your community and offer them $200 gift certificates toward your school's services for their employees and for their elite customers. Distributing these gift certificates to employees will not only enhance their employees' income, but will also show that they care about the employees' health and fitness. Rewarding loyal customers with these gift certificates is also a great way for the businesses to encourage on-going use of their services!

It is important to coach the participating business owners, and to define both your intentions and expectations when you give them the gift certificates. In order for you to enlist their influence as additional outlets for referrals, they need to have a grasp of your school and the benefits and programs that you can provide to their employees and customers.

Imagine the impact this program can have on your enrollment! If every pizza that the local pizza parlor sells includes a gift certificate valued at $200 for martial arts classes, you potentially can reach hundreds of people in a very short time!

The business owners offering your gift certificate have the benefit of providing their customers with something of value, and you have access to a community of people who may never have taken advantage of your school!

The business owners need to be committed to your mutual goals, so that they actively distribute your gift certificates (rather than just leaving them sitting on the counters). However, they may not feel comfortable explaining the benefits of your school, or perhaps are not confident that all of their employees can do so. Provide them with a simple letter to use with the gift certificate to help to alleviate this concern, and to lessen the time that they might have to take away from their busy days to explain the purpose of their gifts.

The following is a sample letter that can be used by businesses wishing to offer additional incentives to their employees. You may customize this letter to fit the needs of the participating businesses, and your school:

Sample Letter:

Dear Valued Associate;

As an employer, J. Wigets strives to create a professional, personally challenging, and rewarding work environment. We are committed to delivering the highest possible wages, top quality benefits, and any additional perks and incentives we can. We believe that a healthy associate is a happy associate.

Studies have shown that people who participate in health-related activities enjoy increased energy, sharper focus, and higher confidence levels than the average person. In addition, we have found that the level of stress is reduced. A martial arts program can provide all of these benefits. We believe that not only will you receive the benefits listed above but also that you will learn to protect yourself and your family. That's a benefit you cannot put a price tag on. The martial arts teach its students to have a positive attitude, and to set and achieve physical, mental, and spiritual goals.

In an effort to help you, our most valuable asset, create a healthier, safer, more success-oriented way of life for yourself and the ones you love, J. Wigets has secured an exclusive one month membership for you and one family member, to an award winning local martial arts studio. This one-month program is valued at $99, so by taking advantage of this great opportunity for yourself and any other member of your family, you will be receiving $198 worth of benefits at NO COST to you.

You can activate the free membership by contacting (martial arts school) at the number listed below. We hope you will take advantage of this incredible offer, and enjoy all the benefits of being an integral part of our winning team.

Sincerely,
Store Manager
J. Wigets

By utilizing an idea such as this one, not only are you building networking relationships within your community, but you are also creating new opportunities to make a positive impact on the people who live and work around you! Of course, this can be done with any business – the goal is to develop the relationship and be clear when you strike a deal with the business owner that they will be behind the campaign as if it were their own. In return you can do the same for them.

Maximization - The Serious Marketing Campaign

Not long ago I attended an unbelievable seminar with marketing guru, Jay Conrad Levinson, the author of *Guerilla Marketing*. Have you ever seen the cartoon where the light goes on over a person's head in a cartoon drawing? Well, if I were a cartoon, I would have had that lit bulb above my head at this seminar.

The interesting thing about learning something new is that most of the time it is not something that you have never heard before. The saying "When the student is ready the teacher will appear" is totally true. You must be ready. So I am hoping after reading this the light bulb goes on above your head, too.

Good marketing is not about the most exclusive, expensive and well planned campaign costing thousands of dollars and running for a few weeks or months per year, it is about a consistent campaign that runs over an extended period of time. When developing a marketing campaign and advertising your company you must remember this one golden rule: Consistency is everything. Many of the people who I consult with regularly have one thing in common. The simple fact is that if people are experiencing growth, then they are doing something right, and that is being consistent with their strategies. So why is it that many people are still treating marketing as if it was a single roll of the dice at some casino. I believe the answer to be lack of education. Remember I spoke before about the analogy of a generator? A successful campaign is one that is consistent just like the power from the generator.

Now by lack of education I'm not referring to formal schooling. I don't mean people need a degree in marketing. In fact a degree in marketing doesn't always make the person competent at developing new business for others. I have had my share of issues with so called marketing experts only to find out I know more than they do. Granted, I could probably start my own marketing company due to the many years of experience I have with building businesses. What I mean is people are not sure what consistency really is. How much is too little? How much is too much? There are some people who have opinions one way or the other, but mostly people don't recognize what consistency looks like.

I want to share with you a lesson that Gene Simmons from the band, "Kiss" taught me. Now I don't know him personally but I watch his television show every Monday night. His wife and child tricked him into taking a weekend off from work to go snowboarding. They needed to trick him because he is a workaholic. He reluctantly agreed, and then he set up a host of appointments while he was there. Amazingly he immediately started thinking of how he could spin the weekend, making appointments with the mayor of that town, the snowboard company, and the ski resort. It was amazing how his mind worked. I was shocked. The lesson I learned was that opportunity is not limited; it is everywhere as long as you think with that entrepreneurial mindset and thought process.

What are the opportunities that lie in front of you? How can you get people to recognize your school? Do you need to run the traditional advertising in the local paper? Do you need to do what you normally do? Or can you come up with something innovative? Can you do a cross-marketing campaign with other businesses that share in the same health-minded goals as you do? What is it that makes you and your business unique and yet ties it into other businesses with the same mindset? Who do you know who is under your nose who may be of help to you? Do you have a student who is a marketing genius, web developer, direct mail specialist, or public relations person?

It's time to start thinking about what it is that you can do to turn your situation to gold. Who can you call upon, who can you utilize to help you? What avenues do you have in your local community? This is just food for thought. So why is it that certain schools in the area or businesses such as yours do so well, while others don't really do that well at all? I believe it is all in your frame of mind and in maximizing whatever marketing you do through consistency.

Design an Unforgettable Ad

For years, marital arts schools and companies have spent billions of dollars trying to make ads that are memorable and bring in clients by the hundreds. What are the big boys doing that we can do as smaller operations?

Grab the customers' attention: The more time a person spends reading an ad or the more time that ad stays in the person's mind, the better the chance to get that person as a customer. "Vivid processing leads to better storage of memory," as stated in a study from the University of California, Irvine. "The best ads get the advertiser or brand into the minds of the prospects as they consider different possibilities." To the layman what does this mean? Well, in its very basic form, you need a good ad with the right message. It is worth taking the time with a professional and spending the money to design the correct ad and to get it right the first time. I personally believe that to move from ordinary to outstanding doesn't cost very much. I get full color flyers produced in lots of 10,000. Sometimes it costs pennies on the dollar to make the jump to high quality.

How do we get customers to spend more time with our ads? The most memorable print ads have messages and images that grab the reader. They include headlines that contain a benefit and have a strong visual focal point. A lot depends on your choice of media. In a magazine, one large photo works the best, but in a local paper, many photos may work as well. It is commonly felt that the better the pictures and the more space dedicated to illustrations, the better the recognition rates. Good pictures and placement may improve recognition by 50%.

Adding color and contrast for magazines and other publications such as brochures will boost recognition by more then 50%. In a study with two identical ads for a vodka company – one with a white background and the other with a black background, twice as many people remembered the one with the black background, even though the ads were identical. Testing has shown that on average, larger ads in print media are more memorable; however, a creative ad in a small space can be more memorable then a so-so larger ad.

Colors increase recall in print media by up to 20%. Some colors, such as sky blue, golden yellow, and shades of blue-green, are more noticed than others. Red is a good spot color, but full color ads earned a 24% higher recognition score than black and white ads or spot color ads.

Communicate frequently: Repetition is the key to success. Many times a person will run an ad, not get the desired results, and then give up. We call this the "chickening out" period. Far too often an advertiser gives up long before the ad campaign gains momentum. Mark E. Wheeler at Washington State University School of Medicine performed a study of memory in which a word was paired with a picture or sound many times over several days to test subjects' recognition rates. He found that repeated exposure to information in different contexts helps people remember the information. So when you see a message in different formats, such as a print ad, a billboard, and a TV commercial, he says, "You associate the different impressions, and that helps you retrieve the information when you need it."

Use memorable benefits: Ads that grab and hold a prospect's attention are those that immediately communicate a benefit that answers the question "What's in it for me?" The bottom line is that features aren't memorable, benefits are. If you have a headline that states a benefit, people will read it, remember it, and even clip it out of the magazine or newspaper and hold onto it.

Not sure if this approach to advertising is for you? While this doesn't strictly fall under your consulting package, it may be of interest to some and can definitely help many small and large school owners. Or you may simply want to apply the principles to your newsletters for students. Either way, it's worth considering.

"When is this guy going to get to some of the top marketing ideas?"

Well, I am going to do that now, but first I want to explain why I believe "synergy" to be the biggest word in marketing. I want to explain this in a clear, easy to comprehend, no nonsense way. Marketing is a scary word. When we think about it, it sounds much more detailed than it really is. Why is synergy the biggest word in marketing? Simple: no one method works independently. Synergy means the combined action of many components. I have followed unbelievable marketing experts such as Jay Abraham, Jay Conrad Levinson and many others. From them I have borrowed many ideas and have now come up with my Ninja Marketing Concepts.

Ninja Marketing Concepts flows directly off of the myth of the Ninja. Once shrouded in secrecy, these ancient warriors - by the way I am one - (oops - I just blew my cover) were able to manipulate armies and shoguns. The goal with Ninja Marketing is to market to your clients without them knowing it while covertly getting them to help you market and refer other clients to you.

If you have ever been on one of my Teleconference Calls or have listened to any of my recorded Teleconference Calls you have heard a recurring theme, and that is to put a referral program in place. The goal is to generate referral business, no matter whether you run an ad in the local paper or you meet someone at a restaurant. The concept of Ninja Marketing is that the first contact is your only chance. We only have one opportunity to make a first impression. Our goal is to market to everyone, I must repeat that - EVERYONE - who is not an existing client in your business.

Toot Your Own Horn

Just recently I was thinking about all the things that go on at our schools. I thought to myself that there isn't a person in the world who couldn't benefit from all we do. I also thought to myself that if this is the case, either we are the world's best kept secret or people really don't know the power they have
at their fingertips. While I was writing this, I thought "Will people think this is bragging?" Then I realized that our students and the families in our schools know us and realize that we are sincere about what we do: how could anyone think that? So I decided to write this. Considering all that I do and all the times people have said to me that I have changed their lives, I thought maybe it was time to talk about it. I know it sounds as if I am tooting my own horn: some may even say I am cocky or bragging, but to be honest, sometimes things appear to be obvious but in reality they are not. I believe that all school owners should take the time to educate their students and the parents on the reasons why the Martial Arts is so special, but most importantly why *you* are.

Here are a few things I wrote and sent to my students: this example may help you.

Did you know?

Did you know that we have promoted hundreds of Black Belts in the last 15years?
Did you know that this November 9th will be our 18-year anniversary?
Did you know that Jared, one of our Black Belts, started training with me 16years ago at the age of three and just left for college this year?
Did you know that we have 100 active training Black Belts and that some of them started as young as three years old?
Did you know that most of the Black Belts you see teaching started as children or young adults in our program and that it takes a minimum of five to six years to acquire a Black Belt in my school?

Did you know that all of our Black Belt instructors and all of our under Black Belt instructors have gone through our rigorous 10 - week Instructor Training Program? Did you know that Sensei Frank Olmeda is a fourth-degree Black Belt and holds the title of Renshi and has been training for over 17 years with Kyoshi Allie?

You get the point, right? The goal here is to educate the students and parents about the important things going on within our schools. If you don't let them know, then how will they find out? Not all of them have the time or desire to become investigative reporters and researchers. Simply put, they only know what you tell them. You can also use this method to pre-frame your clients for special events and seminars. This is a good subtle way to market future events, create a culture within your school and build excitement.

Here is an example of how you can do this:

Many activities go on in our school and sometimes even I am amazed. In the last 14 months we have had some of the top Ultimate Fighting Champions - UFC, Pride, and Fightzone champions - teaching at our headquarters school in West Islip, N.Y.

To name a few, we have had the privilege of training with Frank Shamrock, Dan Severn (twice), Rigan Machado, Bart Vale, Cung Le (twice) and as if that wasn't enough we also had other world famous instructors such as Sensei Okada from Japan, Ian Thomas of the United Kingdom, Randy Weekley from Colorado and from Long Island we had Soke John Olshlager, Shihan Andy Stigliano, Renshi John Busto and Sensei John Broncato. Wow ... all right at our school! Can you imagine? My good friend John Olshlager has said "to touch the hands of a master will change your life forever. My students are the luckiest in the world.

You may then go on to reinforce what your school represents by stating facts and reinforcing your goal. This is how I wrote about my schools:

Fact:
L.I. Ninjutsu Centers International is the largest Ninjutsu School in the world. L.I. Ninjutsu Centers has had schools in Costa Rica, Bermuda (still), Michigan, Puerto Rico, Brewster N.Y. Kyoshi Allie has been training in the martial arts for 40 years (as of 2008), starting at the age of three. L.I. Ninjutsu Centers is one of the largest martial arts organizations in the world. We are still one of the only classical Ninja Schools in the world with over 1000 students.

Goal: Our goal is to help all of our students achieve what they desire in life. To say the least life-skill that is matched by no other activity. I have seen the results firsthand and know that what we teach enables people to "gain the power to change their lives forever."

The more you communicate with your clients the better it is for both you and them. Believe it or not, there are so many things that they do not know about you and will ever know unless you tell them. Heck, half of them don't even know how hard your task is and how many hours you work. If they did, many would treat you differently. There is nothing wrong with educating them. Education is the key to success – a more educated client is a better client. In our schools we teach "in order to get respect you have to give respect." Many parents may be respected in their particular fields of business, but they may not realize how hard you have worked to become who you are. They may see you as a fighting machine or a part of the killer elite. They may not see you as an expert in child development or a specialist in physical fitness. The more you educate your clients and establish yourself as a professional and an expert, the better you are understood. The goal is to continually talk about what you do and how well you do it. You should also take time to talk about your staff, telling the students and their parents how skilled they are or possibly about how they have become who they are, what training they went through, etc.

The ultimate goal is to build your credibility and create a desire in people to want to be with you. It all boils down to marketing. If you don't market you will remain the world's best kept secret. It is your duty to continually educate parents, students and clients alike on the many benefits your school has to offer. So I say don't be embarrassed "Toot your own horn." *Beep, beep* ...

Getting Over The Marketing Blues

This topic is powerful, interesting and beneficial in more ways then one. Many years ago I stumbled on a book, called *The E-myth*. The author is Michael Gerber. Many of you know him from his articles in *MA Success* magazine as well as because he is one of the most prolific writers on business systems, selling millions of books worldwide. Mr. Gerber was the keynote speaker at the MAIA show in Las Vegas some years ago. When I first read his book, it struck a cord and opened my eyes. Since then I have changed my life.

The E-myth describes the entrepreneurial myth. It describes things we believe to be true that are not true at all, the things we are led to believe due to simple chains of events, things that happen to formulate our opinions about everything we do.

For example, we tend to believe that summer is a bad time for martial arts schools. While this may be true to some extent, we must realize that when business is slow, we shouldn't sit back and wait for it to pick up. I had an interesting conversation with the owner of a new fish market in my area. I had stopped in to talk to him about co-op advertising. He seemed very receptive to doing it, except he asked if I could check back in the fall because his summer business is slow. I asked if he advertised in the summer. He said, "No." I then asked when his business dropped off. He said early June at the end of school, about the same time as he stopped advertising. I asked him to think about it for a second; no advertising, no clients. Do you see a direct correlation to what was happening? With a peculiar look on his face he said, "Ok." Then he told me to come in the following week to talk about advertising. He had bought into the myth. Hopefully you have not entirely bought into that myth as well. Granted there are times of the year that may be slower than others, due to the nature of the time of year or your community.

Changing gears from generating your own activity during slow times is the key to success in marketing.

50 Ninja Marketing Tactics Arsenal

1. Have a back-to-school week day. Here is how it works: Print a flyer and post it in your school. Ask all of your students to bring in their buddies. Give each of your students 10 passes to give to their friends. On the back of each pass print a waiver and disclaimer that the guest's parents must sign before their child comes to the school. Include a place for all their necessary information, such as address, phone number, e-mail, etc. Then teach exciting classes and let the in-house marketing frenzy begin. Don't forget to offer a 10% discount if they sign up within one week of the class.

2. Produce a series of inexpensive name branding items, such as book marks, book covers, pencils etc. Give them out freely and of course with each gift offer a free week of classes.

3. Have a college safety course for women. This may not lead to many students, but it certainly *could* be a great income generator or create good will within your community. After the course offer a sibling discount to anyone else interested.

4. Send a letter to all the school teachers of your students early in the year before the school calendar is booked. Let them know that you are available for school talks, visits, seminars, etc. This will open the door for you to become the most well know martial arts teacher in your community. Let the kids know that you are available for special person days and to visit their classrooms.

5. Start your back-to-school marketing way before the end of summer. Others are already planning their back-to-school strategies. Choose the newspapers, stores etc. that you will be marketing in. Remember, preparation is the path to success. Start setting your goals now and you will be that much ahead of the game. In fact, put together a marketing plan for the next six months, so you can efficiently implement your plans for that period of time.

Now let's talk about activities for the next few months.

What are we going to do over the next few months? Typically this is a very busy time. You may have picked up this book in the dead of winter, you may be snowed in, or you may be in the height of your summer season. Irrelevant of when you are reading this, the goal is to get to work on the ideas that are relevant to you.

Key Activities to Build Name Recognition and Business in the Upcoming Months

1. End-of-summer and fall fairs.
2. Special events within your community, such as fundraisers, concerts, carnivals, any place where groups of people gather. They are all great places to advertise and market.
3. Radio interviews. Go to local stations and local talk shows and offer your expertise to the hosts of the shows in case they ever need a martial arts expert. You can talk about health, fitness, child abduction, awareness, philosophy and self-defense issues.
4. Speak to the sports coaches for spring, summer and fall activities. Offer them your services to help them improve their players' performance. This is a great way to get you foot in the door. Offer them a commission on all cross-over members. Consider becoming a sponsor of the teams.
5. Contact the schools, via the Letter of Intent to promote. (email me for a copy)
6. Do a gear sale. Get rid of all old gear by selling it to students at low prices, and use the proceeds to help buy new equipment. Build a great deal of excitement and remember to "Toot your own Horn" telling clients you are constantly upgrading and adding new equipment to your school.
7. Start planning a special event. It could be a holiday party, a bowling night, or any other special night that will build cohesiveness among the students and staff in your school.
8. Get your students motivated for upgrades by pre-framing them through discussions and other announcements of upgrade opportunities. Then do a two-week membership sale. Give a 10% discount on all upgrades during those two weeks.
9. Get everyone excited by hosting a special seminar with someone famous. Make sure you do a good job of advertising the event. Remember all the great people we had into our school.
10. Push your referrals. Do a membership drive.
11. Make sure you have sound business systems. As I teach on "Next level," we have a trial class call and follow-up system, 2-, 4-, 6-, 8-, 10-week call system, referral system, perfect attendance system, business appreciation system and $0 cost marketing system.
12. Make sure your staff members are doing what they are supposed to. If you don't have a staff, you need to start now. Again, "Next level" has "how to" information available to you.
13. Stop looking for the "goose that laid the golden student. Stop looking for miracles. Stop gambling. Get a concrete plan and work it, endlessly. Do not give up, be consistent and be good at what you do.

14. Work hard at what you do, give it 100 percent of your energy. Stop spreading yourself too thin. Be an expert at what you are an expert at. Stop trying to be everything.

15. Last but not least, realize that there are no secrets. If someone tells you something, learn from it. If something sounds like a scam, usually it is. No one has built a business empire easily. Granted, sometimes people come up with grand ideas, but in order for those to succeed; hard work must be a part of the equation.

16. Re-evaluate Your Understanding of Marketing: Marketing your school needs to be an ongoing effort. Too many small business owners consider marketing an expendable part of the school's budget, or don't consider the true definition of marketing itself. Without your school being constantly in the spotlight- and a positive spotlight at that- your bottom line will suffer the slings and arrows of too little enrollment.

Marketing does not just refer to flyers and advertisements. There are many things that are left unconsidered in marketing plans. The following tasks should be built into your on-going marketing plan:

17. Find your product or service niche - This is also known as positioning by those who love buzz words. It refers to the segment of the market you want to call your very own. If you specialize in tournaments, children's curriculum, life skills, no-holds-barred fighting or fitness you need to directly target this market. Discover and identify your niche and what makes you different than your competitors. This is critical in knowing the direction that all of your current and future marketing will take.

18. Keep Your Marketing Consistent: When creating your school's identity all things must be considered. Create a logo that matches your niche and the market that you're aiming for. Everything that leaves your office should have the same logo. This form of branding will create a consistent trademark or symbol that prospects and students will relate directly with your location.

19. Create Your Total Package- Your "package" refers to the proverbial "box" that your product comes in. Your salespeople, and most importantly- you, are that package. The way that you present your product will either attract or repel your customers and prospects. If you are selling positive life skills do you "walk the walk"? The entire staff's attitude, attire and personal habits need to mirror your product. A school that touts a life skills program will not stand up to scrutiny if your staff members are slovenly, rude and inappropriate.

19. Service Should Come First AND Last- Consumers consider service or lack of it to be one of the four most important influences in selecting a business from which to buy. Service will always win and lose customers. If you have a swinging back door your front door eventually will lose the race. Provide the service you sold after the sale. Follow up with your students continually for feedback so that you can ensure that your costumers feel that they are getting the product that they were promised!

All of these tips are imperative for creating an environment where your school will not only survive- but thrive! Analyze your staff and marketing procedures today to see where you're missing the boat. If you are not already performing all of these tasks, create an action plan and set a goal to begin using them immediately!

20. Systemize Your Referrals- If your school and programming are professional and run well, then many of your students do, or should come from referrals. The simple fact is that referrals remain to be one of the best sources for new students, but in order to utilize this to the fullest you need to have reliable systems in place to manage, maintain and optimize. Put your referral program together now. You should have the following ready to launch immediately:
21. Direct mail to existing students to encourage referrals
22. A referral script to use at the time of intro and enrollment. Including verbiage about how referrals are encouraged, appreciated and rewarded will allow you to begin to incorporate this script naturally into your intro process.
23. Create a reward system to accompany your referral program. Perhaps a discount off of their next upgrade, a free gift from your pro-shop or a discount on special events. Set up a display area in your school that showcases some of your referral prizes. Explaining the benefits or you can follow my referral program.
24. Ask for referrals regularly. This is something that your entire staff should be well versed and comfortable with. Referrals do not often come without encouragement and management by you and your staff.
25. Organize and institute a Back To School Advertising - If you have not begun your back to school advertising, or it is not the right time of the year it doesn't mean you should not put time into this now. This is something that needs to be taken care of immediately. Create flyers and prepare ads based on your back to school specials. Highlight how the Martial Arts can assist students in getting better grades, etc. Be ready with a complete campaign.
25. Contact Your Local PTA- Offer to assist in yearly fundraising events, and offer your services for special programs. A PTA connection can offer you a gold mine of access to potential new members!
26. Buddy Weeks - Run an entire week of buddy days for both kids and adults. Encourage them to bring a friend to class, and be sure to emphasize the rewards they can receive for their referrals! Do this on a regular basis, I recommend every 5 weeks. Run additional contests within the buddy weeks an award prizes for the person who brings the most buddies.
26. Purchase Back To School Supplies with your logo-pencils, pens, notepads and back packs will be flying off the shelves for the Back To School rush. Creating items with your school name and logo will provide exposure in the exact place where you want it!
27. Remain Focused On The Back To School Market: It doesn't matter if school has been in session for 1 week, or 3 months. Now is the time that parents are looking to give their children an alternative extra-curricular experience, or are starting to recognize difficulties that their children may be having in school. These difficulties could be anything from bullying to bad grades. This puts you in an excellent position to refocus your advertising as an effort to ensure that students will have their best school year ever. This is prime time to re-frame those sticking points and difficult situations that parents will find themselves involved in.
28. Door Hangers - If done regularly and using professional high quality door hangers <u>you will get a respectable response</u>. You should do door hangers weekly.

29) General Advertising - Run print ads in the newspaper, phone book, flyers etc. General advertising is a good source of leads but can be costly. If done properly it can still yield cost-effective student inquiries. Be careful of your budget.

30) Radio and Television - I don't recommend radio or television due to the high cost of the advertising unless you have a budget. Many agencies pitch this advertising as a low cost way to reach a large market if you do it in 15-second spots, and some marketing companies will sell you a package and even do the commercials. However, I have not heard many success stories from this form of advertising. With this type of marketing money has to be spent consistently and your campaign must run for quite sometime to gain momentum.

34) Business Appreciation - Work with other local businesses; you advertise their businesses and they advertise yours. We spoke about this previously.

35) Co-op Marketing - Approach local businesses to advertise on the backs of your door hangers, flyers etc. The other businesses help pay for the advertising. This is something many people do not think about. If you are going to advertise and you have a blank side of a flyer, door hanger or postcard you can sell the space to a local business making them a partner in the marketing venture. With the cost savings you may be able to double your advertising dollars and develop and nurture a relationship with another business owner that will benefit you ten fold. We have done this and made a profit from it. If thought about you can actually make a profit on this or end up doing your advertising for free.

36) V.I.P. Passes - If you are not doing these you are operating in the stone ages. V.I.P. passes are simple, no nonsense business cards inviting people who you, your students, or your staff meets to a free trial class or trial week. I have a friend who sends his staff to the supermarket to give out passes as they go through the aisles of the grocery store and load their shopping carts. They then go back down the aisles and put all the products back, give out more passes and then leave.

37) Week Free Passes - This kind of pass should be given out to all your new students to give to friends. This ties directly into your parties.

38) Birthday Parties – Many school owners shy away from Birthday parties. At first I was leery of them as well thinking I was selling out or becoming a glorified baby-sitting service. I have come along way and started doing parties and really teaching quality martial arts within them. I am currently doing a large amount of parties per year and actually making good money doing it.

38) The Un-Birthday – I came up with this name based on the fable with the Mad Hatter. The concept is to give away free parties to who ever is interested. The party got its name due to it not being necessary for it to be someone's Birthday. The goal is to get the student in your school, having fun with their friends. The goal is to get one existing student to host this for all non-existing students. The more people you meet the better. I have had clients that have done this for adults and hosted a self-defense party and had wine and cheese afterwards. This is something you must make personal choices on, but irrelevant it is a great way to get people through the doors.

39) Two, Four, Six, Eight, and 10-Week Calls - This is marketing in the best form. These calls are something that I have begged and pleaded with school owners to do, but many seem not to take me seriously. I know clients who have quadrupled their

businesses using this. The goal is to talk to the customers and find out what they are thinking while preparing them for many things. The goal is to open communication with them, but this is also used to ask for referrals, and also pre-frame them for upgrades and other events and business opportunities.

40) Stationary Advertising - This is a plastic holder with your flyer or any other form of advertising on it which can be left on counter, shelves or any visible areas in <u>local stores and business within your community.</u> This can be tied into Business Appreciation.

41) Lead Boxes - Lead Boxes are a great way to market. I have found that many of the leads are dead leads, meaning that they had no intention of coming to the school, but even if you only get 1 out of 100, it is <u>still worth it</u>.

42) Any Kind of Community Marketing - Exhibit at fairs, local events etc. We had great success with a minor league baseball team called the Ducks last year and are doing a campaign this year for the entire season. We signed up about 25 yearly contracts at $1,500 each from this one source. That's $37,500.

43) Free Special Seminars - Anything you do to <u>reach out to your students or to your community</u> can result in leads. The goal is to give the seminars as a service, so people come in and benefit, and then because of that service people are motivated to inquire or stay on.

44) Anyone Who Asks You to Advertise or Donate - You can turn these people making requests into your Ninjas. If a local PTA or organization is doing a fund raiser, instead of taking an ad in the local journal (which never works), give them passes to distribute at their event. If it is a sit down dinner, give them a pass for everyone sitting at every table. Also, if they are doing a Chinese auction, raffle off a three-month membership or a membership of your choice. Your <u>cost is minimal</u> and the activity is guaranteed to get someone through the doors to experience your class.

45) Meet with Larger Businesses - Businesses that have many employees and offer to give a free seminar. Then offer each employee a free membership of your choice - either one month or three months. Let management know the value of the free memberships and let the owner sell in a Ninja way. <u>The owner will be giving the memberships as a gift</u> from him or herself. This takes teamwork. The owner benefits from the employees' good will and you benefit from the new leads. It works best tied into a seminar.

46) Hold A Spring "Talent" Show: If dance schools can do recitals why can't martial arts schools? Highlighting your students' talents is always a good idea. Plan a school "spectacular" that allows parents to take part in their children's activities, and to see the benefits of your curriculum in action! This type of activity is also a great way to include the community and promote your school.

47) Host a Fundraiser – this is a great way to help a cause of your choice, I have raised over one hundred thousand dollars over the years for charities such as the Carol Baldwin Breast Cancer Research Fund, St. Jude's Children's hospital, Project Action Foundation, Muscular Dystrophy, American Cancer Society and the list goes on and on. I find this to be the responsibility of a martial artist or a business owner but I won't go into detail about that. In any event, there are many positive attributes of doing a fundraiser beyond the normal visible such as press and community good will and synergy.

48) On site Questionnaires – Ask one of your most personable employees to go out and stand in a busy area of the community and ask questions such as have you ever been in a dangerous situation, have you ever felt un-safe, do you exercise, would you like to exercise more…you get the idea. At that time ask the potential client if they would be interested in a free week of classes at your martial arts school.

49) Cold Calling – this is one of the toughest for any sales person and it takes determination and tenacity. The goal is to start at the letter A in your local phone book and work your way through the letter Z. You will find a large amount of rejection but there will be times when some people show some interest. This is simply a numbers game.

50) Host A Halloween Costume Party: Halloween Costume Parties are some of the best income generators ever. Make sure that the party is set up for kids aged 4 years and up through your adult population. You may find it best to hold the adult costume party on a different night from the children's party. These events always turn out to be lucrative and fun. My recommendation would be to charge anywhere from $30 to $50. This cost should include refreshments and a prize for best costume. The party can include bring a friend for half price or free. Immediately turning a retention tool into an immediately advertising source.

Being I like to undersell and overprovide I am adding in one more which is:

51) Halloween or any Holiday V.I.P. Passes: Make sure that you are gearing up to hand out Halloween V.I.P. Passes but this can be done for any holiday. This is an entire marketing campaign in itself, and you can encourage all of your students to hand out these passes along with the candy and treats that they give to visiting trick-or-treaters or during the Christmas holiday as a gift to a friend. You should plan to have enough to give a minimum of 30 passes to each of your students.

Most of the time people think of marketing as immediate. The thought is if I run an ad, I should get some sort of response which will end up in new business. There are many forms of marketing, some are immediate response while others are branding. Establishing your name and keeping it fresh in the customer or potential customers mind. There are other factors which are essential to your marketing campaign which are.

52) Quality Control - I have spoken about this as much as I have spoken about my referral program and two, four, six, eight, and 10-week calls during my tele-seminars and one on one personal consulting. This is the only reason why we are in business. If you are not over-providing and under-selling, then it is inevitable that you will be out of business in a few years. The goal must be to take all your clients and create unbelievable motivation about your product. A happy client is someone who will continually stay with you, spend money, and be a raving fan. Given the opportunity a

happy client will talk about you continuously. That client will refer you every chance he or she gets.

53) Establishing synergy - among all your marketing components is the most important thing you can do this year to maximize your marketing efforts. One component will not work without the others.

Your heads are probably spinning by now. I've given you quite a lot to think about! The good thing is this list is not going anywhere.

Here are some things you can do on a yearly basis.

54) Take an inventory of all of your school equipment: Pull all of the gear that you currently use within your school and get rid of it all. Yes, you heard me correctly: "Get rid of it all." Order all new kick pads and hand mitts. Sell your used equipment at low cost to your students and family members. The old stuff may be dirty and smelly, and can really can drag your students' perception of the cleanliness and safety of your school downward, but for a discounted price there are many student who would love to purchase it. The goal is to help them start on building their home practice gym and continue their training outside your school. Make sure you build this up to create a buzz within your school.

55) Get Honest Advice: Ask your students and parents to tell you honestly what about your school should go or stay. Ask them for decorating advice as well. As we have said so many times before: "Perception is reality." That wall of throwing stars and swords might look cool to you, but may be ominous and frightening to your students! Your students' ideas of safety and comfort need to be your top priority!

56) Clean It Up: Organize a cleaning day and have your students volunteer. Get into every nook and cranny and make sure your school is absolutely spotless. Remember that the appearance of your school is a representation of you. There are not many people who enjoy training in a facility that appears, or is, dirty and run-down. Initially this may not seem like marketing but if your school doesn't reflect an environment which is sellable, then it doesn't matter how many students come through the door, you will be working against yourself.

57) Analyze Your Statistics: You need to analyze statistics consistently. Look at the full picture at the beginning of every season to allow yourself to see where you are lagging and to make short-term corrections before things get too far out of control. This information will also give you a good perspective on where you need to focus your seasonal advertising, and where you should alter the schedule for the coming year.

58) Having Trouble Tracking Your Stats? Use Tracking Forms: **If you are not tracking stats then you need to get started! Use standard and daily forms, and add the task of tracking to your daily calendar to help to take the challenge out of tracking your stats. There are many sources for these types of forms, and you can easily locate a variety of different stat tracking forms in the premium section of www.TakingItToTheNextLevel.com.**

59) Give Your School a Makeover: I mentioned this briefly but changing the color of paint in your lobby area and training rooms can make a world of difference. Most design changes get positive reactions. Changing the color scheme of your decor or the layout of your furniture can add to the comfort of your students and parents, and will give them the sense that you intend to continue to update your school and maintain its friendly and inviting environment. This also applies to your Pro-Shop items. When you always display the same set up of Pro-Shop items, they seem to be design fixtures, not items that are for sale. Remove or move items on a continuing basis. Consumers desire items that are "hot" and constantly on the move!

60) Design a Student/Parent Questionnaire: Remember that it's important to ask the tough questions, too. You cannot be afraid to ask questions whose answers you may not want to hear! Ask parents and students their opinions of your curriculum, the gear that you've sold them, the appearance of your school, and if they feel that they're realizing the benefits that they were promised! Give them the opportunity to hand in the questionnaire anonymously and you will receive answers that are truly honest.

61) Email marketing – this is an area that is overlooked very often. I think many people are afraid it may take a great deal of work and you have to be a computer expert to do this. I have worked with many companies and there are many on the market today that make this as painless as possible. When emailing make sure not to send too many emails and emails with content that doesn't pertain to the client. For example if you are sending a parent of a 5 year old classes on "Pit Fighting" you may lose their interest. In essence what you will do is train them not to listen to you. The goal is to get a captive audience and possible send specific emails to specific clients. Adults may be on one specific list while others may be on another. Do not inundate people with things they do not want, you will lose them quickly.

62) Push Your Fall Pro-Shop Line: Start advertising sales on your fall gear and clothing that every school should have available for their students. Backpacks, sweatshirts, long sleeve T's and school supplies should all be on hand. If you are not currently stocked with any of these items, please email me at Renshilininja@aol.com, or visit www.TakingItToTheNextLevel.com today for more details.

Chapter 5
Systemization of your Business

One Thing In Life Is Inevitable – Change!

The beauty of change is that regardless of whether or not it's something that you had wanted or planned for, it presents you with a wealth of lessons that can enable you to grow and expand your comfort zone. If used to your advantage the end result of change can always be a positive one.

For many years I have enthusiastically shared concepts and my ideas with some of my best friends in this industry. My perspective has always been if the ideas that I have implemented have been successful, then why not help my friends to experience that same success without the hurdles? It is my goal as a consultant to continue to push all of you past your comfort zones and help you achieve levels of success professionally, personally and spiritually that you have never before imagined.

Many of us live and work within comfort zones containing routines that have become second nature. What most of us don't realize is these routines can often cloud our perspectives and keep us from trying new things and thinking "outside of the box".

My goal is to encourage you to take a hard look at the processes and activities within your school, eliminate those that aren't working and implement new things to make your school grow, turning a focused eye on shifting your perspective and breaking free of your routine. After exploring 10 items that are crucial to the growth of your business, each of these items will be drilled down and analyzed in detail to allow us greater insight into the importance of why specific tasks and information contribute directly to your success.

The following is a list of 10 items imperative to the growth of your school:

1) Finalize your trial class numbers - Compile an accurate list of all the trial classes that were booked this past year. Be sure to note those who attended their appointments, and those who enrolled.

2) Compile a list of all memberships types sold - If you have a variety of different membership options, list those that your students are currently enrolled in. Pay close attention to the program that has the most enrollments. Your goal is to build enrollment in those programs that have not been as populated. If you do not have a variety of programs, begin working toward implementing more membership options. Also, make note of who is in each program. For example, 3-5 year olds, how many of them are in that specific category and what is the breakdown male and female. Go as far as to analyze what belt they are and what belt or rank you may have a large drop out rate. The fine details you should be looking at are the whether there is a large number of any specific category dropping out. This may be for a variety of reasons, but identify the loss first and then decide on what the reason is.

3) Note all of the sources of advertising that contributed to enrollment - When looking at your active students list you should have a list that indicates which source of marketing brought these students to your door? This information will give you further insight into how to best balance your advertising and marketing budget going forward this year. Those students who were brought in by referral should have noted the name of the person who referred them.

4) Compile a list of all members - that are currently involved in longer term contracts or specialty programs - How many of your students have upgraded to Black Belt, Masters Club, Leadership Team etc.? These programs help to build retention and easily increase your monthly income! If you are not currently running these types of programs then you need to make a plan to implement programs such as these within the next two months. If one of these programs has been more successful than another, drill down and investigate why. If you are not experiencing success with these programs at all, then you should focus on the steps you are taking to enroll and upgrade to these memberships. Are you not "selling" these programs well? Do you need to review the quality of these programs, what they have to offer, convenience of membership? Having a list is the first step to further analyzing how to improve this area of your business.

5) Know your numbers - Building financial goals is the keystone of what you are attempting to do. All of your other goal-setting is directly related to this one piece of information activity. Begin a file of your current accounts receivables and set immediate goals for the next month, three months, six months and year. This number is a stepping-stone to creating a healthy monthly budget, so this list needs to include all of your paid-in-full contracts and where that money has gone, or is going!

These are just the first steps to knowing where you are, and making a solid and fairly simple path to achieving your goals and breaking out of your routine. How many of us come into our schools every day and run through the same routine, then at the end of the day sit back and wonder why we are not as successful as we know we have the ability to be? A great deal of us don't take the time to think about what we need to do to get the edge we need to be successful entrepreneurs and how we can achieve the results by moderating our daily routines! Remember, as we learned in our chapter on goal setting, you must have a plan and take consistent action.

6) Determine Your Goals - Once you know the details of all of your current stats, it's time to sit down and determine your goals for new members, renewals, and upgrades. Set these goals realistically. Your goals should be challenging yet attainable. These goals should reflect your overall yearly objectives, and should also break the objectives into monthly numbers. Be sure to factor in your attrition rate.

7) Create a Calendar - I cannot overstress the importance of having a detailed calendar for all of your school engagements and important dates. This calendar should be set for the entire upcoming year, leave room so you can be flexible should you need to add something mid-year. Distributing this calendar to your students can help them to know what is expected of them by the school, and can also help them set their own goals for the year. Put the calendar on your website if you have one. This will create a way for you to drive people to the site, a well for other information. The digital version is much cheaper and will save you tons of money in the long run.

8) Determine the Make-up of Your Class Roster- What category do the majority of students fit into? Are they aged 3-5 years, 5-8? You should analyze this information on a regular basis to determine which programs need to be enhanced, or where you should be shifting your focus.

9) Build a Resource Library- Build a library of all of the consulting and marketing resources that you have used in the past, or feel would be effective in your school in the future. A reference library is the quickest way to refresh your staff and your motivation. Gather as much information as you can. You may not think that focusing on "Paid In Full" contracts is of vital importance to your school operations now, but as your school grows you will find you are ready to implement more advanced systems so having this information to fall back on is imperative. Keep your library as organized as possible nothing is worse then going back to look for something and not be able to find it.

10) Get A Business Coach - Without your instructor you might not have made it as far as a Martial Arts trainer as you have come! Sadly many instructors are not good business people. When it relates to being successful as a Martial Arts business professional, working closely with the people who can help you to achieve your business goals is no different! The Martial Arts industry is chock full of people who have "been there done that." These individuals can lead you down the right path and help you to avoid common business pitfalls. As Member of www.takingittothenextlevel.com you have access to me on a continual basis I also do personal one on one "Elite Consulting" for a select group. Utilizing someone's experience is as easy as picking up the phone! Make time to expand your knowledge monthly; just like eating proper food is conducive to become healthy, knowledge is the key to your success.

Using this information can mean the difference between your business staying static or experiencing significant growth. In order to take the next step it's important that we know exactly where we stand, and in which direction we should go! Really it is all about making decisions. I believe wanting is not enough, many people want and even yearn, but never take action. It is up to you to take action.

2, 4, 6, 8 and 10 Week Call Process for New Students

How many of you have heard of the benefits of a 2-4-6 week call program intended to activate and retain new students? We are sure you have heard of the process, maybe even started to implement it, but are you using it effectively? Is it working for you? This is intended to help you master this important process and protect one of your most important assets, a new student resulting from your hard earned sales success!

2-4-6-8-10 Week Calls develop a line of communication between you, your students and their families and drives customer retention. We all know that retention is one of the keys to a success in any business, but particularly in the case of martial arts schools. Some rather strong analogies used in reference to retention are: Plugging holes in the bucket and keeping the front door wide open and closing the back door? Incorporating something as simple as a disciplined and repeatable 2-4-6-8-10 week call process will encourage higher retention in your school by keeping the lines of communication open. You will also have additional chances to understand and overcome any objections as they arise.

However, as the old saying goes: it is easier said than done. Advertise, bring new students in, teach exciting classes and they will stay forever, right? No, wrong! In reality, schools with a shorter curriculum fare much better then schools with a longer, more intensive curriculum. Statistically speaking a school with a 2 year course to reach Black Belt might yield 75-85% retention while a school with a 5 year course to Black Belt curriculum may only show 50% retention. The key to success here is to understand your school's cycles and implement systems that will drive student satisfaction and retention. This will allow you to be financially sound while incorporating systems that foster consistent growth.

Here is an overview of the goals and objectives of each call.

The 2 Week Call: This first call is a great way to open a line of communication between the school and the student or parent. This call will lay out some of the basic rules, guidelines and expectations of the school. This can also be converted to a 2 week appointment or an orientation and review. This call should also be used to begin to identify and solidify the key motivations and interests that the parent or student was looking for when they joined your program. With these clearly identified, you can more effectively stress accomplishments along the way that reinforce initial motivation and interests and keep your students coming with a positive and excited attitude. At the end of your first call you can now ask for your first referral. If you meet with resistance now is the time to establish trust with the client and after that trust is developed ask that they give you a referral.

The 4 Week Call: Students accomplish a great deal within the first three weeks of training and need to be recognized for their efforts. A critical goal of this call and the continuing call process is to transform your new student from interested party to dedicated student and school advocate. Use the 4 week call to highlight and recognize the student's progress and also to encourage them to participate in more school events. The 4 week call is also a prime opportunity to get referrals, or to plant the seed for future referrals. Help your students be an advocate for you and your school by leveraging their excitement and progress over this initial period. Make note that either the 2 or the 4 week call is your time to make a connection and open the lines of communication but most importantly educate the client as to why the martial arts and your school is one of the best buying decisions they ever made. Also, at the end of this call you should be receiving some referrals. If the client felt funny on the initial 2 week call they promised to have at minimum one referral for the 4 week call, make sure you establish that trust goes both ways. If they make a promise they should keep it and so on.

The 6 Week and Beyond Call: This call continues and enhances open communication with parents and/or students. Use this call to repeat and re-establish rules and guidelines, anchor the benefits to the parent or student's initial goals, request referrals, invite participation in special events and lay the groundwork for upgrades and renewals.

These calls should continue on a monthly basis after the 6 week call has been completed. Keeping communication open throughout the life of membership will guarantee you at least the opportunity to hear and overcome objections, and will lead to increased overall retention.

Each of these calls should be scripted and strictly scheduled. Just as you perform your introductory and attendance calls on scheduled days, the 2-4-6 week calls program and schedule needs to be executed in a disciplined and consistent manner. A script should be built for each of these calls to encourage consistency among your staff to make the desired results happen. You can find full scripts for each of these calls on www.takingittothenextlevel.com that can be easily tailored to fit your needs.

Detailed notes should be taken on each call and filed with the student's information for further reference and to be sure that any issues or challenges are immediately addressed. The notes from these calls can be shared during weekly staff meetings for further consistency and awareness across your entire school team.

2-4-6-8-10 week calls are a simple task to accomplish once you incorporate a consistent process into your business schedules and team goals. Forcing this discipline on yourself and your staff will help you to stay consistent and yield better retention and create the kind of dedicated student and family advocates that every Martial Art School hopes for!

Systemizing The Trial Class Intro Call

The trial or intro class is one of the most important steps in the enrollment process. This introduction to your school can make or break the decision for the potential student or their parent. It's important to keep in mind, however, that all contact with the prospective buyer prior to the intro or trial class will be the deciding factor in whether you will schedule the trial at all!

Setting up the trial class should be handled in the most professional and systematic way in order to ensure that you have the opportunity to set up an introduction to your school. Don't forget that it takes a great deal of money in advertising to get your phone to ring, do not waste your hard-earned dollars.

There are 7 top priorities to setting up the trial class:

Script the Phone Call: Set up a system for answering the phone. Have a phone interview sheet and trial class waiver immediately available to all staff members. Rehearse your script with your entire staff until it becomes second nature, and make sure that anyone who answers the phone does it as well as you do!

Trial Class Book: Have a trial class book set up to maintain your trials. Verifying and maintaining your trial class book should be part of your daily routine. Self-discipline is key, and reminders and re-schedules will enable you to keep your new enrollments at an all time high.

Set Up Reminders: Make sure that you are following through on your reminder phone calls. For instance, if Mr. Smith has set up a trial for Friday the 15th, you should be calling him on the 14th to remind him that the staff will be prepared and awaiting his arrival. Follow up and follow through are integral parts of your intro system. If Mr. Smith cannot make it you now have the opportunity to re-schedule, and begin the reminder process again.

Trial Tracking System: Develop a system to track your trials. I detail this information on my video Taking It To The Next Level: A Complete Education for the Serious Martial Arts School Owner. This of course is just one idea on how to track your trials. There are appointment systems in many software programs that will allow you to automate your schedules. You can easily track both your trial class book information, as well as your reminder calls through both of these systems.

Checks and Balances: Put together a set of checks and balances to monitor your trials. In other words, you have to be able to track the trials that you set, the ones who attend their first class, the ones who miss their first class, the ones who show up but don't sign up, and those that enroll. Be specific on which program the trial student enrolls in. This system will allow you to track which marketing is performing effectively for you.

Don't Let Unprofessional Behavior Lose the Sale: Do not settle for unprofessional behavior- or should I say untrained behavior. I cannot reiterate this enough. If you are receiving calls, then you have assurance that your marketing is working and you are one step closer to increasing your enrollment. In any case, a lack of professionalism will drastically decrease your chances of enrollment success. Do not let a lack of professionalism waste any opportunity!

These systems are simple to build, incorporate and maintain at any school. I am, however, always surprised to see how many schools have no systems to maintain their calls at all! If you are not using systems you are already one step behind.

Progressing Students through Levels

We have already touched on some very important stats and issues. We now realize that we should track everything, from the phone calls, trial classes, enrollment, and programs, from the time students sign up throughout their memberships. Otherwise we will have many holes in the information that we need to know in order to make our schools strong. We need to be aware of where we are, and of our strengths and weaknesses. Then we moved on to keeping statistics about our students: their ranks, their ages and the position that they attain within their age group; when students quit – at what age, what rank, after what period of time, during what program etc. This information lets us understand exactly how we are doing with the curriculum, about the excitement within our curriculum, and its difficulty or lack of challenge. We need to find out clearly what motivates our students in order to keep them interested and involved.

In our school we look at all of our students as though they are "lifers," people who have the potential to teach and who will want to run a school. This may not always be the case, but this is how we approach our students so they all may reach the highest potential. In our organization we have four levels of students.

Level 1 - Our new students are considered "Level 1." It all depends on how long it takes from beginner to Black Belt as to what amount of time this level will be. This is the time when students are looking for you to help them overcome fears and doubts as well as indoctrinate them into the ways of your school and the most basic of philosophy. You also want to make sure they avoid injury.

We treat these students as though they will eventually move on to one of our other programs. This is a transient stage of their training and a very sensitive stage that should be handled carefully. We need to track these students and follow up on them as though they were the most important people in our schools. It is imperative to give all new students our highest attention. Of course we want to do this will all of our "veteran" students, too.

Level 2 – Students enrolled in one of our specialty programs, such as the Black Belt Club, are considered "Level 2." These students show dedication and the desire to put more time and effort into their training. They want more and are willing to "step it up." This period is one of the most exciting times in a students training. Everything is new and their motivation is high. At this time we need to track Level 2 students and monitor their stats so that we can effectively upgrade them. Doing this encourages better retention and therefore builds our accounts receivable. This is the time for us to educate our students and their families as to why the martial arts are such a great life-decision. We should take as much time as necessary to guide the parents and the students, giving them all the tools to make educated decisions. Normally a student may misunderstand our motivation, so it is imperative to be clear as to why you are working so hard to get them to see why this level is so important.

Level 3 – "Level 3" students are enrolled in our Masters Elite program. In our school there is no set time period before they may enroll. Eligibility is determined by whether students show dedication, tenacity and the desire to really devote significant time to their studies. This is the most intense program with regard to training and physical dedication. It is also one of the most progressive programs, giving students the highest discounts on seminars, gear packages and uniform options. We love to see all of our students advance to this program.

Level 4 – Students in our Team Leader, Character Development, and Instructor Training programs are considered "Level 4" students. These programs are designed to help students develop the necessary techniques to become teachers. We look at all of our students as potential teachers of the future. We never want to exclude any students from consideration. Some of our best teachers were not the top athletes or the most outgoing in their early student days. They often were the people who were quiet and simply trained. But eventually they started to shine and moved out of the shadows in to the limelight. All of our instructors have been through either our Team Leader Character Development program, and our Instructor Training program. In fact no one can be an instructor with out going through one of these programs.

These four Levels of students are the lifeblood of our schools. Progressing students through these Levels gives our schools the ability to grow, and even to expand into more locations. The "Four Level" concept is taken from the way I organize my schools and is a working model, but the philosophy can be customized to suit you.

Statistically speaking, compiling data and tracking your students' progress enables you to have a business plan and to keep your focus on the big picture. Your vision must not be just an idea or concept; it needs to be a working system. Your system will allow your students to have a future and a dream. They will know how they can progress in rank, and they will know that they can improve their futures, whether they use their martial arts training in their relationships, at their jobs, or by becoming a martial arts instructor or school owner. All of these outcomes give them worthy goals to shoot for.

Stats! What's all the hype about?

Many years ago when I began teaching Martial Arts I had a 400 square foot school and a 4 inch by 6 inch file box where I kept my records. I was far behind the times in regard to computers, but at least I was keeping records! My main focus was to know when students were due to pay their monthly tuition. I had made an arrangement with my 30 students. Each one of them was required to call me if they couldn't make it to class. This was a great way to keep in touch, find out their reasons for not being able to train, and overcome objections as they arose. This was fairly easy to maintain with only 30 students.

I added on another 100 students right away once I had moved into a larger location of 6100 square feet. I initially kept the same philosophy with everyone continuing to call if they were going to be absent. This was so time consuming that I found myself barely doing anything aside from answering the phone for the 25 or so people that weren't able to come in each night. It was time for a change - No more calls, I was going to place all of my focus on teaching. But as a result I lost touch with the students. I needed to start tracking them in a different way. I instituted a few items such as we miss you calls and postcards once a week, but these were not half as effective. People can ignore you much more easily if they don't have to speak to you directly.

Suddenly I found myself wondering what direction my school was taking, and why enrollment was falling stagnant for months at a time. I needed information and I needed it fast. I sat down and began to develop systems that would allow me to keep a finger on the pulse of my school, and enable me to keep statistics in areas that were pertinent to the growth of my business. These statistics will contain crucial information that needs to be maintained in order to run a professional school and at the same time foster growth.

10 Top stats to keep!

Incoming Calls: What marketing resources encouraged them to call, and the time of day that you are receiving these calls both need to be recorded. This information is pertinent because it will not only give you information on which marketing sources are the most successful, but what times during the day you should be building staff coverage. If you are receiving all of your incoming calls from 10am-12pm and you are not there at that time, you need to rearrange your schedules to have phone coverage at that time.

Scheduled Appointments: Once the initial call is completed and you have scheduled the intro or trial class you will need to track confirmation of appointments, and whether they come in for the scheduled appointment, how many appointments have you set and how many have actually shown up? How many have you translated into enrollments?

Tracking Membership Style: Tracking the length of contracts that you have enrolled is a very telling process: For instance if you have a 3 month, 6 month, 1 year and 3 year membership and you find that you have most members currently enrolled in your 3 month membership you will need to redirect your focus on selling longer-term memberships. Remember, the longer the membership the less work for you in up-sells and upgrades. Quite often it is a matter of believing in the program and selling what is really beneficial to the student, but no matter what I say you must realize it is the right thing to do for both you and your student.

Tracking the Details of the 2-4-6-8-10 Week Call: Once a student has enrolled the 2-4-6 Week Call process need to begin immediately. This process becomes worth its weight in gold as you begin to track the details of each of these calls. Pay close attention to the attendance trends of these members and the noted objections. Keeping these stats will give you insight into where the students are most excited in their training and where stumbling blocks, drop rates and de-motivation are occurring most frequently within your program. This will give you an opportunity to be proactive and make changes where they are most needed.

Tracking Rank: How many black belts do you have that still actively train? How many have actually made it to black belt? At my schools we have eight belt levels to reach Black Belt. About 5 years ago, out of hundreds of students we had only a few brown belts and one or two black belts. I needed to rearrange the curriculum so that more students stayed actively training past black belt. I sat down and developed a curriculum that was conducive to long term growth. I now have over 80 active Black Belts and at minimum 75 in each other ranking. Our goal for the next five years is to produce a minimum 30 black belts per year.

Tracking these trends will allow you an opportunity to improve the areas that are needed, and also maintain healthy contact with your students and your business.

Promotion Tracking

Keeping track of the progression of your students is imperative to maintaining high retention, and even to increasing your enrollment. Sadly, many schools do not pay close attention to student promotions, or maximize on the benefits of constant attention to this information.

For many martial art schools, promotions stem from the same systems used for student attendance. Many software programs have great ways to track promotions. However, when focusing on tracking promotions the first thing that you must decide is the actual amount of time between each belt level. There are 4 different levels or criteria that decide promotion at my schools:

1. Time Period: This is the minimum time that a student must remain in a belt level before they are allowed to move to the next.

2. Number of Classes: Promotion directly relates to the minimum number of classes that a student is required to attend during the time period in order to be eligible for promotion. Make special note that I said eligible, not that they are going to receive their next rank.

3. Ability to Perform Curriculum: The student must be able to perform all of the criteria taught at their current belt level before promotion is viable or I will even schedule their belt test and ceremony.

4. Lastly – Physical requirements: At each rank we have a set of physical requirements each student needs to perform. These physical requirements are simple push-ups, sit-ups, jumping jacks, etc. We start off slowly with only a few building on their physical ability at each rank. In my school when a student is a Black Belt Candidate they have a brutal physical test which consists of a 6 month training course, a 3 mile run and hundreds of physical exercises.

By putting these criteria into place we are at the very least guaranteeing a higher retention between belt levels. For each school the promotion schedule may be different. But having your criteria documented, and maintaining detailed information for each student at every level of your schedule puts a simple "checks and balances" system into effect. In this way the studio can ensure quality control and track the ability of each student. It also assists in leading into other things such as the sale of private lessons or "special help" classes for added income.

We track this information through our software program, but it can also be maintained through a hard copy attendance card system (though not nearly as convenient). Once this major criteria is met and the student is ready for promotion there are a few other items that are linked to retention and quality control.

Letter of Intent: Before scheduling a student's test date we give them a Letter of Intent to promote which must be completed by two parties, their school teacher and the parents. This letter not only ties in the student's progress at school, it also emphasizes to the parents and school teachers that the Martial Arts Location takes education very seriously. This helps to open the door for increased contact with local schools, and becomes a viable way for us to secure new students through "school talks", etc. This

Letter of Intent remains to be a guiding force in helping us get our message out to school teachers and parents throughout the community.

Group Testing Dates: Once the Letter of Intent has been filled out and turned in the student will be scheduled for the group testing date. At Long Island Ninjutsu we bulk all of our tests together. This is a great way to turn your test into a vehicle to drive the benefits of your school home to their friends and family. Bear in mind that it doesn't matter whether the student is a child, teen or adult. All age groups can be handled in the same way. Each test should be carried out like a well performed demonstration to sell your services and concepts, as well as your upcoming events and future programs to potential students.

Private Lessons: Testing dates are a prime time to talk to students and their parents about private lessons. Usually a student or parent would like to get a little more preparation in before any test. Private lessons can be a huge income generator for the studio.

Promotion Tracking Checklist: Maintain a promotion tracking form to track the students who are testing and ensure that belts are ordered, certificates prepared and to make sure that everyone's Letters of Intent are completed and turned in. This insures us that each test will go off without a snag, and that we are as professional as possible. The testing experience has to be one that is memorable to each student and their parent!

Promotion Envelope: We developed this as a hand out after the promotion that is handed to the student and or the parent after the ceremony along with the student's certificate. This envelope includes a discount on gear if purchased within two weeks of the test as well as the new information pertaining to their next belt level, the student's and the parents' responsibility as well as any other information beneficial to the student. You can also include any schedule changes or discount for upgrade programs and upcoming events.

Remember, the idea of a belt test it to make note of the progress of the student. The more memorable you make the event for the student, the family and the guests, the longer you will keep that particular student. You are not only testing their abilities, but also priming their guests and parents for future sales.

Weekly and Monthly Checklists

Checklists

Weekly (or twice weekly, based on available time and volume)

2,4,6,8,10 week call process begins and is maintained.
Place "We miss you "calls and "Attendance" calls.
Make confirmation calls for trial classes and missed trial class appointments.
Place "Review" and "Renewal" calls.
Call people who have been referred by students.
Call students who made referrals. The calls should let the student know whether the referral joined, and the status of the student's "free time for referrals" account.
Follow up on delinquent billing.

Monthly

Mail or e-mail newsletters to students and others on the school list.
Provide the head instructor with an updated list of student e-mail addresses.
Send a mailer to students who have stopped within the past month.
Call students who have quit within the first six months to stay in contact and say hello. Try to determine why they quit. This may give you important insight into ways to improve retention.
Mail birthday flyer including three months of birthdays. This lets each student appear on three fliers. (For example, a student whose birthday is in October will appear on the "August, September, October" flier, and also on the next two fliers.
Two weeks before the start of each month, mail birthday cards to students whose birthdays fall within the following month.
Call schoolteachers who gave their numbers on letters of intent. Set up appointments and file into your database.

These checklists provide just a starting point for you to develop your own. Keep track of each function you do on a regular basis. Decide the frequency that will work best for you. Write down each task, and you will be sure that it will never be inadvertently forgotten. Stay organized to get the routine tasks done with the least amount of stress.

Conquering Time - the Ultimate Adversary

Life is not always as you had envisioned! At times our dreams and goals seem so close yet so far, and even though they appear to be within reach they are sometimes elusive. In particular, time is the ultimate adversary we need to defeat.

There are only 24 hours in a day; using our time productively *and* joyously is our ultimate triumph.

When I opened my first Martial Arts school, I built it up to 30 students within months, but many things stopped me from reaching higher levels. I have often at conventions as the keynote speaker and on conference calls about the many problems that continually plague Martial Arts school owners. The pitfalls are sometimes very elusive and frequently lie in the shadows like Ninja.

For years I tackled my own billing, and before I knew it I was dedicating more than 20 hours per week toward the collection of my hard-earned money. I was approached by a billing company several times but I continually put it off, thinking that I was saving money by handling billing myself while also building my school and making smart business decisions. When reality set in about how much time and money I was losing by "saving," I realized it was time to make a shift. Imagine having four hours extra a week to teach privates at $100 per hour - that's another $400 every week in income, $20,000 per year.

Before I go any further let me explain to you what scenarios I had considered. I thought – heck if I am paying a billing company, why not just hire a full time person and pay him or her. Not only would I be able to utilize that person for other functions if there was some time left over, I would be able to keep my entire operation in-house. I even tinkered with the thought that if I was good at collections I could do it for other schools. Then, like a sledgehammer hitting me over the head, I realized that I would rather put all of that time, effort and energy into growing my school. I further realized that the small percentage of money that I paid to my billing company would be made up in added students, special events and customer retention. Another factor was that I didn't have to deal with any negative energy. And most importantly, I was defeating time; I was putting precious, irreplaceable time back in my life.

One of my good friends once told me that when people are mad at you, they usually owe you money. When I was doing my own billing and encountered people who were upset, it was usually because they were either behind on their bills or they didn't want to pay in the first place. Using a billing company has saved me thousands of dollars worth of stress and therapy. Of course, that's the billing companies job and business, so the company's employees are the ultimate professionals at it as well.

The decision to hire a billing company was probably *one of the best*, if not *the most important*, business decisions that I ever made. I am so committed to the Japanese approach in Martial Arts that I was a bit surprised that a Western thought - an efficient billing company - could help me in one very important way to defeat our ultimate enemy - time. But then I realized that it is the mark of a brilliant fighter to be flexible and use his environment to his advantage.

The DNA of your school

Each school should have a standardized way of answering the phone. In my school, I answer, "Good afternoon, L.I. Ninjutsu Centers, Kyoshi Allie speaking. How may I help you?" This is the first line of attack and is also the most important. Remember, there is only one chance to make a first impression. I am finding that many people have really buckled down and are doing a better job at this. After you learn how to answer the phone properly, you must then be able to get a prospect to schedule a trial class with you. I don't recommend giving a lot of information on the phone. Take the time to quickly give a prospect times, never prices, and schedule the appointment. I always say, "The best thing for you to do is come in and try out a free trial class, and at that time I can sit down with you and go over all of our programs." The goal is to get prospects in to experience the program and see your school.

The next question: is your school a disaster site or is it a masterpiece? The goal is to enlighten you about what you don't normally see; things that may not bother you at all, but may bother or offend others. Smell, look, upkeep are what the prospect experiences next. So the link between your call and the sign up has many components.

Next, when a person comes into your school, how does he or she perceive your staff? How is your staff dressed, how do they look, how is the client greeted? Does it feel comfortable? Remember, for a new student, coming into a Martial Arts school can be a scary experience. Nowadays there are so many mean looking Martial Artists out there (just kidding).

Who greets the potential student, what do they say, how do they make someone feel? The answers are important to the sales process, to the sign up. What do we do if a prospect doesn't sign up? Again, we have a system for follow-up and follow through. Each prospect is first scheduled for a trial class, and then called to be reminded of the appointment. When the prospect shows up, we are ready with the trial class waiver and we immediately talk to the prospective student and get him or her ready for class.

Once the prospective student is in the class we have a system to talk to the parents, go over our programs and show them what we are all about. In fact, we call the whole process our "Sales Binder." We also have a digital DVD on our computer and for the parents to take home with highlights of our school. Hopefully by then we have signed up the prospect, but if not we schedule a second free trial class and give the parents our DVD, hoping for their return. Again we follow up and follow through by using our systems that we call our trial class call system.

We also have a stat tracking form to let us know our important sales history. The most important stat is the one that tells us who showed up and who didn't, who came in for a first trial class and who didn't, who signed up on the first class and who didn't, who came back for the second class and signed up and who didn't. This enables us to clearly see what is going on with our instructors, and it helps me learn if the program manager is doing a good job or not. The goal is to find out through these stats what is working and also what we need to work on. The goal is to get better. If we can push up what we do by 10% we will see a 10% increase in our bottom line.

When new students sign up in my schools we have a "Welcome to the Family" packet that we give them, an 18 page full-color booklet that shows all we do, answers all the normal beginners' questions, and tells them what they have to look forward to in the future. In this packet we also include our five buddy referral passes for two weeks free. Also included is a flyer on birthday parties and a host of flyers from local businesses that tie into our "Business Appreciation" system, which is a way for us to include local businesses in our marketing plan.

We then schedule the first of our two-, four-, six-, eight-, and 10- week calls. The first is actually a face-to-face appointment which we consider our "Student Orientation" that we set up on the day of each student's enrollment. The goal is to go over the "Welcome to the Family" packet and to explain our way of thinking. We take the time to show them that we are not just like anyplace else. We make sure they know that we are a professional "life-skills" institute. Our goal is to very clearly explain the responsibilities of a student as well as of parents. We make sure they realize that we are not a glorified day care center and that what we teach is not just a hobby. Martial Arts are clearly a life skill.

After the appointment is set, the student is on his or her way to be incorporated into the school population. We have a system to put billing information into our billing program and send the information off to the billing company. At that time we fill out an attendance card. Each card is color coordinated with the program that the student signed up for, so when we are doing class attendance we know who is Black Belt Club, Masters Elite, Team Leadership, Character Development, and so on. The goal is to have the cards ready for the first class so we start tracking attendance. Attendance is key to monitoring students' motivation. It links to another of our systems for perfect attendance, which is a rewards-based motivation system that we use. If our attendance tracking tells us that any student has missed an entire week, we get on the phone and place what we call our "we missed you" calls. We want to know why the student didn't attend class. If we don't reach anyone we leave a message and send a "we miss you" card. The goal is to let students know that we are on top of what we do and that we care about whether they are training, not just about whether they are paying.

We know that each student is either one step closer to Black Belt or one step closer to quitting. So we take the time to go over all this with them on the two-week appointment. We immediately insert them into the general population but by all means they are not lost in the crowd. The attendance cards tell us which students have the necessary gear, the classes they have attended, whether they achieved perfect attendance or if they brought buddies on buddy day. It also keeps us up to date on the pulse of their training. Training is like a heart beat - it goes up and down. But it's a big problem when it flat-lines. The closer it gets to flat line, the more chances of quitting you will have. So if attendance is three days one week, then one day the next week, then two days the week after that, before you know it you'll have no days. But you can identify the start of a downturn in attendance. This is when you need to make that call or make an appointment to find out why. Did something happen in class? Is the student having a hard time with the schedule? Is the student simply too busy? These are all things to look at. Just follow the attendance card. Consistently use the information on the cards for perfect attendance awards and other retention tools such as "we miss you" calls, postcards, and appointments.

The simple goal is to watch and watch closely. So two-, four-, six-, eight-, and 10- week contacts are the vital link to communication - the two week is a face-to-face, the rest are on the phone unless there is a lull in attendance, and in that case I suggest a personal appointment.

Do you see how the little things start to link together? It is not about crazy software programs; the growth of a Martial Arts school usually comes from the inside out. An inside-out company focuses on the customers it already has and is not always just focused on marketing and new clients. The reality is that if you want your company to be referral-based you need to have raving fans. The only way to do that is to be inside-out, not outside-in. You must focus on quality rather than quantity. Remember, the quantity will come once you ensure quality by way of these processes.

The next step is to use your scheduled calls to build your referral system. In addition to using each call you make to cement the idea of your philosophy and of the benefits students will receive if they follow it, you also want to ask for a referral each and every time you speak to a client. The goal is to get students to embrace the concept that the culture of your school includes referring new members.

Next, start looking at the **DNA of your school**, tracking what you are good at. Our stat-tracking system is a very powerful tool. If you don't have such a system, you need to develop one. We track all trial classes, all sign-ups, all upgrades, all renewals, all cancellations and students who quit. We watch promotions, how many people attend specific classes, how many people are referring other members.

These basic systems and procedures take care of the "little things" for our students and give us a complete picture of our students and their progress through the years. Systems such as these are the fundamental systems you need to keep your school flourishing.

Of course, what we've covered here is only the foundation. There are a host of other "systems" that you need to have in place in order to insure that your businesses continue to grow and prosper.

Here are a few of those other systems.

1) Marketing: This system is open-ended. It must be very thorough and really has many levels.

2) Business Finance: The front line of this system is your billing company, but the other components are your accountant, your lawyer, your investment broker, etc.

3) Financial Plan: This could be developed with a financial planner, but I have never personally found a financial planner who gave me sound financial advice. I have found most of them to be glorified insurance, stock and other investment guides. They are not really asking, "Hey, what is the source of your income, what can we do to save you money?" They are not business savvy. They are investment savvy at best.

4) Business Mentor: I just recently started working with a few Elite Consulting clients. I am helping them in many areas of their business and personal lives. I am helping them to see "out of the box" so to speak. The goal is not to see just the mountains in front of you, but to see the all the hidden jewels inside the mountains. Sometimes it's worth the cost to pay to speak with someone. I am fortunate to have many successful business people as friends. Whenever I have a tough question I can call them and say, hey, what would you do with this employee or what would you do in this situation? I recently was able to quickly help a person I know out of a situation that seemed rather dire. I saw a solution in two minutes. The person was too involved and couldn't see the answer from where he was standing. If you know people who can help you, seek them out. If you don't know anyone who can be a mentor, work to network and establish the relationships that will help you.

This may seem like a host of minor activities, lots of "little things," some of which you may be doing 100%, while others you may not being doing at all. The key to running a successful school is having all the components. So I cheer you if you are successful and doing things correctly. I want to point out, however, that just because you are doing well doesn't mean you shouldn't look within to see if some aspect of your business could be fixed, tweaked or improved upon. Sometimes we are doing so well we become complacent. Complacency is dangerous. Trust me; I have been there - fast cars, millions in real estate, swimming in my built-in pool while doing business, lavish vacations. It doesn't last forever unless you stay on top of your game. You need to continually follow the principal of Shibumi - Japanese for the pursuit of perfection. It is like a dog chasing its tail: you will never be perfect, but the pursuit will propel you toward the end result.

Tony Robbins said it best - strive for C.A.N.I. - Constant and Never Ending Improvement.

Here are normal functions of a school:

1) Open the doors and prepare and teach
2) Monitor students' progress and promote
3) Keep classes exciting
4) Collect tuition
5) Pay bills
6) Repeat process each month

The small details that are often missed are now being looked at as systems. The systems are what make a school tick. The systems or the functions of a school are the lifeblood of the school, the DNA so to speak. What we do in the details enables us to build our schools so that we don't continue to run small schools and make just small profits. Taking care of the details enables us to turn our dreams into actual flourishing careers.

There are some things that get done every day, week or month like clockwork. Perhaps because they are there staring at you, perhaps because they are priority level items, or maybe we just enjoy doing these more than some other tasks. All of us got into this industry because we love the Martial Arts, and we love instructing our students on the way of our Art. The following are items that are often overlooked in our daily processes. Take this time to read through these items and determine which of these are not getting completed, or need some work!

Here are some examples which I think about regularly.

Clean House: Sift through all of the operations in your school. Analyze all the systems that it takes to make your school run and see if there are any cracks. For example: are you not performing your 2-4-6 week calls? Do you not have a scheduled day to send out birthday or "we missed you" cards? If there are gaps in your process take the time to fill them in. The slightest misstep in these simple processes allows students to disappear from sight.

Get Rid Of All Safety Hazards: Take the time to identify any dangerous areas of your school. Things like sharp edges of tables or walls, loose nails, leaky faucets, or ripped mats can be a serious liability. Another serious liability can be a bad employee. Remember, if someone is not doing their job or talking negatively or has a terrible attitude that is just as dangerous as a broken mirror. Make a determined plan to fix all of these items so as to protect yourself against any potentially harmful situations.

Take A Hard Look At Your Curriculum: If a majority group of students are quitting at 12-year old yellow belt, for example, maybe the curriculum is not exciting enough or too challenging for that age group. Perhaps you have a teacher instructing class that doesn't mesh well with children of this age. This type of information can only be figured out with intense analysis and research after your stats have revealed where the majority of your age group or groups drops out. It is also important to interview past and present students within this group for their opinions on the program.

Open The Lines Of Communication: Start investing the time into getting your student's email addresses and phone numbers. Communicating regularly through email, newsletters and the phone plays an important part in retention. This is also an excellent way to market, build referrals and to just keep a finger on the pulse of your school.

Each of the items above are an integral part of the processes of a successful school. Being informed and proactive in instituting and repairing these systems within your school can mean the difference between simply opening your doors each day, or achieving the successes that every Martial Art School Owner has the power to achieve.

Building a resource library

Build a library of all of the consulting and marketing resources that you have used in the past, or feel would be effective in your school in the future. A reference library is the quickest way to refresh your staff and your motivation. Gather as much information as you can. You may not think that focusing on "Paid In Full" contracts is of vital importance to your school operations now, but as your school grows you will find that you are ready to implement more advanced systems.

The Details: Begin by writing down every function performed at your school. These tasks should include everything that goes on in the school from the moment you unlock the doors, to the time that you turn out the lights.

Some tasks to include:
-items for opening: unlocking, checking messages, returning calls, confirming intro appointments, making sure the changing rooms and restrooms are stocked.

-items for training: checking needed equipment, lesson plans, any written/marketing material to be distributed to the class, etc…

-items for closing: Vacuuming and cleaning the mats, returning all training equipment to the proper storage bins, calculating end-of-day numbers (i.e. enrollments, pro-shop sales, upgrades, etc,) checking that all doors are secure.

The idea is to schedule every task that needs to be performed on a daily, weekly and monthly level and place these in a comprehensive manual. By doing this the entire staff can develop a sense of accountability for completing these tasks like clock-work each and every day.

Documenting daily, weekly and monthly activities may seem like an inane task, but I guarantee that this will help you in more ways then you can imagine. A few years back my entire staff would e-mail me nightly to detail every task they had accomplished. This allowed me to monitor their progress as well see what was being accomplished. After weeks of doing this I was able to begin to notice trends in which functions were being ignored. Then I could take proactive steps to curbing these misses.

Record these items as if you were setting up your own turn-key operation and organization. This also allows you the freedom to take time off and leave an operations manual that will give even the most inexperienced staff-person the ability to step in and complete the needed tasks.

Build a Catalog of Educational Material - We all have been to seminars and workshops, taken myriad notes and then thrown them into a drawer to collect dust. A year later when we decide that implementing a Leadership Team is the best move we could make for our school we find ourselves scratching our heads and wondering where all of those detailed notes that we took at the last seminar disappeared to The answer to this dilemma is catalog all of your notes and other education materials!

By neatly typing out notes from each of the seminars that you've attended, organizing them and filing them according to subject, you will never find yourself searching out last year's steno-pad again.

This also goes for any of your favorite business mentors. Many of us devour books by greats such as Brian Tracy, Tony Robbins and even Donald Trump. But what do we do with all of this information once we've put the book down? Build a resource library! Highlight parts of each piece of material that have made an impact on you and add them to your catalog. You will have a quick reference for whatever project you've started, or quick motivation that you find yourself in need of!

With all of these items documented, systemized and catalogued you leave very little guesswork for you, and your staff. Instead of spending time scrambling to tie up loose ends at the last minute, or letting that great idea slip away, they will all be right at your fingertips!

Chapter 6
Student Retention –
The Goose that laid the golden student

Fix your leaky bucket!

A Monk once said to two of his best disciples, "Carry water and fill that tub." The disciples looked down and saw two buckets riddled with holes. They knew immediately that the task would not be easy. But of course, they would never decline such a request. When the Monk asked them to begin, they ran down a walkway to a pond and filled the buckets with water. As they ran back up the walkway, the water spilled out and only small amounts of water got to the tub. The job took ten times longer than it would have if the buckets weren't leaking, but eventually they finished the task and filled the tub. The happy ending to this story is that in time a beautiful garden of flowers grew beside the walkway because of all the water that had spilled during the journey.

As martial arts school owners we continually talk about the analogy of stopping up the holes in the bucket. We need to stop the students from escaping. We need to build our retention. In our reality as school owners, the "garden" that may grow as a result of the "escaping" students can be a better martial arts school, one that has better retention because it has "filled the holes in the bucket."

Tips for retention!

1) Invest the time to find out why students have left your school. Call former students and ask why they left. Do not be afraid to hear negative comments. Assure them that they are not going to offend you; that in fact what they tell you will help you make your school better. And don't forget to offer them a free month to try your new and improved school.

2) Research your stats to learn when people are leaving. Look at your curriculum as a possible reason – are there areas of frustration or boredom built into your programs? Don't be afraid to make changes.

3) Institute processes to reach your students (and former students) that will contribute to the growth of your school. You can distribute newsletters, either through e-mail or regular mail. Remember "e-news" is free. Put together a website with a parents' section, students' section, and prospects' section.

4) Run community events that are free of charge. These events may include parent shows, repeat grand openings, anniversaries, special seminars, etc. All of them should be designed to build rapport with your community and your students.

5) Put together events that are synergistic to your school, creating an environment of good will and family. Some great examples are beach days, family picnics, movie nights, etc. These are ways for parents to meet each other and for students to create bonds that they'll never want to break.

6) Stay in touch with students and parents. Make sure you communicate with them regularly, either by phone or mail. This is imperative to the growth of your school. Many times we get caught up in the effort of advertising and signing up students. We see new students and think we are gaining, but we lose sight of the "holes in the buckets." If you stay in constant contact with your client base and keep a pulse on what they are feeling, you will be able to increase your retention tremendously. This to me is the most important action you can take. A simple phone call is often sufficient to turn a student around. Set up an appointment if someone is having a hard time, give a free private lesson, write "We miss you" cards and do "We miss you" calls, contact loyal students and just tell them you think they are doing great. You may even want to call or write some students to tell them that you have gone through the same kind of struggles they have been experiencing.

7) Teach exciting classes. I know we all think that our classes are exciting, but here is a formula that I follow to keep students involved. We break our one-hour classes into three segments; the warm up – this could be stretching, exercises etc, then the curriculum – this is the nuts and bolts of the class, specifically what they need to know in order to progress in rank, and then the warm down – most of the time we don't actually warm them down, but instead work them hard with exercises and fun activities. Remember, fluff is fun in the beginning but gets boring real fast. We need to keep our people sweating, smiling and striving for more in each class.

My list could go on and on, but I am positive that you can come up with more on your own. It is my goal to suggest some new programs to boost retention, and to start you thinking of your own ways to make sure that your retention improves. When I speak of retention around the country at different schools, I want the message to get out that there is no single solution. It is something that needs to be continually built and adjusted as you grow. Each new level you reach, each new student you get, changes the dynamics of your school ever so slightly. Your school is a living entity, and you need to continually nurture it in order to succeed. Making sure you stop up the "holes in the buckets" is one important way to do this.

Making the Grade!

Many times throughout my martial arts life I have struggled with raising the bar and not selling out to commercialism. I have come from what I know as the "old school mentality." For the newcomers, this means my perception was that real martial arts are not about money or having a big school or making large profits. Well, coming straight from the horse's mouth, that perception is not at all true. I once had a friend who asked me one question that changed my life. He asked, "Are you helping people or are you hurting people?" With the teaching methods that I was using then, when I look back on it and review how many students that I lost or turned off, I was definitely hurting people. At the same time, I was not making the most of my business. It occurred to me that doing the best for my students and having a big and profitable school might just go hand-in-hand!

I have thought about the words that ring out from school to school. They're posted on walls; they're chanted in classes. The words say, "We Are a Black Belt School." The question is, "Are you really?"

When I speak to school owners about their goals, there are not many who don't say they want to help people to attain their black belts. The black belt is just a metaphor for all the things that we teach as martial arts instructors, from the physical to the spiritual to the mental. When I ask school owners how many Black Belts they have promoted over the years, many of them will reply by saying "a few." The explanation they give is that for one reason or another students couldn't cut it, that it takes a minimum of five years to attain a black belt, and a host of other reasons. I used to say the same thing, but now I realize they weren't reasons, they were excuses. I then ask how long the school has been open. No matter what the owners say, the time usually doesn't justify the small number of people who attain their black belts. (I am not talking about the so-called belt factories that don't have any criteria other then a good active checking account and time.

Here is what I did to become a "Black Belt School." It wasn't easy, and I made a host of excuses before I was able to let go and realize that my students were most important and their success was the only thing that I should be concerned with. I needed to let go of my ego and work toward getting my students to achieve greatness. All the rest follows naturally!

1. First, I sat with my staff on an early summer morning and looked through my statistics. I looked to see what rank and age my students were, and how long the students had been training. I researched when people were quitting. I needed to know why they left, at what age and at what point in their training. Then I needed to seriously look at my curriculum and cross-reference the quit ratios to see if the curriculum was part of the problem. Once I found factors that were relevant, I needed to make changes. I had to eliminate the things that were getting people frustrated, or at least move those components to a rank that would make it easier for students to learn. I needed to fit the movements with the age and mentality.

2. The second thing we did was to institute a striping system in the ranking. That enabled students to monitor their progress more easily, so that they were able to recognize their accomplishments and see clearly were they were, were they needed to be, and what was required of them.

3. Next, we added a perfect attendance system. This helped us to motivate students to attend more classes. We included rewards such as trophies and plaques as well as shirts for parents and stickers for parents' cars. This motivated students and parents alike about their training. It also gave parents a bargaining tool to motivate their children to come to class more often.

4. Then we shortened the time it took to achieve a black belt. Originally, it took approximately seven years to achieve a black belt. We shortened it to five years without sacrificing any standards. This still is very long for a student to wait, but we have found a way to keep them motivated and make it work. On average, schools require about two to three years for students to achieve black belt. We also added in the higher ranks that took longer, multiple stripes, and testing on a more regular basis. There is now one formal for the belts and the other for the stripe.

5. We wrote out our entire curriculum and broke it into four categories: Adults (16 and up), Youth (8–15), Mighty (5-8), and Little (3-5). These curriculums are linked, and from the adult level downward, they are thinned so that by the time you get to the Little category the curriculum is at its simplest form.

6. We added a cyber-dojo, probably one of the only ones on the Internet at the time. We have password-protected areas that are linked to students' ranks. These areas allow students to print the movements and a complete description as well as access video links, still photos, and a chat room. The cyber-dojo has proved to be a great way for parents to work with their children as well. Parents and students are able to stay up to date on all the requirements and methods of training. Students can print their techniques and keep them in their classroom notebooks. This keeps students from getting frustrated and also gives them something to strive for. They are not allowed access to higher levels until they get their belt.

7. Last but not least, we started doing student questionnaires for all testing and striping. Students must fill out complete questionnaires, with their families if they are underage, and answer questions that pertain to their training, their motivation, and their interest in upgrading or in other programs. The questionnaires also help them communicate with us on referrals. We love to ask questions that are not the common ones, such as "Do you feel like a valued customer?"

These are some of the things that I did to commit my schools to "Black Belt Excellence." Now, within the last five years, we have promoted many Black Belts and have a very high active training count.

Perfect Attendance – What is it all about?

As school owners and managers, one of our most difficult jobs is to make sure that our students consistently attend classes. And the results of our efforts often confuse us, because as often as we speak to our students about motivation and teach classes that both excite them and keep them striving for more, we still lose students. We know that retention is of utmost importance to all martial arts schools, but we realize that keeping students is not only about the classes, the curriculum and the lessons. It is about fueling students' inner drive and motivation. How do we get students motivated and how do we keep them there?

There is not any one factor you can point at that motivates all students, or even one particular student, all the time. What seems to excite students today may not do so tomorrow. The fact of the matter is that while insuring that your classes are top-notch, you need to go further to foster the type of motivation that leads to excellent attendance. Understanding this, we need to put systems in place to keep students' interest. One great way is presenting perfect attendance awards.

In our schools we developed a program to reward students for their efforts toward achieving perfect attendance.

Here's how it goes:

We calculate a monthly minimum attendance requirement for each student based on the program in which the student is enrolled. For example, in our schools, a student who may take two classes per week must attend a minimum eight classes per month for "perfect attendance." Once the student attends the required classes in one month, he or she is awarded a 6-inch trophy with a kick figure. For every additional month of perfect attendance, the student gets another 6-inch trophy, until he or she has received four trophies for four months. The student may then turn in the four small trophies for one 12-inch trophy, signifying four perfect months. The student does not need to have four consecutive months. A month may be missed. Remember we are training students to attend classes regularly.

Next, when a student has earned three 12-inch trophies, he or she may exchange them for our 1-year plaque, which signifies one year of perfect attendance. Along with the plaque, the student receives a t-shirt with the school name and number, along with t-shirts for each parent. The student also receives window decals for the parents' cars.

Each student who is awarded a perfect attendance trophy or plaque is also given a certificate to commemorate the award. The certificates are suitable for framing and provide another concrete reminder for the student of the accomplishment.

Our goal is to motivate, excite, and create an environment that gives students an extra incentive to come to class. The perfect attendance program encourages students to work hard and develop good attendance habits. It helps develop a synergy between students and parents, all of whom participate in the awards ceremonies. It creates a buzz of recognition within the school about the students who are receiving awards.

Since we started our perfect attendance awards system we have doubled the number of classes that students attend. Not bad for a few trophies, some time and a bit of hard work.

Retention is Marketing

You've Got Mail!

Quite often I receive e-mails and phone calls from consulting clients asking about marketing ideas. Being a fan of advertising and the lure of all the technologies that go into it I am intrigued by the question. Recently I got an overwhelming response to my simple Marketing Action Worksheet that I developed. As unique as it sounded to people, the worksheet was a simple, no-nonsense tool to track what you are actually doing.

I believe that at times people dabble in advertising and marketing but never truly put together integrated activities that they can call substantial or actually consider a marketing campaign. My school is continually in marketing mode. We have advertised in many areas.

Here are few:

1. We have a booth at a 6,500-seat minor league baseball stadium where we are raffling off five three-month memberships valued at $496 each. We are also offering a free concession to all the runners up. This has been tremendously effective for us, yielding about 1,400 prospect names, as well as 15 new members on yearly contracts of $1,500 or more. We paid a total of $6,600 *for 10 games*. We are still working out leads and we are not done signing people up.

2. We regularly hand deliver door hands within a three-mile radius of our school, sometimes as many as 1,500 per week.

3. We are working with a Public Relations firm gaining momentum within TV and print media.

4. We continually do birthday parties, buddy days, free seminars and special events. For example we recently exhibited at a huge craft fair that we have attended for the last 13 years. We gathered another 130 prospect names.

5. In addition to all the above, we have a referral program in effect all year long. We can actually call this a culture within our school.

With all that said, I am continually in search of new avenues of marketing. My ultimate goal is to always have our presence known within the community. Even with all the marketing and advertising that I do, there are still people who come into my school and ask me when we opened as if we are brand new to the community.

Even with this marketing campaign, the true secret to success is realizing that retention is marketing. Begin with the question: are your students and families satisfied or highly motivated? The difference is what will determine whether you have good retention or bad retention. **Highly motivated customers stay with you.** Even those who leave for external reasons will spread positive word of mouth about your business and will prompt responses. My ultimate goal is to serve my customers and to make sure that they are so happy that they can't think of anything else. I want them to believe whole-heartedly that attending my school is the best decision they have ever made in their lives.

So how do we do it?

1. Look within and ask yourself how you treat your clients. Do they see themselves as being important?

2. Treat every contentious situation as if it could make or break your business. Take care of things in a timely fashion.

3. Make sure that the situation is handled in such a way that the customer is satisfied, not you, but your customer. Because the bottom line is that customers' concerns need to be satisfied or you lose them.

4. Make sure you listen; sometimes that is all it takes. Listening is 50%; the follow up is the rest. If you do not handle customers correctly you risk losing them forever.

5. Don't think like a Martial Artist – sensei or master. Think like the owner of a company and make sure that you and your employees remember that the customers are always right and that they are paying the paychecks. Without customers the company is non-existent.

Why is retention so important? The answer to that goes very deep. Retention is not just customer service but also everything else that goes along with it.

Here is a list of things to consider:

1. Curriculum – does it support long-term growth of the students and the school?

2. Excitement of classes – what is the quality of instruction and how dynamic is it?

3. Follow-up and follow-through – how on top of your game are you?

4. What systems do you have in place to professionalize your school?

5. How effectively are you working the systems? Are they a hit-or-miss operation?

6. What do you do to go above and beyond to make your school stand out?

7. Why will students come to you rather than go to other activities?

8. What is it that you are doing other than your classes to keep people engaged in your program?

9. What do you stand for that makes you special? Are you more than a fighting program? What values do you teach?

10. What is it that parents and students see you giving them? Do they recognize your school the same way you do?

When all of these things are working and you are operating at *minimum* 80% on all of them, you will see results that will be shocking. Your referrals will go up, your quality of students will go up, and overall your business will grow. **So don't get caught up in just running ads; make sure that once students arrive at your door, all the things you need to keep them there are in place.**

Chapter 7
Employee Management –Heartache to riches

It just isn't me, it is everyone else!

About three months ago I attended a seminar by Michael Gerber, the author of *The E-myth*. His seminars are always amazing. If you ever have a chance to attend one, do so. During a portion of the seminar he spoke of the myth that most employers think that their staffs are going to take the time to sit around, goof off, and take excessive breaks. While most of the time we believe that our staffs do a good job, I sometimes know that things could or should have been done differently. I can sum it up by saying that if it were me I would have had the job done already; I wouldn't have made those mistakes and I would have completed the job properly. Any time this is the case, we have a choice to do one of a few things: 1) fire the person 2) retrain the person; or 3) do the job yourself. When retraining doesn't work and you have exhausted all efforts, then the only choice is to let the person go.

I thought it would be interesting to share with you the way things work in my schools. My upper management staff – the people who run my businesses for me - are instructed to stay in contact with me via e-mail. Every evening I review their tasks, their daily projects, the things that they need to do on a daily, weekly, bi-weekly and monthly basis. I do this with all of my top people. They regularly communicate with me via e-mail. I thought that just reading a letter sent to me by one of my staff members would be of interest. I think that this will be a lesson in itself. I hope it serves a purpose and you enjoy and receive some benefits from it.

To set this one up, I asked the question, "Why are your weekly tasks only half done?" I asked why the sections were left blank on the e-mail. He responded by telling me this:

Staff member: The "why nots" were not done because the "whys" were.

Kyoshi Allie: Yes that is the thing; we need to learn to get all the stuff done. Remember there are a number of things that need to be done weekly in order for you to see some sort of synergy. I know that if they are completed the synergy will be there.

Staff member: And the stats were done, it just wasn't marked. I have also been doing upgrades all week. Did you see the results? I've been doing promotions, calls, conferences with students and parents, and private lessons all week. I've also asked a staff member to do more calls. I gave the person a calling schedule to do and she didn't listen to me. This is a problem.

Kyoshi Allie: So we need to retrain. Give her some audio tapes on placing calls and get her back on the ball. Maybe look at what she is comfortable with and have her do those calls only. But it is unacceptable for her to simply refuse.

Staff member: I spoke with her again and I told her that when she finishes prepping the dojo she needs to prepare her calls for after class. She is supposed to come in early on selected days and do calls, which she is not doing. Again I spoke with her so this can get done. I try to manage them without having to complain to you every time I have issues. I understand that I suffer for not enforcing the requirements. I should be harder on my staff when things don't get done.

Kyoshi Allie: This is a perfect example. You don't necessarily need to be harder on them. The idea is to determine the way they work, and if it is not up to standards do whatever is necessary to get them to do what needs to be done. I realize how hard it is. I realize exactly what you are going through. It is not easy. This is my daily struggle. I know that if I had three more of me, and five more of you, we would be unstoppable.

Staff member: I am going to start to document when things are not completed, to show you how many times I have to ask for things to get done. I work hard and have always worked hard to make this dojo grow.

Kyoshi Allie: The deal with work is that you either work smart or you work long and hard. In the beginning you need to work hard, but in the end you need to work smart. Keep focused and keep learning more about managing people. Become a master of people skills. Read the book *Develop the Leaders Around You*, by Maxwell.

Staff member: I know I am responsible for this dojo and I take the responsibility for getting things done. I think that I have been too nice and understanding with my staff (some more then others). You see only the bubbly and professional side of some employees, but I see the other side on a daily basis.

Kyoshi Allie: I don't see only one side, I see both. I am not oblivious to staff members' shortcomings. I deal with them continually. Only I try the "honey approach" with them. It is easy when I only see them once in a while. I realize what you have to deal with regularly.

Staff member: Some employees do the bare minimum and then give me an attitude and resistance when I ask them to do more. I'm getting tired of the results I'm getting.

Kyoshi Allie: This is your choice. Start training or scouting for someone new. Start the process of looking for a replacement. We have large bench strength due to our "Instructors in Training" program, but some of them need to be brought up to speed, especially for your school. You have a thriving school with hundreds of students. We must get the appropriate instructors.

Staff member: This dojo is very important to me. For some people here, this is only a job.

Kyoshi Allie: No kidding? For many it is only a job. For us, it is our lives. Even for some people who have been with me for more than 13 years it is only a place to train. So don't think I don't know that. You are in it for the long haul like I am. But remember how good it's been for you and look how far you have come. Look how great it is to be able to help shape people's lives for a living. You are doing an incredible community service.

Staff member: For me, it is part of my life and who I am. I will work smarter and follow up on the tasks that need to be done. I will make this work so you will not be disappointed in me.

Kyoshi Allie: I am not disappointed in you. Have you ever been unhappy with the results you get from someone you love? If so, you know how I feel. It is not a feeling of disappointment with the person; it is a feeling of disappointment with the results. I realize that you are dealing with staff. You can't control them all the time, but you can be in charge of the results you get. Sometimes it will take longer then other times, but if you are continually getting the same results, then you need to make some staff changes. I do what I do so that you can progress. Hopefully, each time we learn from our mistakes and move forward. If we truly learn, then we don't make the same mistakes again. We need to stay focused on the job descriptions and the results. We're not running a clinic for people who are out of work. That is the bottom line. We need what we need to be where we want it to be.

Becoming a Boss, Part II

Let's take a look at the "nuts and bolts" of the "Employee Zone."

3 Types of Employees

Let's talk about the three different types of employees:

*Contracted Employees
*Part Time Employees
*Full Time Employees

Let's start with the **contracted employee.** *This is typically an employee who works a non-specific schedule and fills in occasionally.* Many times owners will pay employees in this manor for a period of time, but depending on local laws this may not be legal. If an employee has a set schedule he or she may not be considered a "piece worker" or file a 1099 form for taxes. Again, this is why it is so important to have a good accountant. Your accountant can advise you on this all the way.

Next we have the **part time employee**. *This employee can be a student, or even a mom who works for you.* Sometimes people barter tuition or other services as a form of payment, but again, your accountant will advise you on the legal issues regarding this. If money is exchanging hands, then it is important that you pay taxes on that money. So don't try to scrimp and save in this area. Be smart and manage your money in other areas so you don't get in trouble.

A part time employee can be a student who works for minimum wage and has working papers. Or it could be the mom of your student who just needs a little extra cash. No matter what the situation, make sure that the person is qualified for the job. Many times we look for any person to fill a particular position, rather then finding the right person with the right qualifications. The qualified person may cost you more, but trust me that in the long run, that person will make you much more money, with less training and less aggravation.

Finally, there's the **full time employee**. *This person should be a career person.* I don't recommend hiring someone to do a full time position if he or she is already working at another job somewhere else. This can be a drain, and the person will never put in the time and effort required to be the best possible employee. This is not something you want to deal with. You want to be able to get your full time workers' undivided attention and have them work for you with no distractions. A full time employee is someone who wants to make this a career. Avoid transitory employees who are looking to make a paycheck while they look for something else. Look for employees with the qualifications and the desire to make you and your company money.

Compensation of Employees

There are many ways to compensate employees. Of course the most traditional way is to pay them for their services by the hour. This is something that you want to work out ahead of time. In our company we have defined the positions ahead of time, along with the hourly compensation for each position. For instance, an Assistant Instructor may get minimum wage, while a full Instructor may get $10 per hour. This helps you to avoid salary disputes. It also protects you in case you move a person up the ladder with a pay increase, but then the person doesn't do well in the job. You can bump them back down to the original job and pay structure that the person was working in.

We also have many commission structures set up for front desk people, program managers, and instructors. The commissions are based on many variables, but some examples are new students, renewal students, gear sales, upgrades into higher memberships, promotions, and special events. An employee who has a commission structure can earn money based on these activities and special events.

All in all, pay structure is a personal choice and should be looked at from your point of view and the affordability to the company. It is obvious that a new school may not be able to afford what an established school can. So be very careful that you don't over pay someone and put yourself in a dangerous situation. Make sure you think things through.

Your People Are the Key to Your Success! How to Attract, Train and Maintain Great Employees

Within any company, those closest to you will greatly impact your level of success. Whatever the size of your company you must realize that you alone cannot make the company a huge success. So building your staff by attracting, training, and keeping great employees can help you expand your company into an empire. Remember, it doesn't matter where good ideas come from as long as they work toward the growth of the company. Ask for ideas on a regular basis. Get input from those who are low on the totem pole, from middle managers, and from those at the very top.

In most successful businesses, the concept of "team" is very important. The reason that your entire team should be able to contribute to your business is that you have chosen your employees well and have trained them to do the jobs you expect them to get done. Within martial arts schools or any other business there are some very specific tasks that have to be assigned or delegated. If you have devoted sufficient time to training your employees, you should be confident that they are ready to do these jobs and capable of performing up to your standards.

When dealing with situations where an employee is not performing as well as you know he or she should, the first place to look for responsibility is back at yourself. Once you determine the employee's weaknesses then you must make sure to train (or re-train) properly. Of course, the best way to make sure that everyone knows what to do is to start with a great employee-training program in the first place. Sometimes small businesses do not have those programs in place. You can save yourself much time and trouble if you develop training programs to make sure all employees are fully schooled in the functions for which they'll be responsible.

Here are a few tips about how to attract, train, and maintain great employees. They should help get you thinking in that direction.

Hire the right people: that's the key to the success of any company

Why we get turkeys instead of eagles

1. We hire to fill a position, not to find the right person.
2. We take the first person to show up instead of actively searching for the right person.
3. We don't create an environment where eagles want to nest. Professionals need a company that provides real opportunity for success.

Choose the right employees

Hire people with willingness to learn - those who strive for excellence! Look for people who want interesting work and appreciation more than high wages. Most often the people you want as employees will chose exciting jobs over high pay. Remember, quality employees make things happen. They positively influence others. They volunteer ideas and they live up to their commitments while keeping a positive mental attitude. They do their jobs in a way that makes yours easier.

Establish standards

Evaluate employee performance

1. Establish a basic job description that details the requirements of an employee in each specific job. Set the absolute minimum level an employee must achieve in order to stay employed, and then outline the level of performance you expect in order for the employee to progress and move forward.
2. Establish a level of performance expected, including number of hours, degree of dedication, and the level of performance, staff interaction criteria, and the chain of command.
3. Tie salary increases into the employees' actions that increase revenue to your company. Make sure all employees know that as they bring in more students, up-sell programs, etc., their salaries will increase. Make sure they do not expect salary increases as a matter of course. Each employee should strive to reach "achiever status," the level at which an employee is a true asset to your company.

Make sure you "Inspect what you Expect"

Personally meet with under-performers

Always be clear about your expectations, so that employees know what you want. Don't expect them to think on the same level as you do. Understand that your perspective as owner and boss and their perspectives as employees may vary widely. Try these steps to turn around an under-performing employee.

1. Meet one-on-one to consult with the employee

2. Define the problem as you see it. Clarify any misunderstandings that the employee may have about what is expected.
3. Brainstorm alternative means of correcting deficiencies.
4. Choose the best alternative.
5. Develop a plan of action.
6. Move forward with the new plan.
7. Set a time frame by which you expect the changes to take place.
8. "Inspect what you expect."

Recognize good performance

Recognition of good performance is an imperative step in creating a synergy among employees, the boss and the company. It is important to design programs that lead to recognition of your solid performers. While doing this, make sure you remember that the key to having recognition work for you is to be genuine.

1. Determine those behaviors that you want and need to be recognized. These may include teaching ability, sales activity, innovation, etc.
2. Establish the criteria for recognition, and the rewards if applicable.
3. Sell the programs. Make sure that all your employees are aware of the behavior that will be rewarded. Publicize specific contests.
4. Control competitiveness. Design your programs so that more than one employee can be rewarded. If many employees reach the criteria for recognition, it's a win-win situation for them and for your school.
5. Only reward achievers. Never reward inferior performance.

Develop Enthusiasm

This is a key step to getting the most out of your employees. Here are some basic ways to energize your employees:

1. Establish clear lines of communication.
2. Be aware of what motivates your employees.
3. Understand what role you and your company plays in your employees' lives.
4. Find out what your employees expect from your company and from you as their boss.
5. Analyze what you need to do to increase your employees' enthusiasm.
6. Get involved in motivating your employees. Knowledge without action is useless.
7. Show your employees the big picture of your school.
8. Give your employees enough information and impact to share in your vision.

Becoming a Boss

Boo! Did I scare you? Well for some becoming a boss may seem scary. Maybe we can attribute it to being so close to Halloween. But don't worry; I will try to take the sting out of it.

Being a boss is sometimes a very scary thing. It can involve the fear of hiring people, being responsible for their pay checks, paying taxes, dealing with the government and teaching employees what to do and how to help you grow your business.

I realize that doing all of these things can add a huge amount of stress to your life, but supervising good employees can open up a world of happiness for you, and can be a contribution to society as a whole. I look at being a boss as a huge responsibility. I realize that employing people is a huge undertaking, but it is also filled with rewards and benefits.

Here is an important first step you should take when starting to hire employees. I believe some of the best money you can spend is taking the time to interview and hire a quality accountant. This is the first employee you want on your team. The reason you need a good quality accountant is so that you can manage your money wisely. A great CPA can help you make decisions and keep you from making the wrong ones. He or she will make sure you have all the proper insurances, papers filed with the government and also make sure that you are totally up-to-date on all of the taxes that need to be paid on a regular basis. This person will become part of your team and you should be able to totally rely on your accountant.

If you have the approach that your accountant just files taxes and does quarterly submissions to the I.R.S., you are missing out on much of the process. So you need to start interviewing right away.

What should you be looking for?

Five key steps to hiring a good accountant

1. Make the personal connection. Your accountant should be like a friend. You need to feel comfortable with him or her. If you feel uneasy around the person, then you need to look elsewhere. You should be able to discuss the most intimate details about your life, your business and your goals. This person should have some insight and know who you are as a person and a business owner, so he or she can determine what life-style you should be living.

2. Hire someone who is not too conservative, but also not haphazard either. Remember, this person will be managing your money. Sometimes accountants are not willing to spend enough time figuring out your situation. Make a note; people often say "My accountant takes risks." To me this is a big red flag. Don't get an accountant who takes risks. Taking risks could land you in jail. I have a strong philosophy that if you are making money you should be paying taxes. The thing is, if you have a good accountant he or she will know what to pay according to the strict guidelines of the law.

3. Find an accountant who meshes well with your company. If you are a Martial Arts school, but your accountant has no knowledge of the service business, then that person is not the right one for you. Find someone who has experience in a service industry, even if it is with a florist or a gardener. That way the accountant will have experience with a business that is service orientated.

4. Find someone who is up-to-date on all the tax laws as they come out. Make sure that you always go over new strategies with your accountant. If the person is always telling you he or she needs to look into it for you, that person is not the right one for you.

5. Last but not least, find someone who is able to negotiate on your behalf, one who can deal directly with the I.R.S. or other government agencies, and someone who is used to this. You don't want someone who just files papers for tax time and that is it. You want a competent CPA.

I recommend reading the book by Rob Kiosaki titled *Who Took My Money*. This is an outstanding book that will give you some insight on what to look for in an accountant and on money management. The book is loaded with tips that you will find invaluable.

Common Sense Is Not So Common

When I think about the saying "Common sense is not so common," I picture an older man speaking to a younger man reprimanding him for not thinking about his task. He says to the younger man, "What is wrong with you? This just requires common sense," as he shakes his head in disappointment. This situation is not rare: you have probably had this statement directed at you. Sometimes our expectation of common sense seems so natural, but for the person with whom we are working or talking to, it could totally be foreign.

A good example is a jungle worker in some far-off land who should know better than to go to sleep during a lunch break. But I have seen the pictures of such a worker killed by a large boa constrictor. So in that case, common sense wasn't so common. But it's a whole different story when you're talking to someone about a situation which they have no reference. For example, think about expecting a person to know how to run a business. This requires a high degree of skill, and without the correct training a business owner will fail terribly. So what is common sense among business owners?

While consulting with school owners, I talk to them about tasks that I have been doing for over a decade, activities that I believe are the basic core fundamental principles of business. But my words fall on their ears like a brand new discovery. At times what I think to be basic is not very basic at all. So my approach when I consult, no matter how large a school is, is to treat people as though they were starting from scratch. My theory is that if one simple system is not being used, even if it is the most basic system imaginable, it can have an effect on the growth of the school, initially or in the long run.

So what is basic common sense in the Martial Arts business and life? I would have to say with total confidence, no one thing. What is basic to one school owner may not be to another. My approach is no nonsense, experience-based consulting. I learned from personal experience what works and what doesn't. I share what I am using successfully and what I have failed at. I am not afraid to say I tried something and it didn't work. I am also not embarrassed to speak of my mistakes. I remember being very disappointed with Tony Robbins when he got divorced. I thought, *I listen to this man, I believe in him. I have used his philosophies in my relationship. If he can't have a successful marriage, then how can I listen to him about marriage?* Then I realized that I can learn from other people's mistakes as well as I can learn from their successes, so this is why I share openly and honestly with everyone.

I believe in following an owner's manual or script of some sort, although I must admit that many times I have assembled items without using one and have found a few extra bolts when I was finished. Initially it didn't matter, but in the long run whatever was left out came back to haunt me: the strength or the structure was weakened. Your business owner's manual is your blueprint for success. Even though things may differ slightly from town to town, state to state, what works, works everywhere to some extent. At times things may be culturally different, but all in all, concepts are adaptable. A business owner needs to school himself or herself to adopt the concept of common sense. First a business owner must learn what is common, then make sense of it, then learn it so that it is actually usable.

It is my goal to continuously create common sense action principles in a variety of areas that will help the world by arming people with the tools to live their lives to the fullest.

There are the **five Core Fundamental Protocols of business**. Each should have a set of formal rules describing how to perform the functions:

1) Advertising/Marketing - Client generation
2) CSI - Customer Satisfaction Index - Creating a great quality control environment
3) Procedures Protocols - The systems and what functions are included, as well as restrictions on them
4) Core Functions - The nine levels of income

5) Billing and Accounting

Your Program Manager - A Key person on Your Team

"Okay class, on a scale of 1-10, who is the most important person in our school?"

"You are sir!" "No, try again." *"We are sir!"*

You reply, "Yes, you are." But in reality, while the students are the reason for the school's existence, they are not really the most important people in the school. The most important person in the school is the Program Manager, with the Head Instructor being the second most important. Without a totally qualified person in each of these positions, the school would not be able to stay in business, and many schools fail because their owners don't recognize the important jobs that a Program Manager performs.

With a professional, qualified Program Manager your school will soar. The Program Manager's responsibilities are many and without beating a dead horse we have developed a very intricate program managers form we supply to all of the Taking it to the Next Level clients. Here are just some of the program manager's duties:

Weekly Items To Accomplish

1. Making 2, 4, 6, 8, and 10 - week calls
2. Making "We Miss You" Attendance Calls
3. Making Renewal Calls
4. Making Cold Calls and Calls from Missed Trials
5. Placing Referral Calls
6. Placing Teacher Calls from Letter of Intent
7. Calling Parents Regarding Letters of Intent Questionnaires
8. Upgrade Calling from Questionnaires, and Membership Lists
9. Placing Problem Client Calls from Messages
10. Mailing "Keep In Touch" Cards
11. Entering Contracts 2X/Per Week
12. Reviewing Past Due Accounts and Collection Accounts
13. Holding Renewal, Upgrade, and Problem Student Conferences
14. Setting Up and Preparing for Promotions
15. Preparing Financial Stats and Enrollment Stats
16. Sending Birthday "Thank You" Cards for Parties Held
17. Completing Purchase Orders from your martial art gear suppliers
18. Making Event Calls
19. Checking Messages and Making Call-Backs
20. Updating and Organizing Drawer Information
21. Calling to Confirm Trial Classes for Next Day

22. Calling and Mailing Postcards for Current Missed Trials
23. Recording all Money Intake on Spread Sheet

With this list of responsibilities, it's obvious how important a Program Manager is to your school, right? The tasks a Program Manager must perform effectively give you an idea why a person who is qualified to be a Program Manager should be outgoing, charismatic, good at sales, comfortable with public speaking, professional, organized and highly motivated. Wow – is there really anyone out there like that? Yes, of course, there are many people who are in professional careers who can fit right into this category. The Program Manager is the front person, often the first representative of your school that people meet. This person must be able to leave a lasting and good impression on students and prospects alike. With the right person as your Program Manager your school will soar.

Recognition: Giving Your Staff and Students the Boost They Need

When I celebrated my 41st birthday, usually the day would have come and gone like any other birthday, with nothing special happening. This time it was very different. My phone rang throughout the day with calls from my many friends from around the world, and then I started getting e-mails from all different people from my billing company. It seems the owner Joe Galea had told everyone that it was my birthday, or plugged me into some birthday list at the company. Even though I didn't know many of the people, it was gratifying to have people recognize my birthday. With each e-mail and phone call I became happier about what I usually would have taken in stride.

An ordinary day had become extraordinary. To finish the night, I was overwhelmed with a little party that my six-year-old daughter threw for me with one of my dear friends. Recognition sure made me feel special. Imagine a student or staff member feeling as recognized as I did. This feeling really put me into a totally new place and I am still speaking about it today.

Five Tips On Giving Recognition to Staff and Students

1. Always find a way to acknowledge exemplary service. If one of your staff members or students does something great, tell him or her that you're aware of it, either publicly or privately.

2. Send a note or card to let people know how you feel. It will reinforce the recognition.

3. Post notices about great behavior in full sight. Let the world know what the staff member or student did. Make note of achievements both in and out of the dojo. Let everyone know about it.

4. Share with others how to recognize accomplishments and make people feel special, just as Joe Galea did with his staff. It really made a huge difference.

5. Teach others how to share your enthusiasm. Sometimes people need to learn exactly how to show appreciation. For example, it is the goal of the school to share in people's birthdays by sending cards, sending notes, and making special calls.

While this seems very obvious, it often isn't done. Recognizing a significant achievement, a beautiful smile, or a fashionable outfit someone is wearing usually makes that person's day. This small effort really goes a long way. It is very important to do this, especially with your staff and students. I hope that you will take these little tips and utilize them in your school and in your life. Good luck! By the way, I think you are all doing a great job of growing and learning just by reading this.

Fire up Your Staff!

How do we turn a basic staff into an awarding winning team? First we need to establish if we have a staff; then we need to decide how we should motivate them. Very often in Marital Arts schools there is more a lack of staff than an over abundance. During many of my consulting calls I give information to clients about how to hire staff members. We need to examine two important questions: First, how do I get staff members? Second, when I have a good sized staff, how do I motivate them?

When building a team of competent staff members you must first follow these five steps.

1. Find people who are qualified for the jobs. Don't hire a person simply to fill a position. This is a common mistake in our industry. We find someone looking for a job and we immediately place them in a position. Often they are not qualified and will never have what it takes to get that job done. It is essential that you seek out a qualified person, even if they are not currently part of your school.

2. Put together job guidelines and an employee manual. The manual should describe the positions available in the school, what is required of an employee in each position, the pay structure, etc. It is worth taking the time to develop an employee manual and handbook. You'll find it to be some of the best time and money spent.

3. Develop incentives to keep employees active. Some possibilities are commissions, long term insurance plans, and retirement plans. I realize that to many these "perks" are beyond your wildest imagination, but plan today for tomorrow's successes.

4. Start thinking big. This is really the mindset that you need to develop. Without a vision and goals, you will never get to the top. Planning ahead and setting goals are very valuable.

5. Look for the good in everyone. Overlook some things, but inspect what you expect. Do not be too lenient; if you are you will develop a trend for others to follow. Start by training your staff properly and continue to educate them. Don't immediately fire people for not doing their jobs. Retrain to try to correct the deficiency. If after repeated attempts they are not doing their job properly cut them loose.

Chapter 8
In The Trenches – Stories from the staff

In this section you will read a series of articles written by my staff. The goal is to explain things from the point of view of a person who is currently involved in the running of my organization.

Since the opening of Shin Shin dojo – L.I. Ninjutsu Centers, I attribute the reason for a great deal of my great success, apart from following all the lessons Kyoshi Allie taught me, to the fact that I had my daughter and son with me. My early students and their parents still ask me how they are doing. They always tell me that one main reason they trusted me with their children was because I was a parent myself and had my children with me at the school all the time. They must have sensed a feeling of family when they saw us as a team. Since that start, I have locked into that approach and always use that personal family touch.

I recommend the following steps:

1) Know your students' names:

Always memorize the names of all of your students. When addressing the parents, use their first names only after they have insisted. I have always made it a high priority to memorize the names of every person who visits the dojo. Even when birthday parties are held at the dojo, I know every child's name by the end of the party, and when they leave I say "goodbye" using their names. More important, when they come back I greet them with their names. This really makes them feel important.

2) Take a "hands on" approach:

A light pat on the shoulder and a firm handshake always sends a message from the heart. Speaking of coming from the heart, I have always believed that sincerity needs to be the driving force behind all acts of kindness: without sincerity the act is an empty promise.

3) Be one step ahead:

Confront issues before they become dangerous. When something happens in class that affects the well being of the students it must be dealt with immediately. For example, if a student hurts his or her wrist, you must isolate the situation right away so that the involved student is not subject to further injury and the rest of the class is not affected. Then deal with whatever needs to be done to care for the hurt student. Once that is done you must inform the parents. Whenever possible you should take the parents to the side and calmly explain what happened. More important, let them know how you cared for the child and let them know if any further medical treatment is necessary. Next, you must call later that day or at a reasonable time the next day to see how the student is doing. This shows your concern for the child. Remember, you must be truly sincere, or the parents will sense that you are merely "acting" concerned. After all, they, too, are a part of your family.

4) Display your positive personality.

What parents see forms their impression of you. When walking through the lobby and greeting parents you must always smile! Those of you who know me know this is what I do. A smile sends a true picture that you are in the right place. But as I said before, it must come from the heart. I am a happy person and just looking around me I know I have a lot to be happy for. You must find your inner smile and let it show. Know your people. Know something about your students' and their parents' lives. Visit the plays they are in. Go to their recitals. Become a part of their families. Ask how the surgery went, recommend a fellow student or parent who provides a service (dentist, doctor, general contractor) network among your people. This will be like the old-time hometown bonding, when towns were extended families and everyone knew the butcher, the baker, and the candlestick maker.

5) Send courtesy cards and place courtesy calls:

Another great idea to maintain the family environment is to send students cards when they do something great, whether it is in the dojo or at another activity. A job well done is something that all families like to hear about. One way to find out different accomplishments is to read the local paper. There are always articles in the sports section that highlight students' activities. The trick is to look for them. Don't forget former students. A card from you will show them that you still care about what they do long after they have stopped training with you, and you might just win them back. Ask parents in conversation what their kids are doing aside from the dojo. Communication is key; this is how we build the family atmosphere. This is how any relationship grows.

6) Have mat chats:

Take time in class to talk to your students. Pick different topics, such as:

a) Respect: the ways to show it and how to get it.
b) Good manners and how important they are.
c) How to get along with each other.
d) Caring for each other like a family.

These are just a few of the topics that can be discussed. Remember, the more you talk to your students and find out what they're thinking, the better you will know them. These chats will give you invaluable information:

a) You will be able to detect early signs of de-motivation.
b) You will know when students have something on their minds bothering them.
c) You will also know when students are happy about something and have an opportunity to share parts of their lives.

7) Make the calls yourself:

Take the time to call students and parents personally. Even when your staff does a great job of calling, with students and parents happy to hear from them, one thing that will position your school at the top with them is to hear from you directly. Parents always see the head instructor as the top guy, and when the top guy calls it makes the call that much more important. Calling personally will show them that you care and that they are important to you. This sets up the family environment so students and parents will always see you as approachable and they will not hesitate to come to you with their concerns.

Follow these steps and you will be well on your way to making your dojo into a "family dojo." You'll be happy with the results!

Perfect Attendance

Good attendance is a key factor in maintaining and retaining a martial arts student. One way to encourage students to be consistent in attending class is by rewarding them for it. At L.I. Ninjutsu Centers we have found that recognizing the students' efforts has had a great impact. A student who attends 12 to 15 classes in a given month receives a host of different awards including a customized perfect attendance certificate as well as a trophy.

Since we incorporated this Perfect Attendance Award system into our classes, students and parents have gone above and beyond to make sure that they attended class on a regular basis. Often, children, teens and adults practice the Martial Arts because they do not fit into other sports that are out there, or parents recognize that the Martial Arts fills a void that other sports cannot fill. Typically, in sports or other activities, attendance is mandatory but not recognized as part of the achievement. We realize that just showing up is half the battle.

The best way to implement a Perfect Attendance system into an existing school is:

1. Determine how many times per week a student should attend class and then determine a total for the month. In our school, we recommend that children take three classes a week, but many of them only take two. Since most students come two to three times a week, we decided to reward those students who do not miss class and come three times a week. The 3-4 year olds are offered two classes a week, so for their program we offer the Award for attending two classes per week without missing any. That makes the average to receive an Attendance Award 12 to 14 classes per month for students five years old and up, and eight to nine classes per month for three- to four-year-olds.

2. Next calculate how many times each student has come to class no later than the first week of the following month. Then make up the certificates and gather the trophies. At first in our school we used a generic certificate, but after a while we had a certificate professionally designed by a graphic artist. The new certificate made a world of difference to our students, and we have received many positive reviews from parents as well. In my opinion it is definitely worth putting the time, effort and money into professional certificates and trophies for your students.

Since we instituted the Perfect Attendance Awards, the number of students being honored has grown from only a few to a few hundred throughout all of our schools. We realized that this would be a major expense for us, so we decided to "recycle." We offered an even bigger incentive for students. This new incentive pumped even more excitement into the program. We added other "tiers" of awards for attendance. Here's how it works: when you receive four 6" trophies (for four months of perfect attendance), you can turn them in for one 12" trophy; with three 12" trophies, you can turn them in for a custom plaque that recognizes the student for one year of perfect attendance. On top of that, when a student has one year of perfect attendance we give the student a t-shirt and give each parent a t-shirt that says, "My child has perfect attendance at our school" (of course it displays the logo of the school). Recycling the trophies has helped us drastically cut costs and has also helped parents control the number of trophies the students have at home. We have many students who receive Perfect Attendance Awards on a regular monthly basis. We even have some parents and students who compete over how many awards their sons or daughters have achieved.

This kind of program can only help your retention and the growth of your school. Envision happy children who are highly motivated to come to class and who go out of their way to attend class on a regular basis, along with involved parents who are behind your program 100%.

Developing the Attitude to Succeed

The purpose of this is to discuss the personal pitfalls experienced by one of my staff members during the course of a year and also the personal triumphs. This was written on the anniversary of the first year running a school. Since then the student instructor has left teaching and is now a N.Y. City Police officer. It took a while to replace him with someone as qualified but inevitably one of the students who came up the ranks under his guidance took his place.

I will tell you what could have held me back, and then I will discuss the mindset and attitudes that have helped me to succeed. Finally, I will spell out the things that have contributed to my success.

I have had a major amount of growth this year. The obvious reason is I had continual guidance from my teacher Kyoshi Allie and he has a system for everything from marketing to retention. I faltered when I didn't follow these systems. While planning for this article I considered using the analogy of a computer or the human body. Both perform an amazing amount of processes, and a specific component controls those processes – a CPU or the brain. Sometimes, damage to the CPU or the brain results in the failure to perform certain processes, in the case of running a martial arts school, I realized that I am the "component" that controls the processes for growth and success at my school. I found that if I failed to function to my proper capabilities, my school would suffer the consequences.

There were times I found myself rationalizing why I was not achieving better results. I thought that I had to do everything myself. I thought that there were too many things to get done. I thought there was not enough time in the day. I blamed everything but myself. I didn't acknowledge there were times I went into work late, or decided to "do it tomorrow."

I remember a day, several months into running the school at one of our Monday morning staff meetings with Kyoshi Allie, where he went through his activities for the day and the week. I was in awe of how many things he got done. I then got to spend the next day with him as he ran through his daily procedures. I was amazed. It was then that I realized that all of the people he counseled would benefit just from listening to one thing at a time, and implementing the suggestions he gave.

I began to better understand the possibilities, if I simply *followed the systems*. To do this I invested time in a major self-evaluation of everything from my schedule, to my beliefs, to my results. I didn't allow myself to blame anyone or anything else, since at the end of the day, the person I needed to hold responsible was myself. **I then did the following:**

1. Increased my personal organization
2. Increased organization of the school
3. Set goals, with priorities for myself and for the school
4. Tapped natural resources

I increased my own organization by investing in a better organizer, and by following the system taught me to keep my own responsibilities covered. I realized I was not going to be able to manage a school if I was not able to manage my own tasks. When I made organization a priority, I was able to relieve stress that I had created myself, and to pay more attention to the schools' necessities.

Organizing the school was easier than I thought it would be. Perhaps my incorrect idea of how hard it would be was what had held me back for so long from finishing my "Dojo To Do List." *(This was the same way I felt when I had been afraid to make phone calls or to try to upgrade a student. I was afraid of success, and convinced myself that things were going to be harder than they were.)* Once I organized my files, made a calendar of responsibilities and stayed on top of it, I found that I could not fail if I wanted to.

As far as goal setting was concerned, I was taught there was no way I was going to personally achieve what I wanted unless I knew just exactly what it was that I wanted. Setting dojo goals was just as important. If I could visualize the success of my school and set goals to reach that success, then I would be able to work harder to reach them. The decisions I made would be based on my goals.

Finally, in evaluating my lame excuses for not achieving my goals, I looked at what I thought were my problems. For example, I thought that I was by myself, trying to get it all done. I forced myself to come up with solutions and found I wasn't by myself: I had my students; I had a consultant at my fingertips. I found that I wasn't delegating. I was trying to be a perfectionist and to do everything myself. **I was afraid to ask for help in fear that it would look like I was failing.**

In overcoming my fears, I realized any "machine" is an aggregate of several parts working together. Kyoshi taught me being a delegator and asking for help were parts of the job, and that I had to adapt or burn out. I did adapt and found my fears to be unfounded.

Now I utilize my students to help with tasks ranging from cleaning the dojo to stretching out classes and handing out flyers and door hangers. I call consultants when I need specialists in certain areas. There is less stress on me, less time for excuses and more time for success.

After one year of running a school, I've learned that using systems to stay organized is a key to success. At least as important, if not more important, I've learned that delegating and seeking help where appropriate makes you a leader not a failure.

Putting the pieces of the puzzle together

Every Monday morning we normally host a 2 hour staff meeting. This particular Monday the staff meeting was set on organizing some of the greatest systems into a logical order. Without the first system, the next could never be successful. For example, without man and woman there would be no children. There are eight Next Level Phases. Here are the first two Phases along with some of their broad-based sentiments regarding the systems and their results.

The organization of systems that are available on "Taking it to the Next Level" is really not rocket science. Although when we say that we tend to think it is really not that difficult either. I would say you don't have to know the laws of physics to run a martial arts school or organization but you most certainly have to be a great organizer and business person. School owners have made progress by making a long line of mistakes, stepping back, and really learning from them. Ever since you started your quest to be a martial art professional you have worked hard to determine what the right decisions were (making some wrong ones along the way, and learning from them). Through trial and error you must have come up with some great lessons.

Here are the steps for the first two Phases of running a successful school.

Phase One – Organizing and structuring your business

1. Make the business legal. Meet all the expectations of your local town codes code enforcement and the state.
2. Set up a corporation. This corporation is for your personal safety and protection against law suits. Try at all costs to keep your personal name away from anything involving your business. Of course, this is an issue to discuss with your attorney and your accountant.
3. Find the right insurance. Too much coverage is never a bad idea. Watch your costs but never short change yourself.
4. Create a professional layout for your school. Consulting with a decorator or designer is a great idea if you have the money in your budget.
5. Always remember your ultimate goal, even if you must take small steps to get there.

Phase Two - Getting the student and signing them up

1. Plan your marketing objectives and your advertising strategy. We spoke about a number of ideas in the marketing section.
2. Develop a professional staff to answer your phones. Teach proper phone procedures such as how to answer the phone and how to sell your product over the phone. You need to make prospective students want to come in.
3. Design your trial class systems, from scheduling to confirming to following up on missed appointments.

4. Make the initial sale. Have the prospect sign up for a trial at your school, present your program to the client, and make the sale.
5. Follow up on missed opportunities. You can really increase your business by following up on sales not made, converting people who walk out and turning them into your clients.
6. Have ongoing contact with all clients, especially important as the clients' enthusiasm subsides.

The staff noted during that meeting that many of the systems seemed to overlap, with objectives and functions seemingly intertwined. The objective is to thoroughly teach and train each component of each step so that the Martial Arts business owner and staff are able to effectively implement them.

Private Lessons Create Motivation and Revenue

Assets are hard to determine and it's often confusing figuring out what your assets actually are. For instance, people think of their home as an asset, when in my way of thinking it is nothing more then an expense. The only way I consider something as an asset is if it is making you a profit. You home is not a profit-center, even if its value has gone up, unless you sell it.

Now, on the other hand, what is definitely an asset because it makes you money and creates motivation all at once? I say the answer is **private lessons**. Private lessons not only create income for the school but also play a vital role in retaining and motivating students. Every student gets something different from private lessons. One student may want the personal attention while another may want to get ready for a promotion or special event, such as a tournament.

When giving private lessons to our five- to eight-year-olds, I have found that half-hour private lessons work the best. Their attention span is shorter than that of nine-year-olds and up, so at the end of an hour private lesson the younger kids are exhausted both mentally and physically and looking forward to going home. This is definitely not what a school owner wants. The goal is to create the motivation that keeps them coming back for more. Once we started doing the half-hour private lessons, we found that the kids were excited and extremely motivated when the class was over and this has made it much easier to sell the parents another block of private lessons. Teens and adults seem to enjoy the hour lessons, although if taught correctly a 30-minute lesson could give them a phenomenal workout.

A private lesson should be designed for the individual student but not controlled by the student. When first doing a private lesson you may ask the parent and student what they want to accomplish during the private time together. It is important to include them in the planning and it helps to create a bond between you and the student. This bond can be very important in the retention of the student. Once you know what the student wants to accomplish you can structure the private lessons to cover that objective, and get the student to study the curriculum and learn the material that needs to be worked on.

If you see that a student is having trouble in a certain area of the curriculum, you may have an opportunity to up-sell the student into regular private lessons. I use our review sheets to see what students feel they need to work on, and then approach the parents and students about taking private lessons to help them overcome the obstacle or obstacles they are facing.

Students who are consistently coming up on your weekly "we miss you" calls due to lack of attendance are prime examples of students in need of private lessons. If the parents are ready to give up and take the child out, I suggest offering several private lessons for **free** to help motivate the student. This will also prove that you're committed to making sure their child enjoys and succeeds at the program. This type of customer service will come back to you 10-fold. Envision those parents talking to the other parents about how committed you were to the individual needs of their child.

Many times the question arises about what to charge for a private lesson. A private lesson is time taken out of your busy schedule and your time is valuable. So do not hesitate to charge accordingly for a private lesson. In our school we charge $75 per hour, or five private lessons for the price of four, dropping the cost per private hour lesson to $60. I know of individuals who are getting as much as $150 per hour. When I personally do private lessons, which I prefer not to do any longer, I charge between $150-200 per class. There have been students who, due to work schedules and other commitments, want to take only private lessons. For these individuals we usually develop special pricing. For example, we had one student who only took private lessons so we reduced the price to $40 a lesson when he booked two per week and paid for the year in full ($4300).

As you can see, private lessons are a great way to motivate students, create income for the school, and get parents to become your biggest advocates. If you personally are not able to teach the private lesson, see if you can get some of your senior ranks or staff members who have instructional experience to teach them. One way to make it worth their while is to split the profit with them or pay them an appropriate hourly wage for any lessons they teach. The last and final option is doing semi-private lessons with small groups of people. For example, if your goal price is $200 per hour, then why not invite four students at $50 per hour. The goal is for you to get your desired dollar per hour rate and then teach the class for the particular group of students.

All Systems Go!

Any successful business must employ systems in order to continue to thrive and grow. Big companies and many franchises have systems for everything they do. From the very moment they come in contact with a potential client to the sale or service process, and in some cases to follow up after the experience, systems play a vital role in developing and maintaining a relationship with your client. Good systems ensure that all customers receive the same quality and level of service, and demonstrate professionalism on the part of the company.

Before I became a Martial Arts instructor, I worked in an assembly plant that manufactured hand-held bar code scanning devices. The company spent a huge amount of money doing research and testing to determine the best and most efficient way to build the product. Once the system was perfected, the assembly process became quick and simple enough that anyone could learn it in a matter of fifteen to thirty minutes.

Having a good system is crucial to the survival of any business. However, the best system in the world will only help you if you use it. It seems hard to believe that a company would spend so much time, money, and energy to develop a great system and then not use it, but it happens quite frequently.

It is easy to see when a system is not being followed because your results will begin to vary. I could always tell when someone wasn't following the system at the assembly plant because one of two things would happen. Sometimes, when someone stopped using the system or varied from it even slightly, it would throw off the entire continuity of the build process and production would slow down. When this happened the end result was we would not make our numbers and it would take us longer to complete the build. The other indicator that the process was not being followed correctly was that the defect rate would skyrocket and the quality assurance team whose job was to make sure we consistently produced a quality product would slam us.

When these things happened it wasn't too difficult to come up with a solution. Simply getting back to the system and following the process would correct the discrepancies every time.

The Martial Arts industry is no different. We have systems for phone calls, trial classes, for enrollment and retention. There are safety procedures and systems for running a dynamic class. The school owners and head instructors have spent many hours speaking with people, reviewing statistics, and analyzing data to come up with the systems used at the dojo. If the systems are good, everything will flow smoothly from prospecting to promotions, and everything in between.

If you are having trouble coming up with good systems or don't have any systems already in place, don't fret. Your consulting representative is always only a phone call or e-mail away. In most cases the consultants have been where you are and you can directly benefit from their experiences. There are so many great systems available that you can pick and choose elements from several systems and create a customized system that applies to your school and your school's needs. Remember, these are tried and true methods that have generated fantastic results for the school owners that have used them before. They can do the same for you as long as you implement them and use them with enthusiasm.

Don't forget that simply having the system is not going to get you anywhere. You must use your systems like a road map guiding you towards your destination. If you stop using the map you run the risk of veering off course. Sometimes even a few degrees can make a huge difference. So make sure you find and implement great systems, and then be sure to always use those systems and they will be your road map to success.

Program Manager Priorities

"Things aren't always what they seem." We have all heard this expression before. I believe the expression is nonsense. In my opinion, *things are always **exactly** what they seem*. If we use our best intuition, and we're honest with ourselves, we can understand and often predict the way a situation will turn out, can't we?

The best advice I can give you is to do the most important things first. I am stating the obvious, I know, but the secret to your success is really no secret. It is prioritizing. Sometimes we find that school owners, or their staffs, get caught up in all the "busy work," and they neglect to perform the most important functions for building their schools.

The best way to share the benefits of the Martial Arts with the public is to bring new students into your school, and hold on to the students you already have. This is your priority, and the tasks you must do each and every day are the ones that focus on these "Key Result" areas: *new enrollments and retention*. Therefore, your most important tools are your daily planner and your telephone.

Every day, you need to make a list of your tasks and appointments for the following day. Then prioritize your list and do the most important items first.

The daily tasks that are the highest priority for a Program Manager are the following:

1. Take out the trial class book and verify that all people scheduled for trial classes today were called yesterday. Confirm the people in trial classes scheduled for tomorrow, and call anyone who missed a trial class yesterday.

2. Check the phone messages, and write them all down. Immediately call only the people who requested information about classes; set trial class appointments with them and record the information in the trial book. Handle the rest of the calls later in the day.

3. Retention phone calls, such as attendance calls or 2-, 4-, 6-, 8-, 10-week calls can be done on a weekly basis, and should be scheduled in your planner as well.

When list is done every day, nobody will slip through the cracks, and your current and potential students will know that they are important to you. It also becomes a simple and quick process when you make it your routine.

If you are not getting the results you want in building your school, analyze your daily activities to find out why. If you are not focusing on the Key Result areas, then the answer is clear, and "things are exactly what they seem."

Concentrate your efforts on your highest priorities. When the most important things are done first, you will find that all the other tasks get completed as well.

Who Bosses the Boss?

Being your own boss is a wonderful thing. You get to make the decisions, you set the standards, and you reap the greatest rewards. However, being the boss can be a double-edged sword in some cases. When you are the boss you have the most to gain, and also the most to lose.

You see, for a regular employee, the job is not as critical as it is to the boss. If the company does not make a profit, the employee still gets paid. If the company has a cost increase for parts or materials from its vendors, the employee still gets paid. The employee has a nice, safe, virtually risk free environment.

This is not to say that employees never take an active role in the company. If you do your research and ask the right questions during the hiring process, you can cultivate a caring and growth-minded staff that does keep the company's interests in mind.

Even with a top-notch staff, you as the boss must constantly remain vigilant towards your business. When you have a great staff that you can rely on to take care of everything, it is easy to become complacent and overlook things. Even when you implement systems to make your business a turnkey operation, you must keep your finger on the pulse of the operation at all times. Remember, you are there to keep everyone accountable for his or her responsibilities.

Delegation is an important skill to master. Simply assigning a task and then forgetting about it is not good enough. You must inspect what you expect and make sure the task is followed through to completion, and with the results you expect.

So, the question is, "Who bosses the boss?" The answer is simple: you do. I know this is not always easy. There will be times when you will be tempted to stay home or in your office and let your staff handle things. There will be occasions when you will have the opportunity to "duck out" early. You'll even be able to justify your actions by telling yourself it will help staff development to let them run things on their own. However, during these times you must remember that ultimately it is you who will feel the repercussions of these decisions.

Am I saying that you can never take a day off? No, of course I'm not. You train your staff so they can do their jobs to the best of their ability. A good staff using good systems will function efficiently without you needing to oversee every little detail all of the time. Just keep in mind that your company is a product of your vision. It was your hard work and sweat that got you where you are. So when you get the urge to 'blow off work and watch some DVDs" ask yourself this question: "Is this going to help me to achieve my ultimate vision for my company or not?" This is a question only you can answer, and only you can decide when it is time to put your nose to the grindstone and to be the best boss you can be.

Chapter 9
Always be a student of higher Education

Making this the best convention ever

Many of you attend the major martial arts conventions every year. You've probably spent thousands of dollars to meet fellow professionals and benefit from information and techniques that have helped them be successful. But what do you have to show for it? Many of you probably still have a pile of information that you've gathered, notes and paperwork sitting in a closet. You promised yourself that you would go through it regularly and institute some of it a little each time so that you could make your schools grow and become more professional. The problem is, with all the information that you have, the new information that you receive regularly from trade associations, and all that is going on you may not have instituted much. I, too, get caught up in day-to-day activities. So how can we take the cost of the convention and turn it into a pile of gold? Or make the best of the material we get regularly. Well here are **six tips** that will help.

1) First and foremost, there is work that you need to do before you go to the convention. **List the areas of weakness** that you find in yourself, your students and your school. Once you have established the list, you can search out seminars that are related to those topics. Brainstorm with your staff about changes they would like to see at your school. If you are bringing your staff, write a list and divide up responsibilities. Go to the conference with an open mind. Even if you see things that rub you the wrong way or are at odds with your philosophies, seek out a small idea to take home to better your school. One of the biggest mistakes we often make is that we get caught up in the frenzy of the convention and lose sight of our goals. We need to stay focused. Forget the gambling, the fancy dinners, and the nightlife (at least until you are done with the seminars).

2) **Find people you can network with**. Don't just use the convention as a tax write-off and a mini vacation. Remember, if you go to the convention and get a few good ideas, the positive changes to your business may pay for 100 vacations over the next few years. Take the time to go out to breakfast with some heavy hitters and players in the martial arts business. Exchange phone numbers, addresses and e-mails. Bring a stack of your business cards with you to distribute. Don't show up at the convention empty handed.

3) **Make new friends**. Many times, martial artists are creatures of habit. They tend to continue to do what they already do well, and forget to have open minds. They believe

that their systems are the best; their methods are the best; and so on. This mentality is very self-limiting. I think that if you spend the money to travel to a seminar and take the time out of your busy schedule, then you should be open to new people and new ideas. Remember, if you make one friend it may change your life forever.

4) Take the time to investigate. Play your own "spy game." Look at what other companies have to offer. Take the time to see what new successful schools are doing. Look suspiciously at things that may be the next fad." Quick fix schemes and slick money-making opportunities usually don't earn you as much money as hard work. You need to be open to new ideas, but don't jump at every new strategy unless you are convinced it will work for you.

5) Remember the goal. Why are you going to the convention? What is the end result you are looking for? Studies have shown that people who set goals are much more successful then those who do not. For example, I remember about five years ago I attended a seminar in Clearwater, Florida. I walked into that convention with the goal of taking my children's curriculum to new heights. I went to a seminar by a renowned specialist on little children and was thoroughly impressed by her presentation for three hours afterward, four of my top staff and I sat in a back hallway next to the kitchen and revamped our entire curriculum. As you know, I have one of the largest schools in the world today. This is due to that one day of listening and learning.

6) Don't be fooled by the numbers and the fluff. Many times, while attending seminars, people will tell you their success stories. I have found that many consultants have lost touch with the reality of what it takes to run a martial arts school full time. They tell you what to do, send you information, and expect that it is easy to put it into action. Being that I am in the trenches so to speak, I know that you can get it done, but I also know that it will take time and discipline to make it work. I once started a seminar by saying, "This year alone I bought a Ferrari, a Viper and a Mercedes with my earnings." I then asked how many people in the audience would like to do that. I asked the attendees if they would like to see the cars. People looked puzzled. I then reached into my bag and pulled out three matchbox toy cars. Everyone laughed, though some people were annoyed. I think the people who were annoyed got the message. Anyway, don't believe everything you hear. Be a bit skeptical, but look for people with a real track record.

Change or Die

What if you were given a choice to make your life better by changing your behavior? What if it wasn't just rhetoric but really a matter of life or death? Could you do it, would you do it?

Many times people change *temporarily* because of an upset boss or a slick motivational speaker or a self-dramatizing CEO. But we're talking about actual life or death now, your own life or death. What if a trusted source such as a doctor or another authority figure told you that you needed to make changes in the way you think and act or your time would end? Would you have the inner power to make those changes and stick to them?

Some say "Of course!" I would make changes, and so would anyone else who had that choice!" Try again. Here are the odds: Scientific studies have shown that the odds are nine to one that you wouldn't change. The consensus is that many people are sick because of how they choose to live their lives, not because of environmental or genetic factors beyond their control. Many studies have demonstrated that 80% of any health-care budget is consumed by the negative impact of five behaviors. You don't need an M.D. degree to guess what those behaviors are: too much smoking, drinking, eating, and stress, and not enough exercise.

Patients whose heart disease is so severe that they require bypass surgery, a traumatic and expensive procedure that can cost more than $100,000 if complications arise, could arrest the course of their disease before it kills them by switching to healthier lifestyles. Yet very few do, if you look at people after coronary-artery bypass grafting two years later, 90% of them have not changed their lifestyles. Even though they know they have a very bad disease and they know they should change their lifestyles, for some reason, they don't.

Conventional wisdom says that crisis is a powerful motivator for change. But even severe heart disease, which is among the most serious of personal crises, doesn't motivate, at least not nearly enough, nor does giving people accurate analyses and factual information about their situations. What works? Why, in general, is change so incredibly difficult for people? What is it about how our brains are wired that resists change so tenaciously? Why do we fight even what we know to be in our own vital interests? We'll get to that in a moment.

But first let's talk shop. Why is it that even though we have resources at our finger tips and even when we ask for help, we are resistant to helping ourselves? Maybe it is not because we don't want it; maybe we don't want it enough. Think about any success story and you will find that it wasn't luck that led to the success; it was pure dedication and the willingness to work hard and make changes when changes were warranted.

Here are some ideas on how you can embrace change in your life to benefit yourself and your growing business.

Framing Change

Doctors have tried to motivate heart attack patients to care for themselves with the fear of death, but it doesn't work. For a few weeks after the heart attacks, patients were scared enough to do whatever their doctors said. But death was just too frightening to think about, so their denial returned, and then they reverted to their old habits. And when businesses react this way, many of them don't make it. In fact within the first three years nearly 70% of new businesses fail.

Is joy a more powerful motivator than fear? "Neuroscience tells us that each of the concepts we have - the long-term concepts that structure how we think -- is instantiated in the synapses of the brain." Concepts are not things that can be changed just by someone telling us a fact. We may be presented with facts, but for us to make sense of them; they have to fit what is already in the synapses of the brain. Otherwise, facts go in and then they go right back out" reframing to concentrate on the positive results of changing, rather than the negative results of maintaining the status quo, can have a tremendous impact on the ability to change.

Radical Change

Reframing alone isn't enough, of course. Paradoxically, radical, sweeping, comprehensive changes are often easier for people than small, incremental ones. For example, Dr Lakoff says that people who make moderate changes in their diets get the worst of both worlds: They feel deprived *and* hungry because they aren't eating everything they want.

In business, people often hesitate to make sweeping changes until it is far too late. Now is the time to sit down and look at things from a different perspective. If you are not happy with the results you are getting, you are either doing something wrong or you don't have the right people in place to help you succeed. Sometimes a radical change is necessary. Now I am not saying to fire your entire staff, but maybe you can change the way things are done enough to put a fire under their tails.

Research shows that these ideas of reframing and radical change fit perfectly in the business realm. Bain and Co., the management consulting firm, studied 21 recent corporate transformations and found that most were "substantially completed" in only two years or less while none took more than three years. The means were drastic: In almost every case, the CEOs fired most of the top management. Almost always, the companies enjoyed quick, tangible results, and their stock prices rose 250% a year on average as they revived.

Sometimes the choice is either to change or die. To change or not to change, that is the question. The simple fact is that it is entirely up to you.

The Life Trap

I am constantly thinking of ways to inspire the desire and encourage our school owners to be the best they can be. It is inspiring for me to see the growth in most schools I work closely with and also very exciting for me to hear from others that they have instituted ideas and concepts that are helping their schools.

When schools don't succeed, it is for myriad reasons. The most frequent reason is what I have coined, "The Life Trap." This trap is a vortex in the universe that has a pull so much stronger then gravity. It takes motivated individuals and basically reduces them to sheep in a herd. Now this may sound harsh, but be honest, how many times do you actually feel this way? For example, you work hard all day and just can't seem to find enough time to get the most important things done. Or you may have a solid plan of action organized with a set "to do" list and believe that nothing short of a hurricane will get in the way, but at the end of the day, you still haven't finished your projects. This is what I call "The Life Trap."

The good news is there are ways to get around the trap, and they don't involve rocket science. In the book "The Warrior," one of the authors categorizes people in three levels. The first level is the sheep; the second is the wolves; and the third is the sheep dogs that protect the sheep. The sheep are people who are herded every day by the things society has in place for all of us. We listen to the media, believe what we are told, follow fads, styles, cliques etc. My goal is to teach people not to be sheep. You can learn to be the sheep dog or the sheep herder. You can become the master of your life.

Start by not believing all that you hear. Even Buddha said that you should listen and learn and then go out and make you own determination. The goal is not to think in the box or, for the sake of it, out of the box. Our goal is to see the world and our parts of the world as they actually are, and to base our actions on true situations.

How do we keep from falling into the "Life Trap?" Here are five steps

1. Take control. Do not just meander through life as though things will get better tomorrow. Take control of all things that happen in your life. Do not leave things to chance. Try to find out what you can do about a specific situation and then move in the direction of making it exactly what you want.

2. Prepare. Always be the most prepared. How many times have you heard people speak of how their long-lost relatives always talked about getting life insurance or a will but never got around to it? Now their families are out of luck with nothing. Or how about the people who wait until their gas gauges read "empty" and then drive around with knots in their stomachs but never fill the tanks up with gas? Preparation is one of the most important traits of successful individuals.

3. Rid yourself of procrastination. Find the habits that are good and those that are bad. Work on ridding yourself of the bad ones. It takes 21 days to develop a bad habit, but three times as long to develop a good habit. Clearly, it takes much more work to develop good habits. Even though it is easy to fall off track and lose the momentum, do not put off until tomorrow what you can do today about developing those good habits that will help you.

4. Stay focused. Focus is the enemy of the "The Life Trap." Lack of focus is the very definition of why we do not succeed. When we lose focus we lose momentum. We need to train ourselves daily and build a strong foundation of self-discipline. This is not as easy as it seems but it is well worth working on.

5. Last but not least, have balance in life. Balance the activities of your life, and at the same time, prioritize what you want, how you will get it and what your plan of action is. This is a goal-setting activity. Tony Robbins has developed the mentality of "C.A.N.I." - constant and never ending improvement. If you approach each day with the desire to improve yourself, your life and what you do, you will move forward faster then the vast majority of the people around you.

Chapter 10
Life Lessons from someone who cares

Developing Your Spiritual Connection

Bam! Another news report comes through. Terrorists this, hijackers that, people are constantly doing bad things. Why even bother listening to the news or reading the paper: it is just too depressing. In the 21st century we are constantly bombarded by negative thoughts. Statistics show that the average person sees over 10,000 acts of violence by the age of 18 either in the news or on television. How are we not supposed to be hardened to the fact that things are going wrong in our society right underneath our noses and we are not doing a thing about it? Have you ever had tears come to your eyes after seeing an animal harmed in a movie, but those bad guys can get shot and it doesn't even make you feel a bit of sadness?

Well, you can make a difference. It is a fact that if you put your mind to it you can make an extreme difference. Look at Gandhi, the Dalai Lama, Martin Luther King, the Pope and Mother Theresa. All of these individuals had one thing in common; they were all empathetic and compassionate people who believed they could make a difference.

You may ask, how do I do this? I am very busy. I have a family; I work all day and night as well. I spend hardly any time with my family as it is. I am also barely able to open my eyes in the morning already. So I can't possibly fit in one more thing.

Some of the actions you can take won't even take time out of your busy schedule or make you tired. How about recycling bottles or using the front and back of paper before you recycle it? How about picking up a piece of paper that someone else threw on the floor? How about holding a door for someone in the shopping center? How about paying for the person behind you at a tollbooth? Tell a person you don't know that he or she has beautiful smile. Tell your secretary or boss that he or she is a great person.

In my eyes, being a spiritual person has nothing to do with religion. Rather, it is about the development of the inner spirit of love and compassion. Each person may feel differently about this, but to me being a spiritual person is not about how you pray or to whom you pray; it is about kindness and empathy.

Here is an exercise that you may want to practice. Take a bowl of marbles or even a pad and a pen. For every negative thought you have put a black marble in the jar or put a check in the negative column. For every good thought put a white marble in the jar or check the positive column. At the end of the day, tally up and determine if you have been as empathetic and compassionate an individual as you think you should have been. This may take some practice and time. Don't worry; the lesson is the practice. **Practice every day to be a better person.** Develop your spiritual side and live life with love and compassion.

At times we get caught up in what I call the "Mental Blender." The continuous spinning leaves you dizzy and it takes time to recover. Sometimes we look at vacations and weekends as the recovery from our mental blender, when in reality the only way to recover is to change perspective. Rather than trying to hide or run from the stresses and belief systems we have, we should face them straight on and learn to use them as tools to improve our lives. A vacation is only good if you have nothing to take a vacation from; then and only then do you truly enjoy yourself and look forward to coming back to your life.

Live life to the fullest and work hard at strengthening the mind, the body and the spirit. Make sure your goals are to improve your "self" and you will be pleasantly surprised that all the "things" in your life will improve along with it. Life is a series of lessons; the average person doesn't learn from them, so you need to become above average, to become the change in the world that you want. Be the ball (remember the movie Caddy Shack?). When you're constantly working to strengthen your mind, body and spirit, you'll live life to the fullest, and best of all you'll enjoy

Why Not Ignore the Bling?

Every generation is bombarded with the newest and greatest of everything, from jewelry to clothes, hairstyles to shoes, sneakers to cell phones - all things that create the fads about which generations are famous for decade after decade. In the 50's it was greased-back hair; in the 60's it was tie-died shirts; in the 70's it was bell-bottom jeans; in the 80s it was crazy, hair sprayed hair; in the 90's it was the decadent relaxed flannel look; and in the 2000s it's what they call "bling." Bling is a word associated with flash, wealth, and, in my opinion, gaudiness.

When I was younger, life seemed to be slower, with less stress and less clutter. I can only imagine what it was like in the 50's. I am sure the youth of America was searching for the same things - identity, girls/guys, cars and the meaning of life. Why is it that six-year-olds or more often teenagers taking Martial Arts classes turn to me and say, "I am a bit stressed" or "I have a bad back" or "I don't want to do this; I want to quit?" Life's paths seem to have taken some extreme turns in the last decade, and our children are dealing with far more stress and clutter than ever before. But there are some situations that seem to remain constant.

There is a saying "The village raises the child." Our job as parents and teachers is to be very conscious of which village is raising our children. In fact, we also need to be aware of what thoughts are going in our own heads regularly. Recently I hired a public relations firm to work with my company. I had an amazing opportunity to promote a seminar that we were running with a world-renowned Martial Artist. Our PR firm contacted the local news and they said that they couldn't commit a crew to our event and would let us know within one hour of the event if they could spare someone. When I asked why, the PR person told me that the local station needed to have someone available in case of emergency like car accidents, house fires, etc.

To me this is shocking. The station turned down a feature on a group of 75 people getting together to pursue a common goal of encouraging positive self-image and healthy lifestyle in order to report on a negative event such as a car accident. I don't understand this mentality. Have you ever heard the computer term GIGO - garbage in, garbage out? GIGO is something that we deal with on a regular basis. We sort through what we believe is good for us and what we believe is not. The sad reality is that because of all of the clutter we sometimes pick the "garbage" and miss things that could positively change our lives forever.

It is my goal as a consultant to share. Not all of my ideas are going to work for everyone; my goal is to share enough information so that most people find a way to benefit somehow. I started consulting to help Martial Arts school owners and to achieve my goal of sharing - that is, to improve the Martial Arts and the well being of people worldwide. I hope that somehow I have had a positive effect. I also hope that you share in my goal and that through your Martial Arts you will continually improve lives, one person at a time. My dream is to have people recognize the Martial Arts as one of the most positive activities in which they can participate. I hope to be around to see that happen.

So join me in encouraging our youth to ignore the "bling" being offered to them. Let's give them a good alternative. I want to work with the Martial Arts community to enable all people to recognize the benefits that can be realized from the Martial Arts. Let's work together.

Living a Stress Free Life

We sometimes hear people talking about "the attitude of gratitude." Well, all of us need to remember all the things that we can be grateful for. Every few months I like to send out an e-mail teeming with pure positive attitude and great spiritual connection. This happens to be one of those e-mails.

Here are my tips on how to be thankful for life and to gain a spiritual edge. I hope you like it.

"Nine-to-five isn't good enough! We'll work 9-9!" This seems to be the mantra of many working people today. Seven days per week, 12 hours per day, and it doesn't end there. Moms need to be super women – taking care of the family, cooking dinner, cleaning, organizing, running the house and being a wife is just the start. Men need to have some sort of super power as well - work all day, on the train, at home, weekends and that is just to make ends meet. To get ahead, you work on the side. How do you ever find enough time in the day for what you want to do just for yourself?

The key to relieving stress is changing your perspective. Many times people feel overwhelmed, and stress becomes a key factor in their lives. How can we live a stress free life?

Five Tips For a Stress-free Life.

1. Shift your perspective. For example: Two people approach a roller coaster. One is deathly afraid and will be sick on its first turn; the other is elated at the chance to take the ride. How is it that the same ride can bring on two entirely different responses? Well the answer lies in perception. One person has been brought up or born with the desire for thrills and craziness. The other is more subdued and less of a thrill seeker. Try to understand the true nature of a situation and learn to deal with it without getting stressed. Your own perspective truly influences your reality. If you shift your perspective it may entirely enhance your life.

2. Don't take things to heart. For instance, being caught in a traffic jam can really change your day. Don't let yourself get worked up over being late. You can't change anything about the situation unless you have a helicopter on call to swoop down and pick you up. So getting angry, annoyed or even developing road rage to transfer some of the pent up feelings to someone else will do you no good. Take that time to relax and listen to your favorite radio station or a book on audiotape. Think of good things that have happened in your life.

3. Let things go. Many times, disease is a manifestation of internalized emotions. Your body is the most unbelievable machine that can filter and get rid of many toxins. At times, though, it can self-destruct if we are not careful. Stress can create many changes in your body. Look at ulcers for example. The way your mind interprets things can lead to an ulcer. That same roller coaster ride we spoke about previously could lead to an ulcer if a person was forced to go on it in total fear continuously. So understanding your capabilities and letting go of the things that upset you is your best choice.

4. Don't sweat the small stuff – because it is all small stuff. A great book was written with this title. The concept is to not let little things become big things and get under your skin. For example, early on in a relationship couples go through a phase called the extreme love phase. Little things, or personal quirks, may be perceived as being cute.

In this stage everyone has the highest level of tolerance. As time goes by, those same quirks become annoying, because the tolerance level has decreased. So a little thing that was once cute is now very annoying and upsetting. Don't let those little things become big things.

5. Practice compassion and empathy. The Dalai Lama teaches this regularly. We should look at all living beings as if they were the dearest people to us. We tend to treat people differently when we know them and love them. For instance usually a baby can do no wrong. Once, while holding my baby daughter in my arms, she threw up on me. I didn't even think about it. It was okay. In fact it brought me closer to fatherhood. If that same thing happened with a sick friend, I'd need to work at not being upset that they didn't think to let me know ahead of time. But doing so would help me build compassion and empathy.

Living a stress-free life is a conscious choice that we must make and practice daily. If you really want to get rid of the stress you must be in control of your life. You must choose not to let the little and unimportant things bother you. You must grab the stress, control it and get rid of it.

Developing Your Spiritual Connection

In my eyes, being a spiritual person has nothing to do with religion. Rather, it is about the development of the inner spirit of love and compassion. Each person may feel differently about this, but to me being a spiritual person is not about how you pray or to whom you pray; it is about kindness and empathy.

Here is an exercise that you may want to practice. Take a bowl of marbles or even a pad and a pen. For every negative thought you have put a black marble in the jar or put a check in the negative column. For every good thought put a white marble in the jar or check the positive column. At the end of the day, tally up and determine if you have been as empathetic and compassionate an individual as you think you should have been. This may take some practice and time. Don't worry; the lesson is the practice. Practice every day to be a better person. Develop your spiritual side and live life with love and compassion.

At times we get caught up in what I call the "Mental Blender." The continuous spinning leaves you dizzy and it takes time to recover. Sometimes we look at vacations and weekends as the recovery from our mental blender, when in reality the only way to recover is to change perspective. Rather than trying to hide or run from the stresses and belief systems we have, we should face them straight on and learn to use them as tools to improve our lives. **A vacation is only good if you have nothing to take a vacation from**; then and only then do you truly enjoy yourself and look forward to coming back to your life.

Live life to the fullest and work hard at strengthening the mind, the body and the spirit. Make sure your goals are to improve your "self" and you will be pleasantly surprised that all the "things" in your life will improve along with it. Life is a series of lessons; the average person doesn't learn from them, so you need to become above average, to become the change in the world that you want. Be the ball (remember the movie Caddy Shack?). When you're constantly working to strengthen your mind, body and spirit, you'll live life to the fullest, and best of all you'll enjoy yourself.

Chapter 11
Sales 101

Public Speaking – Be Heard or Die

As odd as this may sound, people place public speaking high on their lists of fears. I have seen people actually freeze up and break down in tears with the look of death on their faces when they're asked to speak in public. Studies have shown that people are as afraid to speak publicly or do a presentation in front of an audience as they are of drowning. Amazing you may say. Well if this is your comment, then you are one of the few who really don't mind speaking in public and would do so at the drop of a dime. For others, public speaking is something to be avoided like the plague.

Getting over the fear is harder for some people than for others, but usually it is just a matter of practice. We believe that if you are well prepared you will be able to make public speaking a part of your daily routine, or at least to approach it without any fear or anxiety whatsoever. Some may say "I have no need to speak in public so why bother learning?" But in modern society you never know when you will need this skill. For everyone, no matter what job you have, from accountant to professional athlete, being able to speak in public and communicate your ideas will be a benefit for you. Incorporating public speaking skills into your life will make you a better communicator.

When you speak in front of an audience, your presentation will almost always have one or more of these three objectives: to inform, to persuade or to entertain and capture people's attention. Being prepared is more then half the battle.

Tips on How to Feel Comfortable Speaking in Public

1. Prepare your material so that it is informative, interesting and captures the audience's attention. Remember that the amount of information that is retained is lowered when your presentation is unnecessarily long. So by the end, a great deal of the presentation may be lost. If you are well prepared, concisely present your information, and use tools such as handouts, Power Point presentations, and audience participation, it will increase the amount of retention.

2. Know your audience. Doing a detailed audience profile is sometimes difficult, but the function at which you are speaking will often give you insight into the topics that the audience is interested in hearing about. This is half the battle. Knowing the topic and the clientele ahead of time are keys to your success.

3. WIIFM ("What's in it for me?") Each person in your audience has come to you for reasons of his or her own. Each has a specific reason for being there. Audience members want something from you that is personal, something that they can take home with them and use in their lives. The most exciting word in the English language is "me."

The power to persuade depends on your ability to get your point across. Most people who are good at sales have good public speaking skills. They may not be able to stand up in front of an audience but they are able to verbally communicate benefits to others. As a public speaker you must engage the audience, entertain them and keep their attention. These skills are all part of your ability to be a good public speaker.

Every Good Presentation is Composed of Three Main Parts

1. The introduction: The introduction is a brief outline of what you are going to be speaking about during your speech. It should take about 10% of the length of your speech. For example, if you are speaking for 60 minutes, then your intro should be no more then six minutes. The introduction is your chance to make a good first impression. Establish what's in it for the audience and develop rapport and credibility by letting the audience know exactly who you are and what you stand for.

2. The body: This is the main focus of your speech and should be about 80% of the overall length. The topic that you are speaking about will be fully covered here with supporting information, stories, ideas, quotes, comparisons, statistics and contrasts. You can add analogies, humor, audience involvement and visual aids if needed.

3. The conclusion: This is up to 10% of your speech and should briefly review with the audience what you have told them. This is the last thing the audience will hear and it must be professional and well put together. Your conclusion is the final impression that you leave with the audience. An effective conclusion should go over the key points of your presentation. If you have a product that you are selling, the conclusion should also motivate them to purchase your product. Your conclusion should leave a mental picture in the audience members' minds. Some components of an effective conclusion include suggesting some action steps and ending on a positive note.

10 Steps to Preparing an Organized Speech

1. First and foremost, select your topic to be appropriate for the targeted audience.

2. Limit your topic to one specific theme: don't try to cover too much material in a short amount of time.

3. Do your information gathering. Make sure you are well prepared. Study your topic and research your material. Be ready to answer any questions.

4. Do a formal outline of your key points. Use between three and six key points on your topic.

5. Gather supporting data. Keep people interested with supporting information, examples, stories and analogies.

6. Develop your introduction to include a grabber or a hook. Make sure that the topic and the material are catchy and interesting.

7. Write your conclusion and make it strong and believable so that you leave a lasting impression.

8. Design your final draft using large print, index cards or oak tag.

9. Practice your presentation over and over until you are comfortable with it. You should rehearse it at least six times out loud. If possible, record yourself on audio or video. Review your recorded presentation looking for mistakes or uncomfortable pauses.

10. Rehearse in front of people, not the audience to whom you will give your presentation but rather people who can give you feedback.

The more familiar you are with the material the easier it gets. For those who do presentations regularly and often speak about the same topic, it is comparable to performers doing a Broadway play over and over again. The words flow and become second nature.

With time, anyone can become comfortable with public speaking. You just need to be prepared and practice, practice, practice.

Signing up Problem Students: Do We Want Them?

The question of whether or not we want to sign up problem students has plagued Martial Arts school owners since the dawn of time. Every school owner has the desire to teach and spread the word of whatever style he or she teaches: the goal is to help others. In reading some mission statements of schools, I found them to be more like something that you would expect to read in a church than a mission statement for a school of fighting arts. Many of you probably have had a similar situation to one I've often had: when you are speaking to people and they ask what you do, you tell them you are a Martial Arts teacher. They then respond with, "I don't want to mess with you or Don't kick my butt." This is typical of the impression that the Martial Arts has put out. Along with the stigma of Martial Artists being the tough guys among teachers (and this includes all teachers) we are at the same time considered subservient and thought of as individuals who should be self-less.

For most of us this stigma seems to be part of our DNA – our genetic makeup. To some extent we believe this as well; hence our lack of desire to charge more and believe that we should charge more. The main question here, however, is why do we have the desire to help people? Well, the answer is that as a Martial Artist you are teacher, and as teachers we believe we can make a difference. So we try and try again and again.

What do we do when a parent approaches us with a child who has behavioral issues such as A.D.D., A.D.H.D, A.D.O.H.D, anger management issues, or defiant syndrome? In most cases we offer to help, believing that under most circumstances the Martial Arts can be a cure-all. Now I do think that under the right conditions, with the right family support system of our program, this can be the case. But realize that you only have one part of the equation. So when all the stars are in alignment it is perfect, but when they are not we are in deep trouble.

Take this scenario: Little Johnny joins and initially you see progress. Other then having to call his name 15 times per class and use the time-out strategy and four thousand pattern interrupts, you are good to go. The class bows out and you feel as though you have done your job. You look around the room; kids are smiling and you've taught another class that is considered a success. But when is it really a bad day, not a good day? I have encountered a few situations that have made me change my frame of mind, and this has helped me forge a mentality that we live by in our schools.

Before I go on, I want to paraphrase a story I received on e-mail just yesterday. Of course there is a comical side to the example: There was a hospital that was having a bad string of luck over the last year. Every patient in room 212 in the intensive care unit died at 12 noon sharp on Monday morning. There was nothing anyone could say or do to stop it, nor could they figure out the cause. Soon they hospital staff believed it had to be a spiritual event. On the next Monday all nurses, doctors and hospital staff stood outside room 212 with crosses, holy water and whatever other religious charms they believed in to stop the phenomenon, when in came George, the cleaning man, to do his daily rounds. Everyone continued to pray when at exactly 12 o'clock he reached down and unplugged the life support system to plug in his floor polisher and started to clean. This of course illustrates the concept of how we don't look at what the real situation is. So here are few things to consider:

1. Ask yourself if you are really technically capable of helping this individual. If not, can you recommend a professional who is able to help?

2. Are you doing more harm than good? Sometimes what *we* do really is only a portion of the situation. Behaviorally we can offer a part of a cure, but if the parents are not following up, then it is all lost; it is like a patch, not a cure.

3. Are the parents really working with you and the child? I have found that parents are very busy; being a parent myself, I know it is easy to be in denial. Parents have pure love for our children, and it allows us to overlook a great deal. Sometimes parents are really not that in tune with how severe a situation really is. In order to help a child, you need a complete team: you, the child and the parents.

These last two are the most important of all:

4. Are you putting so much time into this child's needs that it is difficult for you to teach the classes the way they are supposed to be taught? Is this child draining all your energy?

5. Are the parents of all your other students looking at this negatively? Are they upset that you are taking time away from all the other kids who don't have issues? Are they getting their money's worth, or do they perceive your special attention to a problem student as a negative thing? I assume you know without my telling you that most parents are feeling this way. Even the parents with the troubled child will see that you are neglecting your responsibility to the class and will feel embarrassed.

A solution you can offer to the parents of problem students is private lessons. Special classes for kids with behavioral problems have an entirely different curriculum geared toward specific issues.

Most importantly, **you must think about what the end benefit is toward the growth of the majority of students training in your facility and the growth of your school as a learning facility in general.** This is something that you need to be quick to judge, and also good at diagnosing. Good luck and feel free to e-mail me with your comments or questions.

Overcoming Objections!

"I would love to do this but I have to first clear it with my wife," or "I can't really commit to this right now," or "My son has never really stuck to anything for any period of time and I don't want to waste my money," or "I just don't have any time right now." No matter what the situation, the list of objections goes on and on. I am sure you have heard many objections, and I'm here to tell you there is a way to get past them.

Objections are basically a form of client communication. When prospects don't commit to a particular item, sale or program, they are telling you that you have not sold them yet: that you have not communicated the benefits and touched the reason why they came to you in the first place. If they walked through your door (after all this is the hardest part), then they are interested in joining your school or buying your product. So if they walk out with out signing up, then for some reason you have not connected with them.

An objection is a way for prospects to say, "I am not quite sold yet." If you have answered all their questions, there is still a chance that they may not want to join your school or buy your product. Many times when this occurs, you have said something that doesn't appeal to them. Or maybe you have not listened hard enough to what the client is looking for. Diagnostic selling is basically the method of listening to the prospective clients and then presenting them with solutions to the objectives that they want to accomplish. No matter whether the objective is to lose weight or gain self-confidence, you need to appeal to their desires. It doesn't matter who you are, what you do and how cool you are, if the prospects don't see the benefits to themselves then it is a lost cause.

Here are some staff training and mental sales training exercises to help you overcome objections and close the sale:

Drill One: The Benefit Game

This exercise is effective in preparing you for any objections. Write down all the objections that you have heard in the past and then write an appropriate response to each one. After you have done this, practice the responses. Get used to speaking to clients about their objections, using the responses you have developed. For example: a mom tells you that she wants to help her child develop patience. She asks what you can do to help her child. Tell her specifically what components of your program help this situation.

After you have answers for all of the objections you've documented, you and the staff can drill this on a consistent basis and become masters at conveying the information that prospective clients really need to know. Most importantly, don't do it simply for the sake of a having an answer: make sure that you believe in the answer you are giving and practice responding from the heart. Don't be a salesman, be a solution provider.

Drill Two: Become a Better Listener

Learn to listen when someone is objecting, and then restate the objection so that you can be sure you understand the person correctly. I have been in the situation where I restated an objection back to a client and the client said, "Well that's not really what I meant," and so the client then explained the objection differently. It is so important to listen to what the client wants. Always give clients your undivided attention so that you can be a specialist and a problem solver for the sake of the clients.

One of my favorite responses to a client who is not sold is, "In a perfect world what could I do right now to convince you to sign up? If there was one thing that was holding you back, what would it be and how could I eliminate that obstacle for your benefit? After all, our goal is to help our students." This usually gets the client to think about his or her objections and open up a bit. A sale is always possible as long as we continue the conversation.

Once a potential client walks out the door, the chance of a sign-up is drastically reduced. Take the time to listen to the objections of prospective clients and then explain to them wholeheartedly that participation in your school is something that can help them achieve the things they want. To insure a sale, the decision must not be about you or your school: it must always be about the client.

How to Convert the Difficult Sign Up

The battle lines are drawn: you sit across from each other and the only thing between you and the prospect is the desk. A bead of sweat starts to form on your face, and no matter what you say or do, the person counters with an answer that feels like a jab in the face.

Does this sound familiar? Have you ever had a prospective student or parent of a prospective student who, no matter what you say, comes back at you with more questions and negatives than you could ever think of? I used to call people like that "the portals of doom" and think, "Do I really want them in my school?" Now I have a different name for this type of prospect, and it's not @((#*#*)). I call people like that educated consumers.

Consider white noise. As I refer to it, this is the noise in everyone's head, not necessarily sound but rather thoughts, ideas, concepts, past experiences and media. In fact, the media contribute most of the white noise there is. People are getting so good at overcoming this white noise that it seems as though people are often almost catatonic. They are able to function in a semi-conscious outward state. They seem to be listening and appear to be paying attention, but they are still very much catatonic.

So how do we sell to them? How do we get them to realize that what we are about to give them may change their lives forever? How do we really get through to them so that when their children want to quit a year later, they remember your conversation?

Five Ways To Sign Up The Difficult Sign Up

1. Appeal to their desires; don't necessarily sell them on you but rather on what you offer and how it will help them.

2. Listen to what they need. Don't get caught up in how good you are or how good your program or school is. Find out what you have that they need.

3. Do what is right for the student. If people can't afford your program, or seem to be telling you that they don't actually stick with things nor encourage their children to persevere, refer them to someone else. You only want serious people who are looking to give this 100%.

4. Perform diagnostic selling. This is a selling technique that basically is done backwards. Ask the prospect to tell you what he or she wants and you truly, now I mean truly, determine how your program fits into that person's needs and desires, once you have made that clear, you are well on your way to closing the sale.

5. Always know what to say; don't be caught off guard. A wary client is already on heightened alert. He or she is looking to discredit you, but it is not intentional. The person is keenly aware of all the scams and frauds out there. That type of person is not afraid to ask all the appropriate questions.

I recommend that you start to study more about sales. Read books by sales greats such as Brian Tracy, read and listen to Tony Robbins products. Anything that you can do to make yourself more educated about human nature will make you a better "connection person." When I say a better connection person, this is really what I consider myself to be. I am not a salesman, really, although in a technical sense this is a word people could use for me. What I really do is connect people to the activity that is best for them. In essence, you should be a Martial Arts matchmaker. Hey, I think I am onto something here. Match the right students to your school and you'll surely take your sales skills and your school to the next level.

What Makes Someone A Stellar Seller?
Top Sales Secrets

What is the biggest problem in any business? The answer is usually selling more products. We'd all like to have businesses where people are banging down the door to spend their money. The reality is that the better we become at selling the better our business will perform. In our economy there are many ways to sell; the soft sell, the hard sell, the puppy dog close, etc. The question is what's right for you?

How can we turn prospects into long-term customers? Here are my top ten sales tips!

How to Generate Leads

1. How to use cold calls effectively. Cold calls are not the times to make sales; rather they should be used as introductions and a way to break the ice. Don't expect to sell someone without developing some sort of connection or relationship. The first question to ask on the call is, "Is it OK if I share with you what we do and why people use us? Then, we can decide whether it makes sense to go further." Don't plead or beg. Talk to people about your benefits and ask if you can send some more information. If they seem eager to learn more from you, set up free trial classes and invite them in. Ask if they have kids or if they are interested in information relating to their personal health and safety. Send them safety tips for children and adults, and put them on your e-mail newsletter list. Get an idea of how you should categorize the household or the individual.

2. How to get past the locked door. Voice mail is today's lock on the door. The most foolproof way to leave an effective voice mail message is by establishing your credibility. Do so by referencing a referral, your research, or some newsworthy event in your school. Again sell your benefits, speak about the many people in your school who love your product, and talk about what you do. This is very important. Remember, don't push too much. Leave a friendly message and a special offer.

3. How to write a successful sales letter. Make the letter look personal, just like a letter from a friend. Or make the letter very professional so that it is noticed immediately. Most often your sales letter should back up your cold calls and help you develop those relationships. Include an article on safety or one highlighting how the Martial Arts are great for children.

4. How to generate repeat business. Our customers aren't just customers; they are the life blood of our businesses and must be treated as such. We need to keep customer service at an unimaginably high level in our industry in order for people to take notice and take us seriously. Many of us tend to neglect our businesses and the requirements of business that are important. We end up getting caught up in day-to-day activities and forget the big picture.

5. How to offer great customer service. Passionately believe in your product and your staff members. The only way you can do so is to be in a culture that supports and encourages great customer service. Everyone needs to go that extra mile. Behind every transaction there needs to be a personal relationship, and every staff member needs to work for the benefit of the company and the team.

How to Close a Sale

6. How to meet a prospect in person. If you remember only one thing, remember that the prospect is the most important person in the world. Why? Because that person believes he or she is. After all, most sales are geared toward how it will benefit the prospective customer or someone close to him or her. Isn't that why anyone buys anything? There is only one time to make a good first impression. Give your client your most undivided attention. Don't seem scattered. Don't answer your cell phone and don't let staff or anyone else interrupt you. Always ask follow-up questions, clarify what the client wants so that you understand what's being asked, and give feedback that you're listening. You don't want a second to go by where the prospect doesn't feel it was valuable spending time with you.

7. How to make your sales presentation the best ever. Whether you have one minute or one hour, always be organized. Rehearse to the point that you know your stuff cold. You should not need to hesitate or ask another person for information. You want the client to trust and hang on to your every word. You must be the consummate expert in the room. Prospects should be turning to you and joining your school because you have the information they need or the service that they want.

8. How to surpass your goals for the week, month or year. People generally sit back and relax when they've made their quota or hit a particular goal. I believe that meeting your quota should be just the starting point. An athlete can't always be in what we call "the zone," but the only way to stay on top is to continue to perform at a peak level. Star athletes will have short lived careers if they stop performing. When you think you have done enough, do some more. Your actions are much more powerful then your words. You are what you practice.

9. How to schedule your week most effectively. After each day, I spend the evening preparing for the next day. As you sit back and review your day, put the next day's schedule together. It is much easier to schedule this way that to try to schedule while you are in the midst of your day-to-day activities. Sometimes a day will get the best of you. Being prepared helps you stay productive. Every weeknight I recap and go over what I missed and goals that I didn't hit. This is the time I review and recharge. Scheduling this way will give you weekly clarity. This can also be done monthly, quarterly and yearly.

10. How to create customer loyalty above all else. Trust is one of the key components to success in any service business. A problem with our society is that there are many unprofessional individuals in business. This makes people skeptical of the professionalism of every business. Do whatever you must do to be professional at all times, to keep your promises daily, and to deserve the trust of your customers. Remember the days turn into weeks and the weeks turn into years. The main thing to remember is you are only as good as your last impression.

Making This The Best Holiday Season Ever!

Before I start giving you my positive talk, I want to fill you in on a little secret. Even for the most motivated individuals, life has its ups and downs. To give you a little insight, since last October I have been in five earthquakes, one typhoon, had a car accident and many personal struggles. I have had employees steal from me and other business problems. Of course, nothing I have experienced was as horrific as the devastation we've been witnessing on a regular basis on the nightly news. Even though my problems may not hold a candle to the things that I see, does this mean that in my life I'm not experiencing personal struggle on a regular basis. Heck no!

No matter what the situation, there are a few surefire ways to stay positive and live life with smile and a happy heart. If you follow these suggestions, you're sure to have the best holiday season ever!

1. Understanding – In theory we realize that we are not the only people in life with problems. Although we realize this, do we act on it? Sometimes no, sometimes yes! The most important thing to remember is that everyone has a reason for acting the way he or she does. During the holidays, "'tis the season, to be jolly" is a motto for many, but for others this may be a very stressful time of year. Not everyone is experiencing the holidays in the same way. For some the holidays may remind them of better times, times when loved ones were alive or times when they were happily married. All in all, you can't expect that all people will be cheerful and in a positive state of mind.

2. Realistic Expectation – One thing I learned from a very wise man is that you should never let people rent space in your head. Every time you hold a grudge, the person you are holding it against is out tap dancing. The most important thing in your life is learning not to expect others to act according to the way you act. This expectation is unrealistic. Everyone has a different genetic makeup, being raised differently and understanding things from an entirely different perspective. Just because you believe something to be so doesn't mean that others feel the same way.

3. Tolerance – The concept of tolerance has a great deal to do with understanding. Sometimes though, just understanding something doesn't make you tolerant. The thought of someone being rude to you may upset you, but the fact is, if you had a bad day and acted out of context, wouldn't you hope that someone would be tolerant of you. Of course you would! I think if we were a bit more tolerant to behaviors that we are not accustomed to, we would be in a better state of mind to handle whatever we had to face in our lives.

4. Acceptance – Imagine a world where everyone accepted one another for exactly who they are. By displaying understanding, realistic expectations, and tolerance we can accomplish exactly that. I am not saying that you need to agree with everything that goes on around you and just walk away; that itself would be an injustice. It takes a very strong person to be able to let things go and move forward. Usually what it comes down to is forgiveness.

5. Compassion – Compassion is a tool that could change the world. Just recently I was in a situation where a parent in my Martial Arts school acted rudely. He spoke badly and treated me and my staff members with disrespect, potentially throwing years of what I thought to be a good relationship out the window. Immediately I wanted to terminate our relationship for the simple reason that in the Martial Arts he breached all possible protocol. I reconsidered and decided to pocket the insult and forget the entire situation. I gave him the benefit of the doubt, and considered that he may well have been reacting to some aspect in his personal life that had no relationship to me or my school. I was just a handy target. Compassion is not easy at times and takes a great deal of practice but it is one of the most powerful tools available to us in spiritual self-defense.

Sales 101 - The Ninja Way

Today is a day to be truthful with yourself. After all, the truth is what we are all searching for. Although life at times can be difficult, it can also be rewarding as if you were the king. Sometimes all it takes is looking for the little things in life.

Just recently I read a story of a sales person who had watched a competing company's advertising campaign for approximately one year. The television ads were dynamic and the radio worked hand-in-hand with the print ads. The sales person approached the owner of the business where he worked, showed him the ads and explained how he had been following them. His boss asked what the sales person thought. After careful consideration they decided to run a similar campaign. After a few months the store owner approached the sales person and explained that they were losing a great deal of money.

The sales person was shocked and couldn't understand, so he made a bold step and went to the competition and asked them if their campaign was doing well. The competing owner explained that they were not on the same wavelength and that he didn't understand the very essence of the campaign. The sales person was quite taken back but at the same time listened intently. The store owner went on to explain that the campaign was designed for entirely different reasons: the purpose was to gather names for a mailing list to use for future sales and to sell the names to mailing houses. The ads were deceiving but had an ulterior motive. When looking at other businesses' successes, be sure to look closely. The goal in sight is not always the goal in mind.

Being a sales person is a matter of being true to yourself. Every day you make new friends, speak to people, get your point across in conversations, and in essence do some sales. For those of you who are very open to new experiences, you may meet new people and voice your opinions more openly than others. But as a sales person at some point you are selling yourself to someone. Let me be a bit clearer on what I mean.

Even going out of your way to say, "Have a nice day" is a pre-sell for another meeting; being kind is a way to help others and show them that you are a nice person. For those of you who are totally altruistic and always do kind things automatically, you are still selling something: others just don't know about it.

You may be saying to yourself that I am crazy. Why do I associate everything with sales? Well, actually, I don't. What I am saying is that everything is about communication; it is through communication that things are accomplished. The goal is to help others or to get the word out about something that can benefit mankind to help the world. I see sales as exactly that: putting people in touch with the right person, the right product, the right idea, the correct concept. I am merely a vessel to help people get what they deserve and what is beneficial to them. In my life, I see myself as a broker, not a sales person; as a connector that bridges the gap from scarcity to abundance. I do not see myself as peddling something that is not worthy, nor do I see myself as a sales person with all the negative stigmas attached to it.

Selling is a matter of connecting to people in the course of service, but it is a beneficial service to mankind.

A sale begins with the very first contact you have, the very first smile, and the immediate connection between two souls. Sales have a beginning, middle, and no end. A sale is a contact from the start to a continuing relationship.

Contract or No Contract- That is the Question

To many school owners, using contracts is the only way to do business, to others the word contract is feared like the plague. When I began teaching the Martial Arts in the early 80's the very thought of having yearly contracts was taboo. The talk amongst owners was much different back then. If you had binding agreements like health spas and clubs you were selling out as a commercial school. This mentality amazes me to this day! The truth of the matter is that if you charge a single penny for your services you are, in fact, commercial. So, why not be professional about it?

However, the question still arises in a school's business planning: Contract or no Contract. Early on in opening my schools I instituted yearly agreements. We use the word agreement because that is exactly what it is - an agreement between two people: owner and buyer. Since the word contract has a connotation that people fear, we eliminate the word entirely. Of course people are not stupid - we are not fooling them nor do we try! We are just finding a more kindly way to explain the arrangement between the school and student.

I have many competitors in my area that scream proudly in the streets each time a new student comes through their doors that they do not use contracts. Like hundreds of others that have joined my school, one mother had just come from another school and was looking into taking classes at Long Island Ninjutsu Centers.

I have to ask if you are using contracts, she said. I immediately corrected her: "agreements."

Aren't agreements a bad thing? Because the guy down the road talked about them as though they were, shouldn't I be afraid of them?

I explained to her than an agreement defines not only her responsibility as a member of my school, or parent of a member - but also defines the school's responsibility to her and her child. This not only protects the school - but the investment of her and her child's time, training and even health! She knew nothing of what an agreement represented, and my competitor had used the very fact that he didn't have them as a selling tool. At my schools we do exactly the opposite, and it is quite obvious that most cases it worked to our benefit and not his. We use yearly agreements as a selling tool - and it has indeed helped me to take my studios from 50 to well over a 1000 students in less than a decade!

Outline the student/parent commitment: As in any school, there have been students that have contemplated dropping out for one reason or another at some time. Having an agreement saves this situation. By directing the student to the billing company where they will be told that regardless of attendance the payments must continue, you have an added tool for motivation. The school owner- on the other hand- is able to reinforce the idea of continued commitment to training to the parent/student. Aside from that - what parent wants to pay for something they are not utilizing?

Even if the parent/student ultimately decides to not continue with their training, or needs to take an extended period of time from training, having an agreement helps to keep stable revenue flowing in.

Keep Your Cash Flow Stable: During the summer many people take vacations or are involved with other activities. The buyer will justify that if they are taking off two weeks for vacation, they may as well take the entire month off. We realize that breaks can de-motivate students, causing them to never return to class at all. With an agreement in place you are allowing the payments to continue even if the student or their child is not actually training. An extension of time onto the end of the agreement will allow the parent to not feel as though they are losing out on time that they are paying for!

Having an agreement guarantees steady growth, and stable income. If I have 200 students on yearly agreements then I know that 200 people are paying for their tuition. This stable income allows me to focus my energy on building onto that 200 Schools that boast of not having agreements will experience moderate to extreme fluctuations during summer, holidays, and inclement weather. Steady cash flow guarantees you the time, focus and revenue to increase enrollment and other areas of your business!

Making the decision to incorporate term agreements (contracts) into your curriculum structure can build your school's success. But once you've made the decision - how do you battle the common objections that your customers may have to signing a term enrollment?

There are many reasons that incorporating contracts, or agreements as many call them, is beneficial to you as a business owner. But in the same way those benefits may have swayed your decision to use contracts - there are many ways that signing a contract benefits the student as well, the key to overcoming the contract objection lies in how you outline and present these benefits to your members.

Understanding and Explaining the Commitment: We have all trained for many years. We made a commitment to dedicate our lives to the Martial Arts - and without that commitment we could not have achieved our goals. We need to show the student or parent that as instructors we are committed to helping them or their child achieve greater discipline, control, respect and ultimately their Black Belt. Realistically we will be helping them find solutions to the needs that made them look to the martial arts in the first place. This is essential in getting people into agreements.

Consider this - how many public or private schools in the educational system that you know of would allow you to sign up on a month to month basis? The very reason that you sign into a year of tuition is not only for the benefit of the school- but the school also has a commitment to the children that are attending. The Martial Arts also educates and builds a future. It is our responsibility to break this misconception and underscore the life lessons that we are instilling! If a parent/student came to you with a specific need and goal, then a commitment of 1 or more years is an answer to that need - and the only reasonable solution.

Ask yourself - how much do you believe in committing to the growth of your business? With that growth you become a better martial arts instructor and are able to help more students. As you grow you will see the student population grow and you will also see the students stick around a great deal longer, and the contract objection become far less.

Show Them The Money - Many people speak of their enrollment cost in terms of monthly payment. By changing your perspective, the breakdown of your program cost, and laying this out clearly for the member there is a financial benefit to signing a term enrollment with your school.

Here are a few ways to place a price incentive into place for term enrollments:
Waive or Lower Your Registration Fee for Term Enrollment - If you are not currently charging a registration fee, put one into place for those who are interested in month to month payments. This technique is often used in health clubs to encourage patrons to

sign onto longer term contracts. A significant initial savings will appeal to those with tight budgets.

Place Financial Incentives On Longer Term Contracts - Creating a significant savings for a longer term commitment will appeal to a buyer's checkbook. You can achieve this by lowering or increasing your monthly payments by even as little as $5 per month. In length of term a six month agreement is a savings of $30, a twelve month term $60. When compared to one another there is a pertinent amount saved!

Reconsider Your Payment Terminology - Something as simple as changing your explanation of payments can outline the savings that your member enjoys. Stop thinking of your curriculum in terms of monthly payment amount - and instead discuss it in program cost. For example - instead of saying: classes here at All American Martial Arts are $79 per month. Say: A six month program here costs $474.00 plus the $79 registration fee.

By changing your vernacular you are further outlining the financial benefit for the student or parent.

The truth in the contract objection lies in the uncertainty of the member: I'm not sure Johnny will want to continue, or I'm not sure I will like the classes. By having an exciting intro process and curriculum you are overcoming that first hurdle - but outlining the benefits of a commitment and guaranteeing them a savings for a longer term commitment are sure-fire ways to appeal to their needs. Having the billing company there to play bad cop and reinforce their commitment should any challenges arise doesn't hurt either!

Phone Calls and Intro Classes: Making the Numbers Work for You

The Tip: Finalize your trial class numbers - Compile an accurate list of all the people who booked trial classes this past year. Be sure to note who attended their appointments, and who enrolled.

The details: Many school owners assume that they are currently tracking these numbers at their schools, or that these items are not important enough to be considered a top priority. I must stress that these numbers represent crucial building blocks for your school. Without accurately knowing where you stand, your perception of the areas in your school that need the most immediate focus can get clouded, allowing important sectors of your business to begin sliding, and students to slip through the cracks.

Let's assume that you run a school with over two hundred students. You are not tracking enrollment stats, but you believe that you are consistently enrolling new students each month, and that your school is prospering and doing well. However, when you sit down and analyze the numbers you find that your enrollment in January of whatever year is the same as your enrollment was in January of the prior year. To make matters worse, your attrition rate has also stayed consistent throughout the year. In reality, your school has not experienced a bit of growth the entire year!

In my journey through the consulting world I have seen this happening in schools across the country! This type of stagnancy in a school can be avoided by tracking the statistics of almost every aspect of your school.

The following numbers should be compiled in weekly, monthly, quarterly and yearly increments:

Phone calls - Not only do you want to track all incoming phone calls and their sources, but you also want to track the time received, who took the call, and whether the call resulted in a trial class. All of these details are of equal importance.

1) Tracking Incoming Calls and Source - Knowing how many calls you are receiving and their sources allows you to analyze the marketing that you are currently utilizing. If you are not receiving a large number of calls you may need to step up your marketing in general. If most callers indicate one particular source of marketing, you may want to eliminate other marketing ventures that are not paying off.

2) Time of Phone Call- Tracking the trends of the times that your phones are busiest will allow you to organize your schedule to accommodate the trends. If you are receiving most of your calls when you do not have sufficient phone coverage, you should rearrange your schedule or assign a staff member to those particular times. If your calls are going to voice mail, by the time that you retrieve them and return the calls there's a great possibility prospects have scheduled trial classes or joined another school!

3) Staff Member Who Took the Call- Simply put: while tracking this information you may learn that a particular staff member has not scheduled any trial classes. You then know you need to provide that staff member with training in how to encourage prospects to schedule trial classes!

By analyzing these items, you can see the important part that each of these pieces of information plays in your success! These numbers are just the first step. To gain an even more solid grasp on where your school currently stands, it's important to uncover how these numbers correlate to your intro appointments.

Paying close attention to your phone call statistics is a great way to keep a finger on the pulse of your school, and also to redirect your focus. Once you begin analyzing the details of your calls, the next step is to take a hard look at your intro appointment and enrollment statistics.

We will now decipher which intro appointment statistics are important to trap, and why. We will also discuss how to translate these numbers into higher enrollment and better retention!

Trial Classes - Once you have a handle on phone call statistics you can begin breaking down information regarding your trial classes.

1) Percent of Callers Scheduling Trial Classes - Compiled per staff member answering calls, this number will indicate the effectiveness of each staff member at converting the phone calls. Any weaknesses that you identify will give you an opportunity to revise your training and systems for turning phone calls into solid prospects.

2) Trial Classes Attended - Take a close look at the number of people who scheduled trial classes who did or did not attend. If you see a large number of unattended trial class appointments, then you may need to implement more confirmation systems. Confirming intro class appointments gives you an opportunity not only to remind the interested parties of their scheduled appointments, but also to re-schedule should they indicate that they could not attend.

3) Intro to Student Ratios - This information directly relates to improving your sales systems and sales staff in the same way that knowing which staff member receives calls can pinpoint a training weakness. These numbers are also vital when you have different program options for students to choose from. Again, knowing who closed the sale is important to enable you to track whether a staff member does well at selling a particular program. If one person seems to primarily sell short-term programs, you will need to educate and train that staff member on the methods of selling longer terms.

Breaking Down Your Memberships

Having a variety of membership types and programs at your school can be effective in appealing to prospects with a broad range of interest levels and budgets. Keeping detailed information about each of these programs and their enrollment numbers allows you to build more quality into popular programs, to work to increase interest in lagging programs and to eliminate those that are slowing down the momentum of your school.

The Tip: Determine the Makeup of Your Class Roster - If you have a variety of membership options, list the students you have enrolled in every program. Also, list the ages and the ranks of the students and the duration of training they have had in particular programs. Note also the students who have stopped training in your programs.

The Details - Why are these numbers and statistics so important? This information is precisely how I took my school from 300 to 450 students. About five years ago, my top black Belt instructors and I looked carefully at the student actively on our roster, the students' current ranks, their ages and how long they had been training. We realized that the majority of our students were brand new. Again, this information was not obvious before we got it down on paper!

By further inspection we determined that the majority of the students who were leaving were quitting at yellow belt, about four months into their training. The next biggest loss was within our blue to purple belt level – approximately three to four years into training. When we looked further at our Brown Belt numbers we realized that they were practically non-existent.

My staff and I put our heads together to determine what steps we could take to stop this from happening.

Get to the Bottom of "Why"- We polled our student base, even students who had left our school, and asked them to tell us honestly why they had quit. Through this information we learned that many of our students were losing interest in the program due to its intensity and the lack of consistent motivation.

Build The Resolution- To overcome this objection, we immediately instituted a belt striping system and cut our Black Belt course back from seven years to five. The result: Our retention went through the roof! Our students were remaining well past the milestones that we had previously seen, and many were achieving Black Belts. We now have many actively training black belts and on average we are promoting 30 to 40 new Black Belts every year!

The moral of this story is as much in the diagnosis as it is in the analysis that we used to get there. Without taking a hard look at the numbers we could not have seen the gaps in our process. Keeping a close eye on your enrollment trends can increase retention more drastically than you would imagine!

Utilizing "Business Appreciation" As a Source of Referrals

At our schools we enlist many different areas of the community as sources for referrals. Although our students and their families and friends are the largest contributors to our success with referrals, there are numerous other sources of referral revenue that can easily be tapped into. When looking for other sources, I encourage you to reach out to your community for additional support for your business.

One way to build community support is by developing connections to businesses local to your school. The goal is to establish reciprocal relationships where you contribute to one another's success by buying products and by fostering relationships with each other's customers.

Supporting Local Businesses

Patronize Local Businesses to Outfit Your School - The first step in building relationships that are conducive to increasing referrals is by using local businesses' services for the needs of your school. For example, use local pizza parlors to supply the pizzas for each of your birthday parties, and local party supply stores for your birthday party supplies. Become familiar with the employees in all of the establishments that you patronize, introduce yourself to the managers, and let them know that you intend to patronize their businesses continuously.

Building relationships this way will allow you further access to the customers of each business. Having a professional relationship with the owners and managers will make them more likely to get creative when it comes to using their consumer base as a source of referrals.

Provide Local Businesses with Gift Certificates Discounting Your Services - Approach businesses within your community and offer them $200 gift certificates toward your school's services for their employees and for their elite customers. Distributing these gift certificates to employees will not only enhance their employees' income, but will also show that they care about the employees' health and fitness. Rewarding loyal customers with these gift certificates is also a great way for the businesses to encourage on-going use of their services!

It is important to coach the participating business owners, and to define both your intentions and expectations when you give them the gift certificates. In order for you to enlist their influence as additional outlets for referrals, they need to have a grasp of your school and the benefits and programs that you can provide to their employees and customers.

Imagine the impact this program can have on your enrollment! If every pizza that the local pizza parlor sells includes a gift certificate valued at $200 for martial arts classes, you potentially can reach hundreds of people in a very short time!

The business owners offering your gift certificate have the benefit of providing their customers with something of value, and you have access to a community of people who may never have taken advantage of your school!

The business owners need to be committed to your mutual goals, so that they actively distribute your gift certificates (rather than just leaving them sitting on the counters). However, they may not feel comfortable explaining the benefits of your school, or perhaps are not confident that all of their employees can do so. Provide them with a simple letter to use with the gift certificate to help to alleviate this concern, and to lessen the time that they might have to take away from their busy days to explain the purpose of their gifts.

The following is a sample letter that can be used by businesses wishing to offer additional incentives to their employees. You may customize this letter to fit the needs of the participating businesses, and your school:

Sample Letter:

Dear Valued Associate;

As an employer, J. Wigets strives to create a professional, personally challenging, and rewarding work environment. We are committed to delivering the highest possible wages, top quality benefits, and any additional perks and incentives we can. We believe that a healthy associate is a happy associate.

Studies have shown that people who participate in health-related activities enjoy increased energy, sharper focus, and higher confidence levels than the average person. In addition, we have found that the level of stress is reduced. A martial arts program can provide all of these benefits. We believe that not only will you receive the benefits listed above but also that you will learn to protect yourself and your family. That's a benefit you cannot put a price tag on. The martial arts teaches its students to have a positive attitude, and to set and achieve physical, mental, and spiritual goals.

In an effort to help you, our most valuable asset, create a healthier, safer, more success-oriented way of life for yourself and the ones you love, J. Wigets has secured an exclusive one month membership for you and one family member, to an award winning local martial arts studio. This one-month program is valued at $99, so by taking advantage of this great opportunity for yourself and any other member of your family; you will be receiving $198 worth of benefits at NO COST to you.

You can activate the free membership by contacting (martial arts school) at the number listed below. We hope you will take advantage of this incredible offer, and enjoy all the benefits of being an integral part of our winning team.

Sincerely,

Store Manager
J. Wigets

By utilizing an idea such as this one, not only are you building networking relationships within your community, but you are also creating new opportunities to make a positive impact on the people who live and work around you!

Four Tips for Selling Better by Phone

Phone calls can be used with great success to line up new members and to keep existing members coming back for more. You may want to call prospects who filled out questionnaires or left their names and numbers in a lead box. You may want to obtain a list of customers of related businesses (purchasers at sports equipment stores, buyers of health foods or mail-order vitamins) and call them about joining your school. And you may want to contact your existing members who are not signed up for auto-renewal to encourage them to "re-up." Whatever the purpose of your calls, there are some time-proven strategies that will help you make the calls as successful as they can be.

Here are four tips to help you sell better by phone:

1. Control the Conversation
It's up to you to control the conversation. While you should never interrupt the other person when he or she is speaking, you need to be able to regain control when you are interrupted. Once the person has stopped speaking, make a statement reviewing what you said before the interruption, and then continue. You can say "Yes, that's a good point. As I had mentioned before..." and continue with your presentation. But remember that whatever the called person has to say is most important to you, because it gives you insight into what he or she is thinking. Somewhere in your presentation, you should address whatever the prospect brought up.

2. Use the "Rule of Three"
Psychologists tell us that a message is more firmly embedded in the mind when it is repeated three times. If you can present your benefit to your listener three times in succession, it will have more impact. When listeners hear, three times, how they are going to benefit, the idea has a greater chance of sticking. See, it just happened!

3. Avoid the "Send Literature" Stall
We've all used the "Send me some information on that." stall when we don't want to talk on the phone to someone who is trying to sell a product or service. When you're the caller and you're confronted by a prospect who asks for literature to be sent in the mail, respond with one of the following:
"I will. Let's talk further about which points you want more information on."
"I can do that. And here are some points that are best explained while we're still on the phone." "I do have a lot of material I can send. Let's narrow it down so you don't waste time reading a lot of stuff that doesn't pertain to you."

4. Know When to Retreat!
You're not going to be successful on every call. It's good to know when to cut your losses. End a call as soon as you've determined there is no potential. Usually, if the prospect shows no interest after two or three attempts to generate some positive response to what you're saying, you can be pretty sure that you will not be able to sell

to this person. Thank the person for his or her time, and offer a telephone number so the person can get more information in the future if he or she becomes interested. (You might also want to develop a program where, as a last resort, you give the person a special promotion code to use within a certain amount of time (one to two months?) for a free trial lesson.) This will help maintain a positive attitude and give you more time to spend with interested prospects.

Calling prospects and members is an easy and economical way to sell your services. Just remember to stay in control of the conversation, to repeat your message so it's remembered, to avoid delaying tactics, and to concentrate on those calls that have a chance of becoming sales.

Chapter 12
Developing Rules for your business

Why Should It Be Any Different In Martial Arts Schools?

Redskins Get Dressing Down

Redskins' running back Clinton Portis and safety Sean Taylor were fined by the NFL for uniform violations in a Sunday night game against the Eagles. Portis was fined $20,000 for wearing black shoes, which did not match the rest of the team, and for wearing striped socks and an unapproved eye shield. Taylor was fined $5,000 for wearing striped socks.

I have found it necessary to talk to my students about the same kind of issues, without the fines of course. At L.I. Ninjutsu Centers it is mandatory for students to wear complete uniforms. Our uniform includes a kimono style top and bottom called a "GI." Underneath, a student must wear a school t-shirt with our emblem, and shorts underneath the pants, also with our emblem. We also require our boys and men to wear groin protectors, and for all students to wear the footwear known to the Ninja as "Tabi." These Tabi are a split toe shoe and are a must for all Ninja enthusiasts.

At this point some of you are saying, "Wow! That is a lot of stuff." If you think about it, it's not that much to ask of the students. Think about hockey and the amount of gear a person needs to buy to play that sport.

When traveling around the country teaching seminars, I notice many schools with students who wear whatever they want. In the Brazilian Jiu Jitsu community, many students wear patches and slogans from sports companies. Usually the patches represent sponsorship, but now it is becoming a *fashion statement* to wear such patches. In our school we believe in showing individualism through expression and technique, not clothing. So it is very important for our students and parents to realize that the way a student wears the uniform is the first expression of responsibility and respect. As in any private educational facility, students have a mandatory uniform. If students don't wear the uniform, then they get penalized in some way, either through detention or not being able to attend school. I once had a young boy student who attended Catholic school and had a ponytail. The school asked him to cut his hair. The parents refused, so the school refused to allow him to attend. We feel strongly about our need to enforce our rules as well.

Studies have shown that school uniforms reduce gang activity as well as bullying within schools. Sometimes children are ostracized for being different because of the clothes they wear. Schools that have instituted uniforms have found less trouble overall.

We believe that if students are not in full uniform then they are unprepared. If they are unprepared in this way once or twice, it may be a fluke, but we look at three or more occurrences as a flagrant disregard for authority and respect. It shows that the students do not agree with our teachings, and also shows us that they incorrectly believe that the small things are not important.

Some people say, "Well it doesn't matter too much to me, why is it a big deal?" The answer is that if a rule is established then it must be abided by. The reason behind the rule may not be clear, or, in fact, the rule may be totally arbitrary, but the school has the right to establish the rule and the right to expect that people attending the school adhere to it. In the ancient world of Martial Arts, a student could be "Hammoned" (Japanese word) kicked out of a school for not listening to the teacher. Many of us, as Martial Artists, explain until we are blue in the face, often to the point of excess. Yet some people still don't listen. Why? I think it is often a lack of communication. In a small number of cases, it is a way for the students to try to push the boundaries and bend the rules. In any case, if you show students that disregarding rules is not proper protocol and is disrespectful, usually they will abide.

Here are some of the reasons behind the uniform:

1. The keiko gi: The traditional uniform of Japan, the keiko gi is formal wear used by many Martial Artists. Once worn under the kimono, it was considered underwear, but most Budokas (Martial Artists) practiced in it. The clothing that you wear in the school no matter whether you are very traditional or not so traditional reflects on your status and commitment. It is similar to how you decide what to wear to work, where your boss may require you to dress in a particular manner. You are probably required to look neat, to wear no clothing that would offend anyone, and depending on your level of responsibility, even to wear a jacket and tie.

In my schools, if even one piece is missing from the uniform, it is an infraction. I always tell my students that I would never wear a ballet uniform to a football game, nor would I wear a baseball helmet to a football game. One does not go with the other. Just one missing piece makes you unprepared.

2. The reason for under clothing: The t-shirt and the shorts are made to absorb sweat. They also serve a second purpose. The sports short – compression shorts are actually good for you. Most professional basketball players wear these for the protection of their muscles. Full underwear is also important if we take time in class to jog. Students who don't wear underwear as part of their complete uniform are unprepared.

Now let's look at an entirely different aspect of the uniform, the benefit to your school:

Branding! If you are not currently branding your school's name and asking your students to display it everywhere they go, then you are missing the boat. It is imperative to stress pride in your school and in your students' accomplishments in your school. In my schools we sell approximately 500 - 1,000 shirts per year. Students should be proud to wear your school colors. The question to ask yourself is, if they are buying clothing that displays logos, shouldn't they buy it from your school? It is a lot better for them to be wearing your logo then the logo of some far off brand that means nothing to you or to them. Not only does it provide advertising but it also connects the students to the school.

Envision, looking out at a sea of students, all of them dressed identically and looking neat, clean and sharp. When the next prospect walks through your door, he or she will take notice of your students and be impressed with the school. It will look like the scene from "Enter the Dragon" with Bruce Lee.

Rules Apply to all aspects of your school

Even though we have discussed previously the rules of uniforms, many other rules must be put in place to keep your school from Chaos and Anarchy. For each policy within your school you should have a specific standard set of rules to apply to each situation. For example: Make up Policies, what have you establish when a student misses a certain amount of classes within their contract period or training month. Do you just extend the period of time forward into the future beyond the term of the agreement, allowing them time to make up the lost classes? Or are you specific in regards to this, stating you can only make up classes within the period time in the year you are currently paying for?

Question like these arise continuously in a martial arts school. So for every system or program in your school you should predetermine the policy that you will have in effect. Remember, retail stores have a specific return policy. If the client returns the item purchased within 5 days they get a full refund, if they do it after the 5 days they receive a store credit. It is essential to be prepared with this information so you do not have to fall back on your immediate decision. It is also imperative so you do not treat one client differently than the next.

Chapter 13
Ending on a good note
What happens when you are done?

Dressing Your Business Up For Sale
By Mel H. Abraham, CPA, CVA, ABV, ASA

It has been said that more than eighty percent of businesses FAIL to make it to the next generation. Others are sold under duress because of health issues, divorce, disputes, business slow down and death. A business sold under these conditions does not typically return the highest value.

How do you avoid these results? The answer is *preparation*. The quality of the preparation determines the quality of the results. What preparation involves is a combination of dynamic and subtle factors, many of which are obvious but often are overlooked.

Perhaps the most difficult decision a business owner needs to make is the decision to sell. Unfortunately, many owners agonize over the many variables involved in selling without ever making the decision to sell. Others will wait too long to sell, and a large group feel they cannot afford to sell their only source of income.

Poor health, divorce, slumping sales, creditor demands, poor employee relations, lack of operating or expansion capital are often the symptoms of an owner who should have sold but failed to heed "early warning signals." Indecision, or lack of proper planning and preparation, can prove to be very costly to the business owner, but also to the family, employees, vendors and customers.

When an owner understands where the business is today, he or she can better envision what it could be tomorrow. Finding the right buyer starts with a review of *where* the business is and what the business is. Ideally, a buyer will have talents and skills that compliment the current owner's. It is imperative to the continued health of the business (or the improved health, in some cases) that a successor appreciates, and is able to maintain, the strengths already inherent in the business. The best way to insure this is if the owner recognizes the strengths and works out a sale to build upon the strong points. Additionally, both buy and sell sides may be motivated by personal, rather than purely financial, factors.

Buyers look for businesses they can make their own. That is why, as one of the first steps in preparation for sale, the owner must attempt to identify the ideal successor. A buyer wants the opportunity to take ownership in both the concrete and emotional sense, to improve the business and to make money.

Financial data alone will not allow buyers to recognize the full opportunity a business represents. Actually, financial statements and tax returns for most small and private businesses are more like mystery novels. They certainly are not operating manuals. Tax returns seldom highlight the opportunities a business represents.

Financial statements alone may not sell a business, no matter how profitable they indicate a business is or has been. What will clinch the sale is the opportunity the business represents. Do not assume that the "numbers" accurately reflect the opportunity presented by the business. Remember, proven money may only be a secondary motivation, while the prospect of capitalizing upon opportunities may be a buyer's primary motivation.

Finding a buyer is relatively easy. In fact, everyone "has a buyer." People interested in buying companies hire firms to search for companies being offered, network actively with lawyers, accountants, bankers and others searching for businesses for sale. The typical aggressive buyer will look at scores of companies, make several offers and still be looking for a company. What really is going on is that many of the businesses being offered have not been adequately prepared for sale or are positioned as less than attractive opportunities, and many of the buyers are going after companies that are totally wrong for them.

Finding the right buyer for a business can be time consuming and frustrating. When a business demands your full time and attention, and its sale is important, professional assistance may be a wise consideration. Obtaining assistance may be a necessity if maintaining confidentiality is important.

Information about how, and to whom, one should sell a company is available from many sources: newspapers, movies, television and hearsay. Unfortunately, these sources often provide information that is misleading, inappropriate and wrong, particularly when applied to small or mid-size companies. These sources often relate information about sales of large public companies. The process depicted does not at all relate to smaller private companies. There is a world of difference between the large, public companies and small, private ones. No one person owns a large, public company; many shareholders do. Public company accounting focuses on maximizing profits both to satisfy shareholders demands and to allow management to retain their jobs. The emphasis is on maximizing shareholder value in the public domain. Private company accounting focuses on *minimizing* profits to reduce the owner's tax bill in order to maximize the owner's wealth.

Private company owners are not concerned with such issues as hostile takeovers, junk bonds, P/E ratios, or loss of a job because the company did not show appropriate profits in recent quarters. Most business theorists agree that there are major differences in management convention and culture between private and public companies. Because virtually no public information is available regarding the sale process and selling prices of private companies, many business owners, and their advisors, attempt to apply public company methodology and Price/Earnings ratios to the sale process of private companies. This is a mistake.

Surprisingly, financial results are not the most important factor driving a small company's value in the eyes of the potential buyer. Therefore, knowing your customer must be the driving force! The person, or firm, recognizing the highest value in your business will pay the highest price. To identify the best buyer or customer for a business, the owner must first understand both objective and subjective elements about the company. How does the company appear to those looking in from the outside? To whom will the problems appear as merely valuable and exciting opportunities?

The value of a company lies in the buyer's view of its future. Financial results reflect only the past.

Most likely successor identification should be the first item on a list of important information that an owner can use to drive a company's value. Unfortunately, this information usually does not receive the attention it deserves. This is understandable since few of us are able to objectively view ourselves, our businesses, or anything else we are very close and emotionally involved with. Also, business owners and most advisors, although immersed in the business climate, are not familiar with driving marketplace forces or the various types and categories of buyers operating therein.

Potential and opportunity are obvious factors that must be on everyone's list. But what is opportunity? Opportunity is different from potential. Buyers will pay for opportunity but not for potential. Why? Opportunity is perceived as having been created by the business owner and potential is that which will be created by the acquirer. Buyers will not pay you for what they will do (potential). They will pay for what you have done (opportunity). Perception of opportunity will vary depending on the type of buyer viewing it, which makes clear the critical need to know your customer.

Profits factor high on most buyers' lists of important factors. Since most private companies' financial statements are driven by the owners' desire to minimize taxes, reported earnings are usually misleading. The numbers alone, even after recasting or normalizing, will not adequately reflect a firm's true value. The value of a company lies in a buyer's view of its future. It is one of your jobs as the owner of the business and the seller to make the potential of your business very clear to the prospective buyer.

Summary

Face the reality that both owners and businesses are constantly changing. Eventually the needs and requirements of a business will conflict with an owner's lifestyle needs, perspectives and abilities.

Obtaining the best results begins with a timely decision to start planning and preparing. Before an owner acts, he or she should have a plan. To formulate the very best plan an owner needs to know what the business requires of its succession management. The owner should know what the company is worth and that the timing is right. He or she must identify the attributes of a likely successor, the type who will recognize the full opportunity that has been created, will pay the optimum purchase price, and will move the company up to the next level of profitability.

Ultimately, one of two paths will be taken by every business owner looking to sell. Either the succession of the business will be a planned event controlled by the owner, or it will be an unplanned occurrence brought about by outside factors. For the good of the owner, the business, the employees, customers, vendors and family, it is better for the owner to take the initiative and control the process.

2005 Mel H. Abraham, CPA, CVA, ABV, ASA – all rights reserved

Mel H. Abraham is one of the nation's most recognized and highly sought after financial experts (CPA) and a very successful entrepreneur/investor with multiple businesses. Regularly called upon as a forensic expert in financial and valuation issues, he is also a nationally recognized and award-winning speaker having addressed professional conferences on a local, state and national level. Mel's two-fold forte is in providing strategies in financial risk management and in personal/physical, threat management and self protection. His clients span the country.

He has received numerous speaking awards and authored numerous articles. His authoritative book, *Valuation Issues and Case Law Update—A Reference Guide*, has been released in a 4th edition. Recently, he was co-author of the business valuation industry's best selling book, *Financial Valuation: Applications and Models*, released by John Wiley and Sons, Inc. and two additional books *A Healthier You*, (with Deepak Chopra and Billy Blanks) released in October 2005 and *Masters on Success*, (with Ken Blanchard, Jack Canfield and John Christensen) to be released by the end of 2005.
Mel holds the AICPA specialty designation of Accredited in Business Valuation (ABV), is an Accredited Senior Appraiser (ASA) with the American Society of Appraisers, and is a Certified Valuation Analyst (CVA) with the National Association of Certified Valuation Analysts as well as a member of the esteemed National Speakers Association. He has a Bachelors of Science Degree from California State University, Northridge.

Chapter 14
Income Generators
To tip the scales in your favor

The Ultimate in Promotion: The Birthday Party!

Years ago, I would have out-and-out refused the concept of having a birthday party or any kind of party in my Martial Arts school. It went against all that I thought was pure in the Martial Arts. I am sure there are still some people who think of this activity as another way to sell out and not really teach pure Martial Arts. I can see them now doing the "quote" thing with their hands while saying "McDojo." I am a "Ninja." I know even people in Japan giggle when you say that, but for the last 25 years of my life I have been practicing the art of Ninjutsu. I was the fourth highest-ranking student under the Grandmaster in the art I studied for years. The reason I tell you this is that Ninja are known for having influenced situations in history. While reviewing all the silly reasons I thought birthday parties were bad, I realized that I could utilize this activity to gain new students and influence many lives that I may never have otherwise been able to reach. In essence, doing so equates to practicing my Ninja skills.

I have found through the years that our parties are a great way to generate new students. They also are a way for us to reach existing students and their parents subtly and to get a message to them that the martial arts are a positive thing. So if you are having second thoughts about allowing birthday parties in your school, then think no more. Birthday parties will allow you to provide a quality service with many benefits not only to your students but also to the general public.

Here are some facts about birthday parties organized in our schools:

1) The person having the party does not need to be a student. Anyone can arrange to hold a party. In fact, we market this activity to the general public.

2) Birthday parties are only one kind of party that we offer. It could be a general party, one that I will describe later as our Party Lotto.

3) We have different levels of birthday parties and Party Lotto's.

4) Parties are not only student generators; they are also retention tools and a ways to bring extra income into the school.

Question: What do we do in a party?

Answer: A birthday party in my organization is in reality a class. The class consists of many different Martial Arts activities. So it is a reflection of what you teach in your classes. You should make the audience watching aware of that fact. As you teach, turn to the parents and explain that this is a great way for you to build the students' confidence as well as get them to focus better at home and at school. Did I mention it would be best if the students of not only the party host are there but also the guests? You want to pique an interest in the person in charge of signing the student up.

Question: How do I make money on parties?

Answer: The answer is simple; you charge somewhat more that all other party places are charging. Why do I say more? We are not the average everyday party experience. We are highly trained and we have so much more to offer to the partygoers. We have different levels to our parties and charge according to the service provided. We also provide goody bags, invitations and a t-shirt for the party person.

If you think about what parties at other places cost, you'll see that charging a little more for yours is still a great deal. A party at an ice cream parlor can easily run you $700, and what you're paying for is a few games and do-it-yourself ice cream sundaes. You're offering partygoers an opportunity to sample the martial arts, and to embark on an experience that will positively influence their lives.

Question: Am I selling out if I do parties? They are a headache and a big mess, plus, I just don't feel comfortable doing them.

Answer: These are all legitimate questions and easily can give you away to talk yourself out of doing them. My question to you is, isn't it worth bringing in people as well as providing your students with a service? After all, if they are going to pay someone, it might as well be you. Plus, you get to share the martial arts lessons with the people attending. I know that if someone asked me if I would be willing to teach a class for 20 to 30 kids for free for one or two hours, I would do it in a heartbeat. So now if you equate the party to a class that you are being paid for, you would probably say, "Of course I would do it."

Question: What is a Party Lotto or as we also call it The "Un-Birthday?"

Answer: Our Party Lotto is a free giveaway of parties. We have found that parties actually cost us only about $75 dollars. This includes paying one or two instructors and the pizza. So my staff and I came up with this innovative concept and we asked ourselves, what better way to get 20 people in a trial class for that low cost? It's the cheapest marketing I ever did. The only condition is that all the guests other then the person who is having the party must be non-members. We actually call students and offer them chance to win free parties to invite their friends to at our dojo. And in reality, everyone who chooses to play "wins" the free party. Each party includes food, drinks, fun and games. Not everyone accepts the offer; it is hard for some people to envision holding a party for no particular reason, especially a free party for no reason. But there are some who accept it without a question. They love the idea and have a great time.

Question: How long are the parties and do you have upgrades or how do you do upgrades?

Answer: Our parties start at a minimum of one and one-half hours and go on up to two and one half hours. In that time period we do 55 minutes of class for the shorter parties and 75 minutes for the longer ones. We teach the basics of the martial arts and do fun drills with the attendees. We also may have the person who is hosting the party do a demonstration, to highlight the party-giver. In the smallest party package, when we are done doing our part of the party, the parents step up and do all the food. The parents are in charge of serving, cleaning and containing and controlling the children. We stand by ready to spring into action if need be. Some of our other parties include a demonstration by our demo-team as well as a free private lesson, including food and clean up.

If parties are not looking good to you as of yet, think about all the income you could be making. If you charge just $275 per party and you do two per weekend, on the average of three weekends per month, you have the potential to make $19,800 per year in added income, not to mention the potential new students and the synergy it builds within your school. That is equivalent to having 20 more students in your school, not bad, right? Of course not.

Here's how we market our parties:

1) We do three-month mailing cycles. Each student that has a birthday coming up gets a flyer starting four months in advance of his or her birthday. Remember, parties are something that parents plan far in advance. So if the birthday is in April, we mail a flyer to the student in January, then another in February, and another in March. This insures that each student gets three flyers or advertisements ahead of time. We call the student as well.

2) We put a beautiful three-fold color flyer in all the local stores and children's shops, increasing awareness of the service that we offer. Information about parties is also on our website.

3) We advertise our Party Lotto by sending out letters geared toward the winning of a lotto prize. It makes the clients feel like the have been chosen and won the grand prize.

4) We include the "Birthday Party" flyer in our "Welcome to the Family" package in which, during month one, we explain our "Taking it to the Next Level" program. We also include it in all of our promotional information the day of testing or promotion.

I wish you the best of luck incorporating the birthday party into your martial arts curriculum.

Remember if a Ninja can do it, so can you. Go for it!

The Un-Birthday Party

Here is the concept: you are the Mad Hatter at the tea party, you are deciding what rabbit hole to jump into, and along comes Allie Alberigo with another one of his fandangled ideas. Are you ready? *Here we go!*

Birthday parties are a great source of income generation, as well as leads. Have you ever thought of staging an "Un-birthday" party?" Here is the concept:

Take all students who are from the age of four years old on up to adult and print a list. Then pick 10 per month from the list and give them a call. Offer them a free Martial Arts party - in my case the Ninja Party or the Un-Birthday Party. Let them know that there are no hidden gimmicks, no hidden fees; you just want to give them a free party and in the process introduce their friends to the Martial Arts. The only requirement is that they invite at least 15 to 20 people who are not members of the school and who will come to their party. Guests will get one hour of fun, exciting Martial Arts lessons, free pizza and natural drinks, as well as a one month pass.

When it is a children's party you should try to have most guests come with their parents. If some parents can't accompany their children, they must still fill out a permission sheet and a short questionnaire in order for their children to attend. This will cover any liability issues, and will allow you to e-mail parents six months of free of safety tips (or other useful materials) and also to call them periodically to see if they would like to have their children join your school. If party attendees like, they can utilize the month-free pass. If they call within one week of the party, they receive a free uniform along with the free month of lessons.

Goals:

1. Non-members try out your school
2. Non-members get a free month pass
3. Existing students get a free gift and in appreciation for being a student
4. You build a family synergy and gain added communications with parents to explain your referral program to them in more detail

Outcome:

1. You have six parties per month with 20 guests each - totaling 120 trial classes per month

2. You do group class intros, saving you loads of time

3. You do group enrollments for adult attendees or parents of child attendees - hopefully resulting in sign-ups

4. You gain access to parents and potential students via e-mail and communicate with them on a regular basis for the next six months. These communications will enable you to earn their trust so that they either enroll or refer someone else.

5. You give away free memberships to your existing students who hold parties whenever a party results in you signing up five new members (this comes directly from my referral program on takingittothenextlevel.com).

Why is the Un-Birthday Party a great concept? It has a winning outcome for everyone. The attendees have fun and learn about the Martial Arts, your students benefit when their parties give you referrals, you benefit from receiving the referrals and giving the trial classes. Also you gain access to a huge database of interested people through your safety tips e-mailings- helping the community and possibly gaining more students in the future.

I hope this was exciting enough for you to see that there is so much you can achieve with simple little programs like this. It can become a central component of your referral and marketing campaigns. You may be able to change your entire school with this one little idea, yourself.

Chapter 15
Building your empire
Become a Real Estate Entrepreneur

My initial journey into real estate

I began my quest to be a real estate entrepreneur at the age of 17. At that time my Martial Arts instructor was my boss in a job unrelated to the Martial Arts. This situation was unique. I started working for him and his brother as a sales clerk in a video store. This was one of the only two jobs I had working for someone as an employee. People used to pay hundreds of dollars to become members and have the privilege to rent videos. Can you believe it, actually paying money to allow you to pay more money to rent videos? Well, I was the top sales person in the store and later became the manager at 17. Remember I said that the owner was my Martial Arts teacher? Well each and every day was a lesson. We would do class during downtime and it was fun, almost like Kato in the Pink Panther except it was always me on the receiving end.

One day my boss approached me and asked if I would be interested in starting a string of companies. I of course jumped on it, with all the trust in the world. After a year of working 90 - 100 hours per week or more, we decided to buy a home. My investment was to defer my salary and all the money would be put into this house. So I did. Working hard, we bought and renovated a house. After all was said and done, my instructor moved into the home with his wife and that is where it all fell apart. All my money and hard work was basically stolen. That is when I learned not to trust blindly and to look for red flags.

I next started my own landscape construction business and for 15 years learned everything I could about business. I started training with a new teacher and embarked on an entirely new era in my life.

I bought my next home at the age of 21. This was my primary place of residence as I moved out of my parents' home. The interesting thing was I remember paying an interest rate of 17%. Imagine! I purchased that house for $127,000 and later sold it for $185,000. Now it's worth $350,000.00. I wish I had held onto it!

So the "adventures" of the Martial Arts entrepreneur had begun. At the present time, in 2006, I own residential and commercial properties. And I own three out of the four locations that house my schools.

My Philosophy and Business Plan

My goal is to own all the real estate that houses my schools. I currently have four schools on Long Island, N.Y. I want to ensure passive income for my retirement with an amount of income that can support my desired life-style and still create savings for my daughter. Eventually (a long time from now, I hope) I want my daughter to inherit this real estate. My goal is to have this inheritance and my life insurance policy ensure that my daughter has a very comfortable life.

I currently have a good portfolio of commercial real estate, which consists of the following:

1. A 4,100 square foot facility with retail rental offices, a full playground and an outside area for training. This property is currently occupied only by my Martial Arts school.

2. A 6,700 square foot facility with multiple areas, including our Martial Arts school, a 1,000 square foot retail store (A Touch of Zen), and retail office spaces.

3. A 3,200 square foot facility with two separate areas: 2,200 square feet for the Martial Arts school and a retail store front as well as office.

4. A 20-acre ranch in upstate Ellenville, N.Y. used for corporate retreats and summer vacation for the staff and employees of L.I. Ninjutsu Centers and A Touch of Zen.

Summing it All Up

Although my initial introduction into buying real estate was not exactly a success, I persevered in the quest, and now own significant real estate, both residential and commercial. I firmly believer that real estate is a way to go to insure your financial future.

Today I'd like to sum up a lot of what I've encountered and learned along the way to becoming a real estate entrepreneur.

Some Problems You'll Encounter When Trying To Purchase Real Estate:

1. Striking the initial deal: do not fall in love with anything. See the property's potential but don't let emotion drive your purchase.

2. Do not put yourself in a situation that may hurt you in the future. Do not put all your eggs in one basket; make sure you are totally capable of making the deal work. Do not over extend yourself. Take chances but be realistic.

3. Pulling together the deposit may be difficult, but as you saw from my story there are many ways to structure a deal. There are many banks that will be interested in making a deal with you. Do not think that you can't make it happen.

4. Make sure you have enough money to cover the purchase of the building and the renovation, as well as some safety money just in case something unexpected comes up. Remember the movie "The Money Pit."

5. Do not let anyone tell you what to do. Don't listen to the negative thinkers; they can turn your stomach into knots. Everyone knows someone who will try to put a monkey wrench in all your ideas. Stand clear of all of those people.

The Upside of Owning Your Own Real Estate:

1. Owning your own real estate is one of the best investments you can make. Real estate has regularly appreciated in the last 100 years.

2. You pay yourself as the landlord. You also get to write off expenses to offset many profits, which you would never be able to do as a tenant.

3. You never have to worry about a landlord selling or kicking you out of the building irrelevant of the lease.

4. You are building your future and putting money into your retirement.

My 10 Top Tips When Purchasing Real Estate:

1. Never purchase from the heart. Do not fall in love with the building.
2. Never believe that the deal is dead. There are many ways to structure the deal.
3. Never listen to real estate people. Always offer what you want no matter what they say. Do not let them dictate what is going to be acceptable. In New York, a real estate broker must submit any offer you make, even if it is ridiculous.
4. Banks are very interested in working with you. There are thousands of banks out there. Don't give up if you get turned down by one. Sometimes specific banks are not really interested while others would love your business.
5. Try always to purchase under a corporate name.
6. Build a "Real Estate Success Team" that includes your accountant, a host of real estate brokers, an attorney you can trust who will keep your best interest in mind, a really good inspection engineer, an insurance agent and a financial advisor. Start building your team now. You don't even need to have the money.

7. Study extensively: read books, watch videos and go to seminars.
8. Get out there and see many properties. Start researching what is available, commercially and residentially, to get a feel for your area. Dolf Deroos has a saying,

"The deal of a life-time comes around once a week." Keep looking; don't jump on the first deal you see.

9. Become fluent in the language of real estate. Look for a mini course to learn the lingo. Anything you need is in books. I recommend authors Dolf Deroos, Donald Trump, Rob Kiosaki, and Robert Shemen. There are thousands. Join the Trump University.

10. Search the Internet and do research. Check out www.Zillow.com or Realestateshark.com. This is a great website to give you comparisons of price values in your area. They are amazing sites.

Bonus

11. Find a real estate mentor. Contrary to popular belief, successful people are more than willing to give you advice, as well as to share how they did it, how they continue to do it and how they stay on top.

Chapter 16
Developing a Retail Wonderland

Developing a Retail Wonderland

Before I go into this next topic, I want to be clear about the mentality of back to school rushes, holiday advertising, and anything else that seems to be "the thing to do." Remember, if you are advertising in a sporadic style, you will get results in the same fashion. Why is it that most people are searching for the goose that laid the golden students? Why do people look for the next fad, the next cardio quick fix, or the next wave to ride until that one gets boring? I believe in the age old adage, "Slow and steady wins the race."

I advertise in some fashion 365 days a year, whether it's on my website, through my e-mails, through print ads, radio, TV, press releases, special events, etc. The list goes on and on. So my point was that we shouldn't need to rush into the back to school thing. We should develop a yearly campaign and advertising plan. I'm offering this again: e-mail me at *renshilininja@aol.com* for my marketing action worksheet. This worksheet is simple but really helps to give you perspective and focus to put together a unified plan of action.

If you want to increase your children's enrollment in your school, then what are you doing regularly to advertise and market to that specific age group or that specific client base?

Here are 10 quick ideas:

1. Do special seminars for children outside of your location; get in with the school systems and do "stranger danger" seminars.
2. Go to the local Day-Cares and Nursery schools and advertise when classes let out. Ask the administration to make your flyers available to their students, and offer to return the favor at your school.
3. Go to the local Boy Scout, Girl Scout, Cub Scout, and Brownie troops.
4. Meet with the PTA.
5. Give away free Martial Arts class parties and birthday parties.
6. Go to the local Chamber of Commerce and sponsor a "stranger danger" night for the community for free.
7. Have a raffle for a three-month membership, making the offer outside a supermarket. Ask the store if you can set up a booth inside on a busy night and do the raffle there.

8. Go to a local mall and offer a special evaluation on self-defense, weight loss, and physical fitness.

9. Meet with the local Mayor or other town officials and ask them to recommend ways to get in touch with people. You never know what they can do for you.
10. Take the time to call all your existing students and ask for referrals. I continually promote my referral program.

Now that we've covered the issue of the importance of having an ongoing advertising plan, which I have spoken about throughout this book, I'd like to begin a discussion of another path you can take to expand your empire:

Building a Retail Wonderland

I am not only the owner of a successful Martial Arts school, but I also own a state-of-the-art 2,000 square foot retail store with clients all over the world and an internet presence at ATouchOfZen.com.

I have made a point of talking about retail in the past, because people don't see me as a retail consultant but rather as a Martial Arts consultant. My goal as a consultant is to help people reap the maximum possible rewards from their schools. In order to do this, is imperative that all school owners realize that if you are not retailing, then you are missing an important and highly lucrative vehicle to add to your success.

I will go into detail about how to incorporate retail sales into your overall school strategy. I will talk about several ways to make retail selling an integral part of your school's success.

If you don't currently have any retail sales associated with your school, you'll find a whole new world of potential opened up before you. And if you *do* offer some retail selling into your school, you'll discover new ways to maximize the profits you realize from the activity.

Tying in your retail to your curriculum

In my school we have eight levels to Black Belt. In each level we teach a variety of weapons, so at each level it is required that the student buys a specific package of gear in order to progress and learn the material. For example, we have sparring week, grappling week, weapons such as tonfa, sai, bo, hanbo, cane, knife, naginata, bokken, sword and iai jutsu. These are all tied into specific ranks, and each student is told before he or she joins that purchasing equipment is necessary in order to progress.

It is our goal to teach students traditional Martial Arts, but in order for students to do that, they need the equipment. In other sports it is not unheard of to buy $500 worth of gear. Think about the skates, helmets, and pads needed for hockey. Heck, even in non team-based sports such as paint ball, golf or skateboarding there is a certain amount of equipment and safety gear needed to make the experience as successful and painless as possible. Why not benefit from the equipment needed by students in our Martial Arts schools?

In our school we offer discount coupons at promotion and rank ceremonies, encouraging the parents to purchase the new gear within one week. If they do so, then the parents receive 10 percent off. If they buy after the first week, then everything's at regular price. In our school, from Beginner to Black Belt, students will invest (and notice that I said invest rather then pay, because it is an investment in their futures) approximately $500 if they buy just the normal gear. If they buy the top-of-the-line, the investment could go up to $1,000.

But how can we incorporate retail into schools that don't do weapons, don't spar etc? This is where branding comes in.

There shouldn't be a clothing item or sports - or school-related item in your school that doesn't have your name on it. For example, in my school we have school branding on tank tops, t-shirts, sweat pants, sweat shirts, mock turtlenecks, gear bags, back packs, sling bangs, water cooler bags, pencil bags, stickers, dress shirts, towels, school hats, sun visors, notebooks, car window decals, folders, fighting gear, uniforms, spring, summer, and fall jackets, wind breakers, and now a coloring book.

If you don't have a wide variety of branded gear available for sale, you shortchange yourself as well as your clients. I believe that if a student wants to buy a shirt, why not our school shirt? The same goes for hats, bags, etc. I have made *L.I. Ninjutsu Centers* into a brand. Our students think it is cool to wear the shirt of the largest Ninjutsu school in the world: We are that school!

By the way, all of our gear and branded items are available on the web at www.ATouchOfZen.com, or you can call 631 893-4243.

So what do you do with your gear and branded items to turn your school into a Retail Wonderland? First and foremost you have to learn about displaying merchandise - known as visual merchandising.

Here are a few tips on what's needed to insure your success:

1. Have a distinct retail section. This doesn't have to be large; it can be a small wall. If you have open wall space then you can have a retail store.
2. Continually clean and rotate the merchandise. If items for sale are dirty, it is a sign that the items aren't selling. Do not let the merchandise sit for too long or past its season. If you display beach shorts in the winter, people are not going to buy them.
3. Display the description and price of the gear. Offer a lay-away plan. Be available to describe the differences between low-end gear and high-quality merchandise. In my school we allow students only to use gear bought from us. In that way we can control

the quality of items and specifically the safety of fighting gear and weapons. Ultimately, we are guaranteeing the safety of our students.

4. Continually update and blow out your stock. For example, a box of shirts that is sitting in a closet can be converted to cash to buy new and more exciting stuff. So if some item is not selling, offer it for sale at a huge discount, even if you lose a bit of money on the sales. Having the cash-flow and being able to buy new merchandise keeps it fun.

5. The last thing for now is to offer items for everyone. Why not stock items for the siblings who are not training in your school yet, sell impulse items, such as rubber throwing stars, bracelets etc.

Another sales opportunity where most school owners miss the boat is hydration products. I find this puzzling because I, along with other Martial Arts instructors, teach the concepts of health. Recently I removed all drinks with heavy amounts of sugar and limited my offerings to plain water and health-based waters. This is a sure way to add a few hundred dollars to your bottom line. Hydration is essential for students in training, and students appreciate it when we make healthy drinks available to them. If we don't, then they'll just purchase those drinks from the nearest convenience store.

I would also like to get you thinking about the individual pockets of people you have in your school. We can call them whatever you like but specifically you may have a breakdown of many different classes. One example may be your 3-5 year old children. I want you to ask yourself are you supplying merchandise that is age specific to those children and something that a parent would be interested in buying them. The purchase could be something they need or a parent may want to reward their child for great behavior and progress in your school. The bottom line you need to ask yourself are you hurting yourself by not supplying them what they need and want. Do this with all your age groups, and think about it in terms of female and male as well.

I've given you a lot to think about. Retail can dramatically increase virtually everyone's bottom-line profit!

Chapter 17
Developing a Winning Curriculum

Developing the Ultimate Curriculum

Fifteen years ago I opened my first school. I am not exactly sure what motivated me to do it at the time and sometimes I think back and want to kick myself, but overall it has been a very rewarding journey. Initially when I opened my first location I was the spitting image of my American Ninjutsu Instructor. I taught like him, taught what he taught, and even spoke with a Spanish accent. This was the oddest thing, because I am not Spanish and was brought up in a very English-speaking neighborhood. I emulated him because we are all creatures of our upbringing. Somewhere logged in to each of our inner thoughts is an imprint of how we are programmed to react.

My first teacher was a great Martial Artist in the physical sense, but he didn't really have a clue about how to teach or to run a professional school. The school was a dysfunctional nightmare. The normal class consisted of an assortment of whatever he wanted to teach and mostly was spur of the moment. Even though this type of curriculum was exciting, there was no way to monitor success, ability and progress. Each student was at a different level depending on his or her understanding. For example two students training for the same duration of time who had similar physical abilities could be at entirely different levels. The movements, the kata and even the self-defense moves were not required to gain ranking. Ranking depended on how much you showed up for class and how hard you worked. There was no rhyme or reason to the methods he used.

When my school started to grow from 50 to 75 students, and then from 150 to 200, I realized that things had to change. At that time I met my teacher from Japan and was excited about following a curriculum that was "written in stone." To me it was like being in college - we kept notebooks and studied many different family lines (ryu ha) as we progressed through the ranks. Even though I was happy with the precision, I saw flaws in the program as I grew within the ranking. The problem was overload of material and monotony. My Japanese master didn't look at it that differently then my American teacher. As interesting and detailed as the curriculum may have been, it was so overwhelming that many students became frustrated in their quest to develop. Some would learn the moves and cram for the tests but not really master the movements or techniques, forgetting them shortly after they learned them. Too much curriculum is not a good thing either. So where's the happy medium?

Before I talk about developing the perfect curriculum I have to make a few points. Even though you may be set in your ways and comfortable with what you are currently doing, you must constantly be evolving no matter how great you think your methods are working. Take what you currently have and look at it regularly to analyze your stats.

When I developed my curriculum I started with the end in mind. Here are a few things that I highly recommend as first steps toward developing your ultimate curriculum:

1. Start from 1st or 2nd degree Black Belt and work your way backwards. Remember that what you see is not always what others see. So see your program through the eyes of the students.

2. Break your curriculum up and make it age-specific. My curriculum starts at Adult level 4th dan (degree) and works back to beginner level. Then we have three categories – Teen, Mighty Warrior and Little Warrior.

3. You have heard the buzz about how everything should be age-specific and this is 100 percent true. But the fact of the matter is that many of the age-specific curriculums for children are nothing more then glorified day care centers. So give your Martial Arts curriculum some substance. Remember why you started what you started and be true to who you are.

4. Think with the end in mind and don't look at your curriculum through what we call "Black Belt eyes." When I promoted my first Black Belts, the test was difficult, somewhat out of a 1970s karate movie. By the time I did my next group of people, the test was even more difficult. I realized later that I was discouraging all the new candidates, due to the expectation that it would get even more difficult. So I set a standardized test for my students to follow and began a 10-week Black Belt test cycle. Having a set test and letting the students know what to expect is perfect. That's why it's so important to think about your curriculum, and whether you really have a cohesive plan.

The Ultimate in Promotions

There was a time when I behaved like "The Grinch that Stole Christmas" regarding promotions. Many years ago, if a student approached me and asked for a promotion or asked when they would be getting one, my typical response was, "You just cost yourself another six months." I said this seriously, and I stuck to it. I had the mentality that I learned from my teachers. I brought along the baggage that they had, and I am sure their teachers had. I mistakenly thought that being like this would teach the students patience, and give them the understanding that the belt was not the important thing. As the late Bruce Lee said, "The belt is to hold your uniform closed or hold up your pants; it means nothing." While I believe this to be true, the reality is that to a martial arts student, the belt is a symbol of a person's ability and knowledge.

Most Black Belts have had similar experiences. While in a conversation, someone finds out you are a Black Belt. They immediately say something silly like, "Don't kick my butt," or "I don't want to mess with you." I laugh at this response knowing that Black Belts are not the killers that people believe them to be. I do realize that achieving black belt status is a prestigious accomplishment. I have sat at a dinner table with owners of Fortune 500 corporations where I looked forward to discussing success strategies and business tips with them, and all I ended up talking about was the martial arts. People envy the black belt and admire martial artists who have achieved this level.

As the years have gone by, my mentality toward student promotions has changed. In the past, people who were not members of my school were not allowed to view a belt test or promotion. Now, the tests are among the most important open events that I run in my schools. As I write this, even *I* am amazed at the shift in my mentality. Looking back on my old ways, I wonder whether I would have my own child continue in a program like that.

Please allow me to paint a picture of what promotion or belt advancement should be. Look at some of the graduation ceremonies in colleges; we see caps and gowns, flowers being given, marching bands and parties that cost thousands upon thousands of dollars. While I do believe these celebrations have become an industry in themselves, the celebrations mark an amazing landmark in a person's life. Similarly, achieving a new level in the martial arts should be celebrated. In order to achieve any belt level, two to three years of dedication are required. The black belt is in the ultimate achievement, requiring seven to eight years of preparation in some schools. There is an extended level of skills to master in order to achieve the black belt or any belt. It takes dedication through bumps, bruises, frustrations and a host of other physical and mental trials. Many hobbies or sports require only a few days per week, and then there's a long break after a few months. Martial arts are an ongoing experience with lessons that unfold as if you were peeling the layers of an onion. The martial arts to me are one of the only activities that a person can engage in that will change his or her life so dramatically.

If you have chosen the correct school the lessons tend to be holistic and spiritual with true morals and principals. As you can see I am a true martial arts advocate. I also believe that the belt is not a right but rather a privilege, but bridging the gap and using different color belts as a way for our students to monitor their progress can introduce confusion. We want students to work hard, work toward their belts and use the different colors as a way to monitor their success, eventually leading up to black belt, but sometimes it works against us. Parents are pitted against each other wondering why a particular student didn't get his or her belt. They equate it to whether the student is doing well or not. They judge one student's performance against others. In other words, if another child started at the same time but achieved a belt sooner they may be upset or confused. I encounter this on a regular basis and it is one frustration we deal with as martial art instructors.

Here are some things that we do regularly to keep the quality of progression as high as possible:

Three Criteria for the Consideration of Promotion

1) A student must attend a specified number of classes within a particular ranking period. The number varies depending on the belt or the age or the duration between the belts. Each student must meet his or her requirements, no excuses. We also include striping per belt level. Each belt stripe may denote a period of time. If a belt takes longer to achieve, there may be more stripes on that belt. So if it takes a year to progress from blue to purple, then there may be four stripes, while if it takes six months, the belt may only have two stripes. Our goal is to continually help the students to recognize their progress.

2) A student must be at his or her rank for a specified minimum period of time, whether or not he or she has prior experience or learns quicker than others. I have found that there is a degree of maturity that is developed within each rank. We teach people the exact curriculum per belt level, and use the art of disguising repetition to keep it interesting, but we never take people above the level that they are in. Nor do we promote ahead of time. We have found this to be a very good way to retain students as well as to fully teach them their curriculum.

3) A student must know the curriculum. If a student is not up to the level that is expected, he or she will not progress. We realized long ago that there is a bell curve in regards to testing. We look at a minimum requirement for achievement. There are those who are far ahead of others in talent, natural ability as well as understanding. This will always be the case. So we have our outstanding students and we have our average. I established my goals on what I wanted an average student to look like, but I wanted my "average student" to be better then the industry standard.

Once students meet these three criteria, they need to pass a series of physical tests as well. In our school we have a list of physical requirements as well as gear requirements that students must meet in order to be promoted to each belt level, and we have a preliminary checklist ensuring us that each student meets all of the requirements.

When all requirements are achieved, we then distribute our Letter of Intent to promote and our promotion questionnaire. This questionnaire is a great way for us to see what is on the parents' and students' minds. We utilize this also as a way to pre-frame the students and upgrade them. Once the students complete the necessary forms, they are ready to go. Then they are placed on the test list.

The Day of the Test

A test in our school has become quite an event. Knowing that younger children and parents get even more excited than the students, we make each person feel special. All of our events below black belt run approximately the same time period. They are the length of the actual class.

1) The parents are notified well in advance and are asked to bring cameras and videos to record the event.

2) The students being tested then go through a series of moves that are required for their level. We highlight the students within our classes. We do not hold a separate promotion. I have found that it motivates other students to see their peers move forward in ranking.

3) After the class (test) is done, we then do what we call our belt ceremony. We have incorporated a belt dedication. This is explained to the spectators and creates an amazing synergy between parents and students, binding the lessons of the martial arts and re-framing the reasons the students joined our program in the first place. We ask all of students who are being promoted to remove their belts and hang them over their shoulders. I then tell them to pay tribute to the people who have helped them get to where they are today. Of course, their martial arts teachers are a part of that, as are training partners and sometimes even close friends, but most importantly I want them to pay tribute to their families. I then ask them to go and dedicate their belts to the people who are here for them and to give them a hug and say, "I love you" and "thank you." This usually brings tears to everyone's eyes. It is a nice time.

With all of this going on, we then award the successful students their certificates and tie new belts around their waists. We then hand each one a promotion packet. This packet consists of the required gear, the next belt level curriculum, and a special coupon discount for our pro shop. This is another way of us tying in gear sales, as well as keeping the students motivated. We usually end by taking pictures with the students.

A promotion or belt advancement is a very special day. It is something that has dramatically increased our enrollment of siblings and relatives, and is also a way to reassure parents about why they are paying for martial arts lessons each and every month.

Chapter 18
Commonly Asked Questions of the Business Owner

Question

Why is it that others can get away with charging more money than I am? I have problems getting what I am charging, and yet they have no problem getting what they ask for. Why is that?

Answer – This is not a difficult question to answer but may be difficult for me to get people to do. Simply raise your prices to what you think you are valued at. First let me say an average industry standard at this moment in time in the year 2008 ranges from $110 - $139 per month, for a 3 day per week – 45 minutes to one hour program. We also have our program for 3-5 year olds at the same price for 2 times per week and 30 minute sessions. To really clear up the myth, you must ask yourself why you are charging so low. Is it out of fear of losing the sale or your belief maybe you are not worth the price? You have trained long and hard, you have invested tons of time into becoming the consummate professional. Your lessons will most definitely change a person's life, so do not be afraid to ask for the price you deserve.

On another note, just from pure experience consulting around the world from the U.K, Australia and throughout the U.S, it doesn't matter what state you are from and what town you're from, if you market properly you will be able to charge a premium price. Don't get me wrong, if you are in a heavily depressed area you may have to charge less, but you certainly do not have to short change yourself.

Question

What do I do to get people to realize my program is worth what I ask?

Answer – This is simple to answer: be as professional as possible. This is from the moment a client walks through the door, up until you show them your program and sales book to explain your membership costs, benefits and prices. Treat people with the utmost professionalism and you will be one step closer to selling the potential client on your school.

Question

In what direction do you see the martial arts going?

Answer – This is a difficult question and I believe it was really geared toward whether I think the Mixed Martial Arts are here to stay or other things may be coming into play. I cannot answer the question about the Mixed Martial Arts because to me it is just another portion of the martial arts. One of my clients with my Taking it to the Next Level program teaches ancient sword play from more of a knight's perspective, yet with the proper marketing he is doing okay at his school.

The thing I do see is martial arts are becoming a dime a dozen. Now don't get me wrong, I don't think all schools or even a majority of them fit into this category. The public's perception is all martial arts schools are created equal. I recently had a parent tell me if I didn't promote their child they would take them elsewhere. In other words it was their way or the highway. I told them to have a nice ride. They left. During our conversation they told me my school and all martial arts schools were a dime a dozen. There was a school on every corner. I though about this and even though it angered me, I had to agree. If you don't like one fast food place you can certainly go down the block to another, so people need to be educated as to why you or your school is not the average every day school. Take the time to explain why your school is great. You do not need to put down the competition, or even mention them, just sell your school, the benefits and why so many people are happy.

Time Management

Question

How can I be effective and get more done in a work week? How can I be more efficient?

Answer – In the beginning chapter I spoke about this and mentioned many ways to become great at time management and goal setting. The honest truth is the better you become at managing your time, the more free time you will find to do the things you want or the things you need to do. It is imperative to either take a time management program or read books on the subject. This will truly be an investment in your future.

Increasing Your Enrollment

Question

What can I do when my business gets slow to increase enrollment and stay busy?

Answer – Quite simply, the answer to this is to determine when you are slow and prepare way ahead of time. I don't mean cut back on costs or other things to save money, rather prepare your marketing and start months ahead, so in essence you won't become slow. The goal is to continually market your program. Be aware of the times you will become slow and change that by adding on marketing or new ideas. We mention many in the marketing section.

Negative People and Influences In Your School

Question

What can I do to overcome negativity at my school?

Answer – I believe in positive energy. The more positive energy you put out the more you attract. Without this being so much of an esoteric answer, the bottom line is negative people love to be around other people that will listen to them. You should be aware of people who speak negatively and make sure you stop it and nip it in the bud. If you find someone is being negative, talking negatively about the school in anyway, set up and appointment with the person and confront them on it. The goal is to change all negatives into a positive. Sometimes people cannot be helped. There have been many people within my school who I have had to get rid of; they are like an infection that is not going to heal. At that point you have to heal it, and sometimes the only solution is to remove them from the equation.

Implementing Systems

Question

Why is it important for me to implement systems in my school?

Answer – Systems are what is going to make your life easier, help you run your business as well as be the most professional you can be. Without systems it is very hard to grow your business and really become a professional organization. You cannot have an organization without organization. So talk to professionals, both in and out of your field and find out what they are doing. Within the martial arts industry there are numerous organizations that can help you.

Referrals

Question

How can I convince my students to upgrade to the Black Belt/Masters Club?

Answer – This is a simple selling process. I spoke briefly on this in the sales 101 chapter. The goal is to slowly progress your students through the different levels in your school. There should be a natural progression. For example, basic program to Black Belt Club, Black Belt club to Master Program, Master Program to Instructor training, etc. First decide one what order you want the student to progress through then list the benefits of each program and then start educating the clients on why it is the route to take. Another simple answer is to become better at selling.

Chapter 19
The Psychology of Entrepreneur

Information Overload

I began consulting many years ago. It started out by accident. Jeff Cohen, who headed up the former "APS", now Member Solutions, asked me to speak at one of their conferences. At the time they had some very powerful conventions at which they had many speakers and a great track record. In the beginning, as I watched masters at consulting and public speaking such as John Graden and Bob Alexander, I asked myself what they could possibly need me for. Well, after being the keynote speaker at one of the events, I got the bug and really enjoyed speaking and helping people. Being on stage for me was something I was used to. For 18 years I performed around the country as an 80's metal musician. So I could get a crowd going, Bon Jovi style. Even with all that, I still wondered *Why me?*

Finally I realized exactly why: I was in the trenches! I wasn't speaking from theory, I was actually doing it. I was not one of those consultants that teach a seminar on how to have 500 students in a Martial Arts school, while they only have 200 themselves. I realized that I had something to offer because I had proven methods and I had been through all the steps, stumbling blocks and mistakes. In essence I could save a great number of people a large amount of time and heartbreaks. Why not share what I could?

What is information overload? Simply put, it's too much information. Fifteen years ago when I began teaching Martial Arts full time, there really wasn't a huge amount of information available to the Martial Artist. There were a few consultants out there with questionable ethics at best. One or two of them had the Martial Arts ability of three-year-olds, but they were preaching to people who basically had no reference and no experience, so whatever they said was amazing to many people, including myself. Every little bit of information seemed new and insightful.

Today, most mass consulting and trade companies work from the paradigm that they have a great deal of information and they want you to have it. They operate as though Martial Arts instructors will know what to do with the glut of information they provide. In contrast, I realize that many Martial Arts instructors opened their schools on a whim. Some were great technicians, others great fighters, but mostly they just loved the Martial Arts. They saw their teachers helping people and eventually said, "If I love this so much, why not do it for a living?" Very few school owners opened their schools the right way, including myself. For example, most didn't have a sound business plan to establish a business from the ground up, with marketing budget and ideas, most didn't have knowledge of how to run a business, how to deal with clients, parents, etc. So the main thing that I see today is new school owners opening their doors and scrambling to make things work.

It is not uncommon to see many great people not able to really make ends meet, not able to make their schools grow, lacking the information they need to help them. I am continually saddened by legends in the Martial Arts barely getting by, when some suave young entrepreneurial Martial Arts businessmen are securing a future for themselves.

So along come the consulting industries with libraries of information. Here is an example: You get a package filled with great information, one particular section hits you as being pertinent to your school, so the idea process begins. For example: Leadership teams. You get a flyer together, you start promoting the program, and now you have to come up with content. You are committed to the program now and you begin to scratch your head and ask yourself, *what the heck did I get myself into?* The problem with this process is that in the beginning the information seemed right, but once you got started there was no-one to help you determine what specifics were right for you and when was the right time to launch systems within your school. Sometimes getting a lot of information about an idea without the tools to take you through the whole process is as much a hindrance as it is a help. And sometimes, even a good idea can be inappropriate at a particular point in time.

Why not first do what you do best. Most of the time, implementing new strategies before you have the basics fully and firmly in place is putting the cart before the horse. Do you have the time to teach, pay bills, market and deal with students, their belt advancements, parents, etc? Probably not. So are these consultants helping or hurting you by promoting ideas you are not yet in a position to implement?

Most definitely, even one good idea can be worth millions of dollars to you over the years. So of course information is valuable. But the most important thing is to seek out someone who can tell you succinctly what needs to be done and when. Without this type of consulting you are basically spinning your wheels. Why start doing system X before system A. Why put the cart before the horse? Why would you want to have a leadership team when you don't have enough students coming through the door?

My recommendation is to begin by concentrating on two areas in your business: 1) getting students; and 2) keeping them. Now you can have 100 different systems to get these two functions accomplished. Find a consultant who knows the specifics of what you need, one who can help you lead you and guide you every step of the way.

Taking Your Program To The Next Level

I continually ask myself what I do to be a better father, teacher, school owner, business owner, humanitarian and person in general. Sometimes the very questions are overwhelming. Being in the constant pursuit of perfection, or "Shibumi," a Japanese term, is quite de-motivating when you think of it as an item on your list of things to do. However, the goal is not to be stressed or burdened by the idea of moving forward but rather to be motivated by the concept of Shibumi.

Why is it that some people seem always to be on top of their games while others "'can't seem to get there? The simple answer is motivation and consistent action1.

When I say consistent action many of you may say to yourselves *If I put any more time into what I am doing, I am going to kill myself.* But consider the fact that being busy and doing "things" is not necessarily the answer: rather the answer is taking the things you do and making them count. Now this could easily translate into a discussion of time management or organizational skills and we could speak about that for hours, but what I am really talking about here is self-evaluation and the evaluation of what is meaningful to you.

What would your life look like if you could hire a company like Dell to create the perfect computer for you with exactly what you need? What would your life be like if you could contact your mentor and motivator and do the same; that is, get exactly what you need? What would you actually be doing? You need to find the activities and answers that make sense to you.

For example, a personal trainer once told me that one of the most useful things that he had told one of his clients was that the client should stop drinking sugar filled workout drinks. He explained to the client that these drinks could have as much as 500 calories. The client realized all his efforts on the treadmill burned 300 calories. "Stop taking in the calories and you will see tremendous results." Sometimes the simple answer is right there in front of you. It is clear as day.

The business of Martial Arts is not rocket science. Nor is it easy, or else everyone would be successful. But as with any other business, most answers are out there. What I find confusing is that people tend not to seek out those answers. They want to continually be in what I call "research and development" mode. Why reinvent the wheel? Why insist on coming up with new answers for every question? If you try the existing answers and find they don't work for you, then go ahead and look for new answers. But don't automatically think that you need to invent your own wheel. Why not simplify your life and get better results? Why not pay more attention to the questions that really matter. Why not look at what is important in your personal life as well as in your business and see what actions are going to yield the most results for the effort expended. What are the important things you should be concentrating on?

If I were to name the two most important factors in running a successful school, I would say they are getting new students and keeping the existing ones. Ask yourself what you are doing on a daily basis to address those two priorities. Of course many activities are connected to these two tasks, and those activities take time. But ask yourself whether your time is better spent searching the internet for a two-dollar discount on sparring gear, or is it better spent designing advertising or calling old students or students who are no longer motivated? And answering junk e-mails (or even just reading them) could take away time from doing 2-, 4-, and 6-week or "we miss you" calls.

Prioritize and be disciplined about it. Trust me: in the long run you will see why it is so important. I invite any questions you have on this topic or any other topic, so just e-mail me and we can work through them together. This is my way of saying, "Let's refocus." We are half way through the year and I want you to be as productive and successful as you are destined to be. Push forward and make this year a great one.

Living Life in the Fast Lane

As each second clicks away, minutes turn into hours and hours turn into days, before we know it, our lives have passed us by. When we lose time we lose one of the most precious commodities we have. Imagine that you had a bank account, and in it you had $168,000. The deal was that you had to spend all of it each day or you would lose what you didn't use. Would you take the time to spend every penny? You bet! That would be the only way that your account would re-charge to $168,000. I think all of us would take the time to spend every last cent.

In each day we have 24 hours, in each week we have 168 hours. How are you utilizing your time? Are you living life, or are you wasting what is so precious? Before you know it your life could pass you by.

Five tips to live life to the fullest

1. Take the time to smell the roses. Realize that life is precious and take advantage of the small things. See all that goes on around you and appreciate it.

2. Take a different path to work or school and recognize the beauty that is around you. See how you can make an ordinary day into a great one. Practice at it.

3. Don't dwell on the bad things. Realize that life is hard, if it weren't it wouldn't be worth living. Stay positive, always. Sometimes this feels impossible, but with the correct frame of mind you can do it.

4. Be sure to tell those around you that you love them and appreciate them. You might not realize it, but it means a great deal to others. Also, you never know when you won't be able to tell those people again. One of my good friends always taught me that you should give people their flowers now, rather then place them on their graves later. Let the people you care about enjoy your love.

5. Don't worry – be happy. This is so true. A great quote is: "When you are holding grudges, the people you are upset with are out dancing." Don't dwell on things you have no control over. Try to influence things in your life that you can change, but do not spend time on things you can't control. Life is about experience and learning. So do what ever you can to improve and enjoy life to the fullest. Learn from all your experiences. The definition of insanity is doing the same thing over and over and expecting different results.

GUILT: Your Emotional Handcuffs

Many times you hear people say that fear is a debilitating emotion. We work hard to help our students rid themselves of fear, and remind them on a regular basis not to let fear hold them back. Recently an article was e-mailed to me about fear and guilt. Guilt can be just as crippling as fear. Guilt can be your emotional handcuffs, or, as that email called it, the shackle of your lives.

Guilt can mean many things: you can experience the feeling of guilt because of a broken promise, a shattered relationship, or even missed goals you set with yourself. Guilt can make you think that you are not worthy of an accomplishment or can even make you believe that you are not capable of achieving success.

The feeling that you are bad or that you are doing something wrong just because of how you were taught to think can be very dangerous. It often keeps you in an endless loop of self-deprecating dialogue with yourself, leaving you unable to move on. It is the epitome of negative self-judgment. It can figuratively keep you "shackled" to your past deeds and emotions and can be the determining factor that prevents you from succeeding in life.

So what can you do to rid yourself of the negative thoughts and effects guilt may have on your life? First and foremost you must realize that the past is the past and not everything you may have always believed is 100% true. The reasons you are feeling a specific way may not have validity at all. Anchors are usually great for keeping a boat from moving, but emotional anchors weigh you down and sometimes can cause you to "sink." Many times as business owners we live by a belief system that is false and has no real bearing on our companies, our clients, or our lives in general.

For example, we may believe that others perceive our prices as being too high or that if we raise our prices people will leave or think we are in this only for the money. But to believe that your clients will translate your good business decisions into the belief that you are running a "commercial school" or as others have been called, a

"McDojo" is totally ridiculous. Feeling guilty about something, or beating yourself up because you believe you are not doing some aspect of the activity as well as you might does not mean that you are bad or doing bad or not committed to excellence. If you feel guilty about something, look inside yourself to determine why you are feeling that way. Can you remember the basis for the guilt? Was it something you read, you heard or were taught? Isn't it possible that even though you feel guilty, you could be wrong?

Of course it's possible. So now is the time to start thinking positively and believing in yourself and your successes. Stop thinking with limited perspective. It is your duty as a leader and business owner to blaze the trail, think out of the box, and lead your people to success. You can't do that while you are feeling guilt and wearing emotional handcuffs. Rid yourself of fear a little at time by expanding your comfort zone a little each week or month. Try new things, and work on it even if you feel uncomfortable or initially fail. Remember if you fail, keep at it until you succeed.

Maybe What You Need Is To Be Better Looking!

Okay…. are any of you fans of the show *Friends*? I love Joey's "How you doing?" In one episode Joey Tribiani takes on the job of teaching a classroom of up-and-coming soap stars. As he walks into the classroom he looks out and says, "Okay, the first thing you guys need to do is to get better looking." I found it hysterical. As you know, I look for the lesson in everything. Even if I am being lazy, I want to at least be able to say that I learned something. So even while watching *Friends* I am learning.

So here goes today's lesson: Just because you can fight, it doesn't mean you can run a school; just because you won the Intergalactic World Championship, it doesn't necessarily mean you can be a Martial Arts teacher; just because you won the U.F.C 27 million times and are the toughest man on the planet, it doesn't mean you will have people beating down the doors to your school. The one common characteristic of successful business people is the ability to work on a dream each and every day and stay on task. I know being good looking can't hurt, but charisma and good solid work ethics will beat out looks every time.

I speak to hundreds of school owners per month. One thing I find is that many people want to achieve something, desire it so much that it actually causes pain in the pit of their stomachs, and still flounder day after day, not getting even a centimeter closer to their goals. Why? Simple: They are spinning their wheels in areas that are not beneficial to them or they are simply the wrong person for the job. Some people might say that Donald Trump's hair is the most ridiculous thing in the world. Why doesn't he change it? Why doesn't he update and go into something more 2006? Even guys like Tony Robbins, the self-help guru, update their look. Why is it that Trump stays with what he has? Well he's actually put a spin on it and uses it to his advantage. He uses his confidence and does what he is best at doing. So good looks are not everything, but charisma and the tenacity to follow through are.

As I speak to Martial Artists, I find that some people listen but don't actually listen actively. They don't take in the things that they hear or hear what they are saying. For example: I spoke to a school owner the other day. He told me that he has been stuck at 100 students for four years. I suggested that he work on his retention and he told me that retention was not the problem. I said if he just tweaked it by 10% he would grow. He told me what he really needed was marketing help. I asked how many students joined his school each and every month on average. He told me about five. That is 60 new students per year!

If his retention was even at 80% he would be growing year after year. Do you get what I am saying? He didn't hear me; he still wanted marketing stuff to solve what was really a retention problem.

I told him that even if I gave him "the goose that laid the golden students," he would still be at 100 students at year's end unless he fixed the problems he already had. His situation was like taking every $100 he made and burning it, because everything he did to market his school would eventually disappear if his retention was poor.

Why is it that everyone is looking to find the next back-to-school push? Today I did consulting and everyone wanted to know what to do for back-to-school. Now granted, there are a hundred good back-to-school ideas out there that you may not know about. If you implement one, it may bring students in the door.

But if your retention is terrible, then why even bother? Once the rush stops you will be right back were you started. So instead of getting better looking, get better at what is most important!

Here are five tips for your school:

1. As the head instructor, read books on public speaking. Take an acting class; learn how to get your point across. Stop thinking that people care just because you are the deadliest guy on the planet.

2. Take lessons in time management and goal setting. www.FranklinCovey.com is a great place to go. They have seminars all over the country.

3. Start looking in the mirror. Be honest with yourself. If you are not good on the phone, don't make calls; hire the right person for the job. Do what you are great at; hire qualified people to do the other stuff. I know you are going to say you can't afford to do that. Well my answer is that unless you make these changes you'll stay exactly where you are, in the "Catch 22."

4. Build a vision for your school. Don't keep your dreams to yourself.

5. Be all that you can be. If you go to bed at night and you haven't improved, then it was a wasted day. Stop going through life always putting things off until tomorrow. You should only have one goal: to accomplish as many goals as possible. That's my personal goal. You may use it if you like.

I hope this helped stimulate you to put your ideas into action. My objective is to see Martial Artists become among the most sought after experts in human development. Please help me achieve this objective by becoming the professional you should be.

Running Your Business Tactically

Just recently I returned from an extensive training weekend with one of my good friends. The weekend was broken down into two segments: Instructors' Training and Tactical Training. Instructors' Training is a program that I have been teaching around the country. It is based on the theory of what it takes to be an instructor both on the floor and off: dealing with students; dealing with parents; signing up new students; and every other facet of running a school professionally. The Tactical Training session was taught by ex-military personnel and was designed to teach about handling armed combat scenarios and hostage situations. You may ask what makes these programs relevant to each other. I must say everything does.

During the Tactical Training session, our first entry was into an elementary school bathroom, then into a classroom. Each time the adrenaline was pumping as we marched forward in our stack of six, weapons in hand. We watched closely as the point man decided whether we should go in or not, as the second man in line covered the door on the entry. As we entered into the world of the unknown, we knew there was the possibility that an adversary would be shooting to kill. We entered. With our lack of training it was a total mess. We all knew what we were supposed to do, but the minute it "hit the fan," we were like six lost children running through the darkened room. As we looked into the room, we cleared to see if enemy combatants were in the room, but in the heat of it all we didn't notice another room that was the perfect place for a person with an Uzi or shotgun to hide. It was scary as the coach (my friend) yelled out, "You're dead, all dead, you missed four doors, another room, you stood still too long," and so on.

Even though I had my head in the game, I couldn't stop thinking of how similar it was to running a business. The owner is the point man; the second in command is the program manager; etc. My mind raced as I thought, *We entered this room and not one of us stuck to our program.* How many times is this true in running a Martial Arts school? How many times does the program manager forget his or her top priorities, or the administrative assistant forget to do scheduled calls at specific week intervals? Maybe even the marketing doesn't get done as well as it should. The list goes on and on.

What we are doing is similar to running into a school classroom with an active shooter. Think about it: each time you ignore an item on your "to do" list, you are running into a room without a plan, inevitably setting yourself up to be "killed." Each time you do this there's the potential for your business to get "killed." You can't wait another second to make sure you do what needs to be done, perform the tasks you need to perform, and take the actions that need to be taken.

Now I realize whole-heartedly that not every school owner knows what needs to be done. In fact I would bet my life that the majority don't know all of the tasks that are important to their success. I would even venture to say that most of the school owners who do know what needs to be done sometimes ignore the requirements and play the "I will put it off till tomorrow" game, to the point of putting themselves in front of a live shooter looking to kill them. Sooner rather than later, that school owner is out of business or in desperate need of finding a way out of the hole.

My recommendation is to build your strategy wisely, on knowledge and know how. Take the time to get with a mentor, a program that can help you every step of the way. Take the time to find out and to plan exactly what it is needed and when, and then put each plan into action fully, before you move forward. Make sure you are running on all cylinders and running smoothly before you run into the lion's den or the line of fire. Make sure that you are not running into a dark room without noticing all that's around you.

Chapter 20
The Art of Organization

The Art of Organization

Being the owner of a multiple school operation, I have been forced to learn the importance of organization and implementation of systems the hard way. My goal here is to help you build critical structure into your business and identify "leaks and cracks" that may be holding you back from reaching the successes you have planned!

I have done hundreds of conference calls and one-on-one calls in the last two years. Speaking with many people, I have noticed a virus within our industry. If this were a computer virus it would have deleted most hard drives by now; if it were an illness a good majority of the Martial Arts teachers and students would be gone. When I say "virus" what I am talking about is the failure to give sufficient time and effort to two major components that are needed for success in the industry.

1. Business organization and education

2. Discipline to do what needs to be done

Not being able to effectively do these two things is the virus that can infect your business. Without sounding harsh I want to explain what seems like a contradiction. As Martial Artists we are highly disciplined in the pursuit of a goal. We have worked hard to become Black Belts, teachers, and school owners. The simple fact that we are where we are is a testament to our hard work.

The problem for many develops when they attempt to connect business and organization skills to those of the Martial Arts. First and foremost, many of us walk around carrying some antiquated mentality that we are not worthy of earning a good living. Deep down inside a good majority of people don't realize their worth, and even if they secretly know it, they are embarrassed to scream it from the roof tops. The next problem is that most of us don't really realize that running a school successfully takes business savvy, marketing knowledge and a heck of a lot of dedication to the cause. I say "the cause" because we are all preachers. When it comes to the many benefits of Martial Arts, we can all talk about how we have helped people and enhanced their lives for the better till we are blue in the face. But being organized and knowledgeable about the Martial Arts doesn't automatically qualify us to be effective as a business person. That takes more work.

As you know I can go on and on about this, but I won't take more of your time giving you my personal philosophies. I want to get right to the issue.

My question is, "Why do we spend so little time on the business practices of our schools?"

I have five questions for you as a school owner.

1. How much time a week do you still train in the Martial Arts?

2. What are you doing to enhance your Martial Arts skills, if not for your students, then only for yourself?

3. How much time do you put into your business education?

4. When was the last time you read a book on business, philosophy or another topic that will help your students?

5. Last but not least, how much time do you waste and how many excuses do you use weekly to justify why you didn't do one through four on my list of questions?

The answers that you come up with to these questions are so important that I want you to take some time and really consider your answers. Take a week to find the accurate answers to these questions – not just the answers that you come up with off the top of your heads. I think that if you really work on getting accurate answers to these questions, you'll be very surprised at what you've already learned.

Time Slicing - Time Management systems

Imagine a delicious pizza pie coming out the oven, steam bellowing off the top, the aroma of fresh basil, tomato sauce, herbs and spices filling the air. The pizza man with the precision of a master divides it into eight quick slices - enough to feed an entire family. What was once a bowl of dough is now eight individual works of art. Now imaging trying to eat that pizza without a knife and fork and without it being cut into eight individual slices. What a mess and what a difficult task it would be. Well, this is an analogy of "Time Slicing."

Some people are easily overwhelmed by big tasks. Tell a person to put on an event at a baseball stadium, explaining that the person needs to cater for thousands and to personally make sure that all the promotion and event planning is done. And then say "Oh, by the way, at the end of the day if you don't make a profit you are fired." Most people would crack under the pressure, some walking off the job and others simply accepting the fact that they are doomed.

Tell that same person to plan this event but slice it into pieces, explaining each task in detail with steps, and it seems much more manageable. Time slicing is nothing more then taking your time and dividing it into simple little projects.

I have an employee who works ideally in this situation. He has many functions within my company and if you look at the big picture he often gets "analysis paralysis." Yet when I help him divide his time into slices he is a production maven. The reality is that he is getting everything done, but because big tasks are broken up into little "slices" they seem much more manageable.

Here's how you can use the technique of Time Slicing:

1. Take time to organize your day the night before. Decide what you *need* to do and what you *want* to do.

2. Assign levels of priority to the tasks at hand; which tasks are priorities and which ones can wait and be carried over till the next day if necessary.

3. Learn to follow your priority lists. Do not let the busy work take away from the production. It is easy to get caught up in the immediate.

4. Learn to be consistent and set aside time each day for specific tasks. For example, Marketing is done on Monday, Wednesday and Friday from 10 to 11 am. From 11 am to noon you do other items. On Tuesday and Thursday you meditate from 9-10 and then work on your employee training manual or have meetings with your staff.

5. Slice up your time so that you have a more productive work week and a balance of all the items necessary to grow your business and be a productive person in society.

Time slicing is a skill you need to develop; it is not something you are born with. I want to stress to you that you need to teach yourself how to do this as well as develop your self-discipline so that you don't fall off the path. It is easy to do this for a week or so and then go back to the old beaten path.

You need to focus on what is important in your life and then move in that direction consistently. Remember consistency is the first character trait of a leader. I would rather have a fair consistent marketing plan than a great non-consistent plan. Consistency always pays off in the end.

The Event Journal

For years I have been building my schools while thinking up new ideas to keep my students happy. There are things we do as school owners which we call retention tools, such as a special events or give-aways. Our goal as school owners should be to continually make things exciting and new. One of my favorite quotes is "Familiarity breeds contempt." If you think about it, within our Martial Arts schools this is 100% true.

Have you ever had model parents who have always been raving fans suddenly turn on you? One minute they love you; the next they start spewing venom about everything you ever did. They put you under the microscope, analyzing everything you do, questioning your every move. Once your offerings become familiar, these parents' excitement about the activities that once made them happy starts to waver quite quickly. This is similar to what happens in some marriages: keeping a relationship fresh – whether it is marriage, a friendship or even a student-teacher relationship – is the key.

What is an "event journal" and how does it tie in to all of this? Simply put, if you are keeping things exciting and fresh you are continuously instituting new ideas, events, and concepts into your school. What is it you do that excites your staff, your students, and their parents? I know there are probably some events that you have done in the past that were amazing successes, while others paled in comparison. What makes one event different from the other? Do you repeat events over and over again and get a tremendous response? Or are you slowly losing the return that you used to get?

These are all important questions. Have you ever put on an event and gotten good results, but afterwards you thought of 10 ideas to make it even better? Maybe you even jotted those ideas down on a piece of scrap paper and eventually misplaced it. Then the next time you did the event, you repeated the same process and made the same mistakes and as you did the first time, with each mistake ringing a bell in your head as you realized what you had forgotten.

The event journal is a very important system for our school. The concept is simple. We have a formal page for each event, first asking some general questions. Then there are the specific questions: how did we market the event? Did we make a profit? How many people attended? What was the consensus of the event – was everyone happy? How can we spin this into marketing other events? Is this a newsworthy event? Can we use it to send out an article or press release to get more press from this event? The list goes on and on. The question is: are you keeping track of your successes and failures? Do you know where you can improve and if so are you using this knowledge?

Chapter 21
Finding a Business Mentor

A business coach will work with you one-on-one to identify your needs. The coach will help you strip your school down to its bare bones and take a hard look at the systems that you do and do not have in place. He or she will assist you in identifying the shortcomings that are tying you to where you currently stand!

The following are some simple steps to successfully utilize a business coach or mentor:

Step 1: Pinpoint Your Challenges: Are you having problems setting up intro appointments? Are you finding that your attrition rate spikes at a particular belt level? Sit down and think about the areas where your school is having its most critical issues. Fully note what systems you are currently using for these activities and then prioritize each challenge according to which is having the most detrimental effect on your business.

Step 2: Schedule an Appointment: Decide on your mentor and set up the appointment to either talk on the phone or email back and forth. I am always available on email.

Step 3: Take Notes: Take notes during tele-conference calls, seminars or while reading books, highlight pertinent parts you receive, and document your conversations with your business coach or mentor! Then add this information to your resource library for quick future reference!

Step 4: Follow Through: Following through means actively implementing the step-by-step instructions that you have developed with your coach or mentor. Working with a business coach or mentor and not following through on suggestions or plans of action is a tremendous waste of time, and can actually strip you of your motivation! Overcoming your challenges is all but impossible if you do not take the appropriate steps to do so. Indeed it is tough to stay organized while living the busy lifestyle of an entrepreneur, but doing something as simple as writing each task into your daily, weekly, and monthly schedule can help to keep you on track!

Once you have a business coach or mentor you'll be able to develop an aggressive plan to overcome any challenges that stand in your way. You'll find that you can implement programs and ideas that you have always felt would benefit your business, and will hold yourself personally accountable for taking the necessary steps to accomplish your goals.

Warning ... You May Think You Know Too Much!

I have been teaching Martial Arts for 25 years and have been practicing for 40. Interestingly enough, no matter how long I have been training and how long I have been teaching, I still feel that there are people out there who truly make me look like a White Belt. On the other hand, I can confidently say I am great at what I do and I am sure if people will listen, they will benefit from lessons that were not taught to me when I was a student.

After all these years, some people bow and call me master, and people from all over the world seek knowledge from me in the physical, spiritual and also personal development areas of life. Yet when I look at myself in the mirror each and every day I realize I am only a man and not all that special. Over the last 40 years I have compiled lessons from good times and bad, good and bad people, been through all the bumps, bruises, and injuries both physically and mentally, and I am still learning. My school has been open for 18 years, and I am still incredibly in love with the Martial Arts and what I see it can do for a person.

There is an incredibly interesting anomaly that is taking place that I call "the fast food society." People are so accustomed to giving money in exchange for a service and believing if it costs a specific amount it is a fair exchange. Very rarely can you buy something worth millions for only pennies on the dollar. The Martial Arts is that rarity. What is paid for with a few hundred dollars per month tuition is paid back in lessons that change lives and is valued in the millions! While you can put a price on a can of soda due to market share and competition, you can't compare that kind of purchase to Martial Arts classes. Once you have consumed the soda and it has fulfilled its purpose the transaction is done. Can you put a value on lessons that may help someone defeat a drunkard at a party or walk away from a dangerous situation?

Knowledge in its very core is fundamental, but when you combine that knowledge with a mentor, coach or teacher, the lessons become invaluable. The lessons of the Martial Arts keep on coming and can stay with you for a lifetime. I have had many students who served and are currently serving in Iraq. They continually e-mail me to tell me how grateful they are for the lessons they learned in my classes, even though at the time they didn't even remember learning them. Some physical and spiritual lessons have kept them alive throughout their stay and out of harm's way both physically and emotionally. I bet none of those students thought they would use the lessons taught to them in that manner.

Chapter 22
Branding

Can the correct name speed your company's success? You betcha!!

   The right name might not make or break your business, but it can certainly help you succeed more quickly. The next six tips can help you pick a name for your business that will lend itself to branding, and that will provide you with a quicker route to large company growth and the building of your empire.

Step 1: Identify who will have input when you pick your name. Ask for input from friends, students, and your employees if you have any. Whether you are just starting or if you have an established school, take the time to think about what your vision is and what you want the clients' perceptions to be. Do you want to be considered a "mom and pop" school, or is it worldwide recognition that you are after? Remember to think about potential names with the end in mind.

Step 2: Know yourself. Understand the personal significance of your company. Find a hook - something that's compelling about who you are - and choose a name with that perspective. Remember that you are your company and why it is in existence. Your school's name must build a picture that will tell everyone what you and your company are all about.

Step 3: Know your competition. Find out what the big boys are doing. What are the similarities between them and their names? Find out how you can fit in while still establishing your individual identity. Strive to be different. Decide what is unique about your school and highlight those qualities.

Step 4: Be creative. Push the envelope. Try to look past the obvious by not getting stuck in generic naming solutions. Think of yourself as a big chain or franchise. What will make you recognizable? Don't just go with Joe's Karate or U.S.A Karate. There are a million others out there thinking just like you, so make sure that the name you come up with is really original.

Step 5: Do your homework. Before you form an emotional bond with any name, find out if it is legally available for use, and make sure it won't translate oddly or offensively in another language. Don't forget your goal, whether it is a quiet, family-style school or world domination.

Step 6: Pick the name. It's an obvious step but often the most difficult to make. If you're waiting, don't, and don't be afraid to change the name you have. Set a deadline, then choose a name that fits your vision.

Customers value honesty and directness, and want to be reassured you're not trying to deceive them. Sometimes a good basic name is the start you need. Once you pick the name, you can share your vision. You do that with branding, and by spreading the message you want people to hear.

Epiphany Page

Page number   **Idea**   **Notes**   **Action**

Epiphany Page

Page number	Idea	Notes	Action